The Popular Handbook

on the Rapture

GENERAL EDITORS

TIM LaHAYE
THOMAS ICE
ED HINDSON

HARVEST HOUSE PUBLISHERS
EUGENE, OREGON

Cover by Dugan Design Group, Bloomington, Minnesota

Cover photo © Dugan Design Group

THE POPULAR HANDBOOK ON THE RAPTURE
Copyright © 2011 by Tim LaHaye
Published by Harvest House Publishers
Eugene, Oregon 97402
www.harvesthousepublishers.com

Library of Congress Cataloging-in-Publication Data
LaHaye, Tim F.
   The popular handbook on the Rapture / Tim LaHaye, Thomas Ice, and Ed Hindson, general editors.
      p. cm.
   Includes bibliographical references.
   ISBN 978-0-7369-4783-1 (pbk.)
   1. Rapture (Christian eschatology) I. Ice, Thomas. II. Hindson, Edward E. III. Title.
   BT887.L343 2011
   236'.9—dc23
                                                              2011047651

Printed in the United States of America
          13 14 15 16 17 18 19 20 / LB-SK / 10 9 8 7 6 5 4

*Dedicated to Robert Hawkins, Sr., who signed
me to my very first book (Spirit-Controlled
Temperament), and was a faithful supporter
of the ministry of The Pre-Trib Research Center.
The company he founded, Harvest House Publishers,
continues to extend support and has published many
excellent prophecy books that have helped countless
pastors, teachers, and lay people interested in learning
more about the future events that will soon take
place in our chaotic world. Now Bob, Sr. no longer
"sees through a glass darkly, but knows even as he is
known." His lifetime of publishing and distributing
Bibles and Bible-based literature entitles him to rest
from his labors while his works do follow him.*

CONTENTS

CHARTS

CONTRIBUTORS

Wayne Brindle

ThM, Dallas Theological Seminary
ThD, Dallas Theological Seminary
Member of the Pre-Trib Research Center
(PTRC)
Professor of Biblical Studies, Liberty
University, Lynchburg, VA

Robert Dean, Jr.

ThM, Dallas Theological Seminary
MA, University of St. Thomas
DMin, Faith Evangelical Seminary
Member of the Pre-Trib Research Center
(PTRC)
Pastor, West Houston Bible Church
President, Dean Bible Ministries,
Houston, TX

Arnold Fruchtenbaum

ThM, Dallas Theological Seminary
PhD, NYU
Member of the Pre-Trib Research Center
(PTRC)
Founder and Director, Ariel Ministries,
San Antonio, TX

Ed Hindson

MA, Trinity Evangelical Divinity School
ThM, Grace Theological Seminary
ThD, Trinity Graduate School
DMin, Westminster Theological Seminary
DPhil, University of South Africa
Member of the Pre-Trib Research Center
(PTRC)
President, World Prophetic Ministry
Host and speaker, *The King Is Coming*
telecast
Distinguished Professor of Religion, Liberty
University, Lynchburg, VA

H. Wayne House

MA, Abilene Christian University
MDiv, Western Seminary
ThM, Western Seminary
ThD, Concordia Seminary
JD, Regent University School Law
Member of the Pre-Trib Research Center
(PTRC)

Distinguished Research Professor of
Theology—Law and Culture, Faith
Evangelical College and Seminary
Adjunct Professor of Biblical Studies and
Apologetics at Veritas Evangelical
Seminary
Silverton, OR

Thomas Ice

ThM, Dallas Theological Seminary
PhD, Tyndale Theological Seminary
Executive Director, Pre-Trib Research Center
(PTRC)
Pastoral staff, Community Bible Church,
Omaha, NE

Grant R. Jeffrey

MA, Louisiana Baptist University
PhD, Louisiana Baptist University
Member of the Pre-Trib Research Center
(PTRC)
Chairman of Frontier Research Publications,
Inc.
President, Grant R. Jeffrey Ministries
Ontario, Canada

Tim LaHaye

DMin, Western Seminary
LittD, Liberty University
President, Tim LaHaye Ministries
Cofounder, Pre-Trib Research Center (PTRC)
El Cajon, CA

David R. Reagan

MA, Fletcher School of Law & Diplomacy
MALD, Fletcher School of Law & Diplomacy
PhD, Fletcher School of Law & Diplomacy
Member of the Pre-Trib Research Center
(PTRC)
Senior Evangelist for Lamb & Lion Ministries
Host and speaker, *Christ in Prophecy* telecast
McKinney, TX

Michael J. Vlach

MDiv, The Master's Seminary
PhD, Southeastern Baptist Theological
Seminary
Member of the Pre-Trib Research Center
(PTRC)
Associate Professor of Theology at The
Master's Seminary
Founder and President of Theological
Studies.org
Castaic, CA

Paul Richard Wilkinson

MA, Nazarene Theological College,
Manchester
PhD, Manchester University
Council member of Prophetic Witness
Movement International

Member of the Pre-Trib Research Center
(PTRC)
Associate Minister, Hazel Grove Full Gospel
Church
Stockport, England

Andy Woods

ThM, Dallas Theological Seminary
JD, Whittier Law School
PhD, Dallas Theological Seminary
Member of the Pre-Trib Research Center
(PTRC)
Senior Pastor, Sugar Land Bible Church
Associate Professor, College of Biblical
Studies (Houston)
Sugar Land, Texas

~

William C. Watson
(provided the chart at the end of chapter 5)

MDiv, Talbot Theological Seminary
MA, University of California, Riverside
PhD, University of California, Riverside
Professor of history and world civilizations
Colorado Christian University
Lakewood, CO

Larry V. Crutchfield
(provided support information for chapter 14)

MA, Denver Seminary
MPhil, Drew University
PhD, Drew University
Faculty mentor at Columbia Evangelical
Seminary
Buckley, WA

INTRODUCTION

Thirty years ago, while accompanying my wife on a missionary tour to Nicaragua, we were in the home of missionaries Jim and Lenora Woodall. At the time, the prophecy-based fiction series LEFT BEHIND® was placed in my heart by God's grace and later I subsequently coauthored the books with the great fiction writer Jerry B. Jenkins. Already I had been persuaded by the Holy Spirit that His calling on the rest of my life was to use every means possible to promote the clear teaching of end-time Bible prophecies because we are living precariously close to the last days.

Jim permitted me to use his study while the Concerned Women for America missionary endeavor led by him and my wife Beverly was being conducted. On the shelves in his study I noticed the book *Dominion Theology: Blessing or Curse?* by Drs. Thomas Ice and H. Wayne House (both men have contributed chapters to this book you now hold in your hands). Back then I was very engrossed in defending the pretribulational rapture view against the many spurious attacks against it by those who refuse to interpret Bible prophecy literally. I had never heard of either author. Frankly, I did not even know what Dominion Theology was. Dr. Ice, however, knew it well, for he was active in the movement until the Lord opened his eyes to the truth of the prophetic Scriptures.

Soon after God used their book to open my eyes to this

and other dangerous, erroneous teachings about Bible prophecy, I met Dr. Ice at a bookseller's convention. We immediately became soul mates on prophetic studies, and as our relationship matured, I saw in him a younger and highly intelligent scholar who also "loved His appearing" and was committed to heralding our Lord's coming for the body of Christ.

At that time I realized that the many attacks from those who refuse to take the prophetic portions of Scripture literally (as they do other parts of Scripture) were robbing believers of the inspiration that comes from knowing Christ could come at any moment to rapture His church. I was also bothered by the fact amillennialists and posttribulationalists repeatedly claimed that John Darby invented the pretribulation view during the late 1820s. My research, much of which appears in this book, made it clear that the position the apostle Paul called "the blessed hope" of the church dated back to within 20 years after Jesus rose from the dead and ascended to His Father's house in heaven. In fact, His promise to come again and rapture His church was the driving force behind the evangelism that took place during the first three centuries of the church's existence. Many quotations from the early church fathers confirm that, including the words of Ephraem the Syrian, a much-respected Bible scholar of the third century (you'll read more about this in chapter 8).

At that time I was reading about the Albury Park and Powerscourt prophecy conferences held in Great Britain during the late 1820-30s. These meetings had a profound effect on popularizing the taking of Bible prophecy literally, and the pretribulational rapture view has continued to have an evangelizing effect on Christianity ever since. When I mentioned to Dr. Ice that we should set up similar conferences he was very enthusiastic, so we set a date in Dallas, Texas, for an informal meeting of well-known prophecy scholars in the Dallas area. Among them were Bible school and seminary professors, authors, and ministers. In all, 31 came, and we had a delightful time informally discussing end-time Bible prophecies. For the first time I had the opportunity to meet some prophecy scholars I respected highly, whose books I had read and reread, including Dr. Dwight Pentecost, Dr. John Walvoord, Dr. Stan Toussaint, Dr. Charles Ryrie, Dr. Gerald Stanton, and several others, some of whom have since been promoted to heaven. Before adjourning, we decided to hold a prophecy study group meeting in late December each year so Christian college and seminary professors could attend.

After a small board was organized, Dr. Ice and I were acknowledged as cofounders of the group, and Dr. Ice was appointed as the director. We called this new organization The Pre-Trib Research Center. Today, our conferences draw from 350 to 500 attendees each year. It is of particular interest that many prophecy-based ministries have been inspired by our meetings, and a number of prophecy books have been written by those who have attended the conference.

It is incredible how God has blessed the conferences and the Pre-Trib Research Center during these first 20 years. Dr. Ice, who I think has a near-photographic memory (particularly for prophetic Bible passages) leads the conference and adds special insights to every speaker's one-hour presentation, and also helps with the question-and-answer sessions that take place after each session. The conferences are truly an enriching learning experience, to say the least. Many young ministers have been given insights from some of the nation's leading prophecy scholars on subjects they did not learn about in seminary and have come to realize the necessity of interpreting the prophetic portions of the Bible literally.

In 2005, the late Dr. Jerry Falwell invited us to move the headquarters of our Pre-Trib Research Center to Liberty University—making it a part of the legacy he left with regard to upholding God's truth. He told me, "I have found that if a school or professor is right on creation and right on the pre-tribulational return of our Lord, he will usually be right on most other doctrines." The reason for that is clear: If a teacher or institution believes the Genesis account of creation and believes Christ will rapture His church before the Tribulation, it's an indication they take the Bible literally. Consequently, they will take John 3:16 and all other salvation-related passages literally.

During my 37 years as a pastor of local churches, I found that teaching from the prophetic portions of Scripture on a consistent basis has three very practical effects on the lives in a congregation: (1) It stimulates believers to realize the urgency of evangelizing to the lost; (2) it increases their vision for worldwide missions; and (3) it spurs them toward holy living in an increasingly unholy end-times world.

All spiritually motivated pastors and teachers have or should desire these practical effects for their congregation. Nothing accomplishes that better than teaching Bible prophecy regularly. Considering that at least 28 percent of Scripture was prophecy at the time it was written by "holy men of God [who] spoke as they were moved by the Holy Spirit" (2 Peter 1:21), that should give us a sense for how often we should touch on the subject. And I would add that our Lord warned that the last days would be days of deception. A clear presentation of Bible prophecy prepares God's people to discern between truth and error. It enables them to respond to the erroneous teachings that are becoming so prevalent today, and it equips them to understand God's wonderful plan for our eternal future.

This twentieth-anniversary commemorative book assembled by members of The Pre-Trib Research Center is presented to the church of Jesus Christ and to the faithful ministers, professors, and lay people who truly "love His appearing." For according to Bible prophecy, it could take place very soon.

—Maranatha

1

WHY STUDYING BIBLE PROPHECY IS SO IMPORTANT TODAY

Tim LaHaye

I saiah is considered by many Bible scholars to be the prince of Bible prophets. Not only did he write one of the largest of the Old Testament books of prophecy, but more than any other, he spoke boldly on behalf of God, who revealed His messages to him through visions (Isaiah 1:1). Isaiah perfectly exemplified Peter's definition of a true prophet, in which he stated, "Prophecy never came by the will of man, but holy men of God spoke as they were moved by the Holy Spirit" (2 Peter 1:21).

Nowhere is this principle clearer than when Isaiah spoke on God's behalf in reference to the children of Israel, who had committed the ultimate sin of worshipping idols in the holy temple of the Lord in Jerusalem 800 years before Christ:

> Remember the former things of old, for I am God, and there is no other; *I am God, and there is none like Me, declaring the end from the beginning, and from ancient times things that are not yet done,* saying, "My counsel shall stand, and I will do all My pleasure" (Isaiah 46:9-10).

After all God had done for Israel supernaturally—releasing them from bondage in Egypt, rolling back the Dead Sea, leading them daily with a cloud by day and a pillar of fire by night, providing them with water from a rock, and giving them victory over their enemies by granting them the Promised Land—rather than worshipping only Him as He had commanded, they turned to idols that could neither see, hear, nor speak.

Fulfilled Prophecy Proves the Existence of God

Time and again, God has proven beyond question that He alone is God by "declaring the end from the beginning." What He was telling us in context (which is the way all Scripture should be taken) was that *I am going to reveal prophecy to you so that when it is fulfilled, you will know with certainty that I am God.*

Essentially, God was saying that when we see prophecy (which is basically history written in advance) fulfilled, we will realize that He alone is God, and that He alone is able to accurately describe (through His prophets) other events recorded in the Bible, such as creation (for there were no human witnesses to creation). Furthermore, we will know we can fully trust everything He says, including what He has stated about our eternal future.

The magnitude of the statement in Isaiah 46:9-10 is seen in the fact that no other so-called holy book in the world outside of the Bible can prove its own divine origin—unlike the Bible, which is able to authenticate itself through the many prophetic statements that have been accurately fulfilled. Dr. John F. Walvoord, the premier prophecy scholar of the twentieth century and former president of Dallas Theological Seminary, in his book *The Prophecy Knowledge Handbook*, says there are more than 1000 prophecies recorded in the Bible—500 of which have been fulfilled in a literal manner. This is one of the reasons we can claim with confidence that future biblical prophecies will also be fulfilled literally. As documented by Dr. Walvoord, all the prophecies which should have been fulfilled by now have been—right on schedule, down to the minutest

GOD AND BIBLE PROPHECY

Creation   **The Flood**   **Christ's First Coming**   **Second Coming**

Ages Past   **Future Ages**

Old Testament

Genesis   ⬛   History   Psalms   Prophets

The New Testament

Prophecy—"history written in advance"
Eschatology—the study of last things
Over 1000 prophecies in Scripture
Over 500 have been fulfilled

Only God can predict the future and have it come to pass!

of details! No other book in the world has such a perfect track record, with a 100 percent fulfillment rate.

The skeptic will ask, "But what about the prophecies that have not yet been fulfilled?" That's easy to answer. As God said through Isaiah, "I am God…declaring the end from the beginning." "The end" refers to the end of days, the latter times. The disciples questioned Jesus about this in Matthew 24:3, just after He had predicted the destruction of the temple during the Tribulation: "What will be the sign of your coming and of the end of the age?" Note how the disciples equated the Lord's second coming with the end of the age. Many of the signs preceding the second coming have already been fulfilled—including some right before our very eyes. For example, over the last several decades, many Jewish people have returned to the Promised Land after being dispersed all over the world for more than 1700 years. And in 1948, Israel was recognized as a sovereign state by the United Nations. No other nation in history has survived more than 300 years after being uprooted from its national homeland. Why Israel? Two key reasons are to fulfill the end-time prophecies about Israel, and to prove the existence of God.

Daniel—A Great Hebrew Prophet

About 100 years after Isaiah, God raised up Daniel, another Hebrew prophet. Daniel was but a lad at the time he was taken captive along with many other Hebrews by King Nebuchadnezzar of Babylon. One night the king had a dream that he realized had great significance, but by morning, he had forgotten it. So he called all of his kingdom's prophets, necromancers, stargazers, and soothsayers before him and demanded that they recall and interpret his dream or else he would have them beheaded. But none of them could fulfill his request. When Daniel found out what was happening, he asked the king "to give him time, that he might tell the king the interpretation" (Daniel 2:16). Later, Daniel came before the king and said,

> The secret which the king has demanded, the wise men, the astrologers, the magicians, and the

soothsayers cannot declare to the king. But there
is a God in heaven who reveals secrets, and He has
made known to King Nebuchadnezzar what will be
in the latter days. Your dream, and the visions of
your head upon your bed, were these: As for you,
O king, thoughts came to your mind while on your
bed, about what would come to pass after this; and
He who reveals secrets has made known to you
what will be (Daniel 2:27-29).

Daniel then prophesied about the world governments to
come, and to this day his predictions clearly demonstrate the
hand of God in the affairs of men. They also show the accuracy
of God's divine Word and prove beyond doubt that He alone
is God. In Daniel 2:27-29, note Daniel's three references to
secrets. Again, prophecy is *history written in advance*. It comes
only from God and is revealed to ungodly people as "secret"
information about the future so that when it does comes to
pass, it can convince those who have heard it to put their trust
in God. That is exactly what happened to King Nebuchadnezzar (see Daniel chapters 3–4 to read about his response to God).

This chart titled "The Times of the Gentiles" portrays one
of the secrets that has been accurately fulfilled over the last
2500 years. It depicts how the end will occur after a time of
governmental weakness (see Daniel 2:41-47).

Note the following four points about four successive world
kingdoms that, in time, would decline in power. These four
kingdoms were the Babylonian Kingdom, the Medo/Persian
Empire, the Greek Empire, and the Roman Empire.

1. Since the fall of the Roman Empire, many would-
    be world conquerors have appeared on the scene.
    But they have all risen and fallen, just as God
    said they would. We have seen the four succes-
    sive kingdoms as described by Daniel.

2. History is unfolding exactly the way God said it
    would, and could very well reach its zenith in the
    twenty-first century.

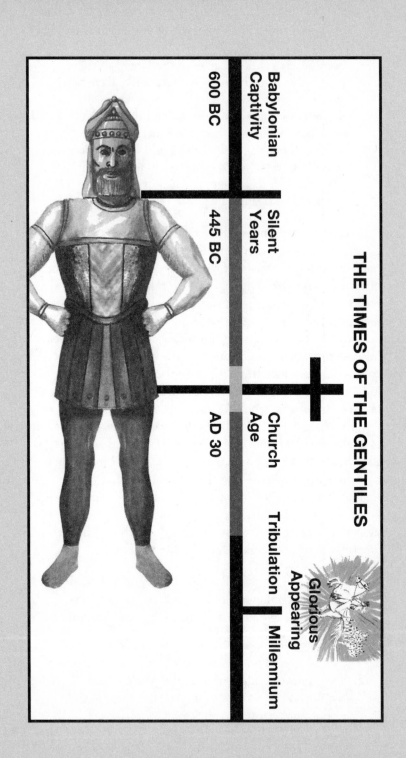

THE TIMES OF THE GENTILES

Babylonian Captivity

600 BC

Silent Years

445 BC

Church Age

AD 30

Tribulation

Millennium

Glorious Appearing

3. There is coming a burgeoning world confederation that is as weak as iron mixed with clay, as described by Daniel.

4. The period of time described in Revelation 6–19 will be followed by God's millennial kingdom, which will grind all the futile governments of man to powder. As Daniel says, the wind will blow them away and the Rock of Ages, Christ our Lord, will set up His kingdom and rule over the whole earth (Daniel 2:35).

Whenever I see the title *Holy Bible* on the spine of a Bible I often think this is the only book in the world worthy of such a name. No other so-called holy or religious book contains prophecies that have been fulfilled with complete accuracy in the manner as those found in the Bible. Over 500 of the predictions in the Bible have been perfectly fulfilled—thus affirming the credentials of the author, the God of heaven, who described Himself to Moses by proclaiming:

> The LORD, the LORD God, merciful and gracious, longsuffering, and abounding in goodness and truth, keeping mercy for thousands, forgiving iniquity and transgression and sin, by no means clearing the guilty, visiting the iniquity of the fathers upon the children and the children's children to the third and the fourth generation (Exodus 34:6-7).

While no one has seen God at any time, it has never been easier to understand Him than it is today, for He gave us an incredible demonstration of Himself by sending His Son into the world to be the "express image" of God the Father. The inspired writer of Hebrews stated:

> God, who at various times and in various ways spoke in time past to the fathers by the prophets, has in these last days spoken to us by His Son, whom He has appointed heir of all things, through whom also He made the worlds; who being the

brightness of His glory and the express image of His person, and upholding all things by the word of His power, when He had by Himself purged our sins, sat down at the right hand of the Majesty on high, having become so much better than the angels, as He has by inheritance obtained a more excellent name than they.

For to which of the angels did He ever say: "You are My Son, today I have begotten you"? And again: "I will be to Him a Father, and He shall be to Me a Son"? But when He again brings the firstborn into the world, He says: "Let all the angels of God worship Him." And of the angels He says: "Who makes His angels spirits and His ministers a flame of fire."

But to the Son He says: "Your throne, O God, is forever and ever; a scepter of righteousness is the scepter of Your kingdom. You have loved righteousness and hated lawlessness; therefore God, Your God, has anointed you with the oil of gladness more than your companions." And: "You, LORD, in the beginning laid the foundation of the earth, and the heavens are the work of Your hands. They will perish, but You remain; and they will all grow old like a garment; like a cloak You will fold them up, and they will be changed. But You are the same, and Your years will not fail." But to which of the angels has He ever said: "Sit at My right hand, till I make Your enemies Your footstool"? (Hebrews 1:1-13).

If you would like to know and understand God, then study the life and person of Jesus Christ, as He is "the express image" of His Father, the God of the universe. If you want to know how God feels when His children face troubles and concerns, study how Jesus responded to those of His generation. When Mary and Martha wept at the death of their brother Lazarus, "Jesus wept" (John 11:35). That expresses how God would respond. If you would like to know how God would respond to penitent sinners, read the story of the woman caught in the act of adultery. Jesus was quick to forgive, and so is our heavenly Father. So it is with everything Jesus did. He revealed the Father; it is through Christ that we can know God's nature.

Fulfilled Prophecy Authenticates the Uncaused Cause of All Things

We are living in a day when the followers of "the wisdom of this world" (1 Corinthians 1:20) are questioning the matter of the origin of the earth. They deny the biblical account of creation and advocate varying theories of evolution that push God out of the picture. Such error-filled "knowledge," which has been programmed into students through a secular educational system, rejects the view of God as creator of all that is. Little do these people realize that Scripture's perfect track record of fulfilled prophecies prove man is wrong and the Bible right! Man did not originate from an accidental spark that created life (something man has been unable to reproduce in the world's most scientifically advanced laboratories) which eventually evolved into human beings. Man was created from the dust of the ground and God "breathed into his nostrils the breath of life" (Genesis 2:7).

How can we know this? Fulfilled prophecy authenticates the Bible, and the Bible declares "the end from the beginning" (Isaiah 46:10). Whenever one is confronted with "the wisdom of man" that questions the Word of God, he had best take God's Word for what it says, for only the Bible has the unmistakable qualities of being supernaturally inspired and eternally accurate. The Bible alone contains "the words of eternal life" (John 6:68), the true history of man's origin, and the answer to his current spiritual dilemma in the face of the most confusing times we've ever known.

The Fulfillment of Messianic Prophecy Proves Jesus Is the Messiah and Savior

When Jesus asked His disciples, "Who do men say that I, the Son of Man, am?" He followed their answer with the most important question that could ever be asked: "Who do *you* say that I am?" (Matthew 16:13-14). Here, He brought us all face-to-face with the question that, when answered, determines where we will spend eternity. Our prayer ought to be that everyone can answer with Peter and say, "You are the Christ, the Son of the living God" (verse 16). Peter did not think up that answer on his own. Even though he had been with Jesus for three-and-a-half years, had heard Him preach to vast crowds, and had witnessed the healings of many, it was God the Father who revealed to Peter the answer given in Matthew 16:16.

Today we have even more reason to believe that Jesus was the "only begotten Son" of God (John 3:16). We can look at the 109 messianic prophecies Jesus fulfilled during His lifetime that prove beyond all doubt that He alone was and is God's Son. For Jesus of Nazareth is the only person who ever lived who healed every person He met who was in need of healing. As a healer He stands in a category all by Himself. As Matthew said, "When Jesus went out He saw a great multitude; and He was moved with compassion for them, and healed their sick" (14:14). No man has ever been able to heal as Jesus did.

Jesus' Fulfillment of All 109 Messianic Prophecies

Space does not permit listing all the prophecies Jesus fulfilled during His brief time on earth. However, the following examples are more than enough to prove beyond a shadow of doubt that He is the one and only Messiah:

- Bible prophecy said He would be born of a virgin woman, without a human father (Isaiah 7:14). The fulfillment is recorded in Matthew 1:22-23 and Luke 2:6-7.

- Seven hundred years before Jesus' birth, the Bible said he would be born in Bethlehem (Micah 5:2). This prophecy was fulfilled (see Matthew 2:1-6), and contains an added miracle within it. When

Mary was close to giving birth, she had to travel on the back of a donkey or camel more than 90 miles over primitive roads and rough terrain. Amazingly, she did not give birth before arriving in Bethlehem—a real miracle in and of itself.

- In Hosea 11:1, God said, "Out of Egypt I called My son." This prophecy stated that at some point, Jesus would be brought "out of Egypt." When King Herod ordered all the little male children in Bethlehem to be killed, Joseph fled to Egypt with Mary and Jesus (Matthew 2:13-15). After Herod died and Joseph brought Mary and Jesus back from Egypt, Hosea 11:1 was fulfilled.

- Isaiah 61 predicted Jesus would have a healing ministry (verse 1). Hundreds of years later, Jesus quoted this passage in a synagogue in Nazareth (Luke 4:16-19), then said, "Today this Scripture is fulfilled in your hearing" (verse 21).

- There are over 50 prophecies having to do with Jesus' death and resurrection, and every single one was fulfilled perfectly. For example:

    He was betrayed for 30 pieces of silver (Zechariah 11:12; Matthew 26:15)

    He was betrayed by a friend (Psalm 41:9; Luke 22:47)

    He was slain between two thieves (Isaiah 53:12; Matthew 27:38)

And the list goes on...

The amazing thing is that Jesus fulfilled all 109 Messianic prophecies that would clearly point to Him as the one and only Son of God. That it is legitimate to use such fulfilled prophecies in order to verify His identity is seen in the conversation Jesus had with the two disciples on the road to Emmaus following His resurrection. They were returning home greatly discouraged after His crucifixion, and He said to them:

> "Ought not the Christ to have suffered these things and to enter into His glory?" And beginning at Moses and all the Prophets, He expounded to them in all the Scriptures the things concerning Himself (Luke 24:26-27).

Later the two disciples returned to Jerusalem and said to one another, "Did not our hearts burn within us while He talked with us on the road, and while He opened the Scriptures to us?" (Luke 24:32). I have found that studying the prophecies Jesus fulfilled gives us a warm heart toward Him and His Father.

No One Else Comes Even Close

Not a single one of the 13 billion or so people who have lived on earth could even come close to fulfilling the 109 prophecies that Jesus did. Being born a male child immediately cuts the possibilities in half. Being born in the lineage of David cuts it down many times more, and being born in the little town of Bethlehem after a 90-mile ride cuts it down even further. There may be some who claim to have fulfilled five or six of the 109 prophecies, but Jesus fulfilled all 109! Jesus is the promised Messiah of God, for He fulfilled all the predictions required of Him. No one else even comes close!

Fulfilled Prophecy Guarantees God's Plan for Our Future

A few hours after Jesus was apprehended, He was illegally tried, falsely accused, and crucified. Earlier, He had promised His disciples that He would go from them to His Father's house, and would "come again and receive you to Myself; that where I am, there you may be also." This is not just a promise to rapture His church to the Father's house in heaven. This reveals God has an eternal plan for our lives in the next world. That is why He put "eternity in [our] hearts" (Ecclesiastes 3:11)—so that we could anticipate in this life the wonderful plan He has for us in the future. The chart, "God's Wonderful Plan for Our Future," portrays this plan in an easy-to-understand manner.

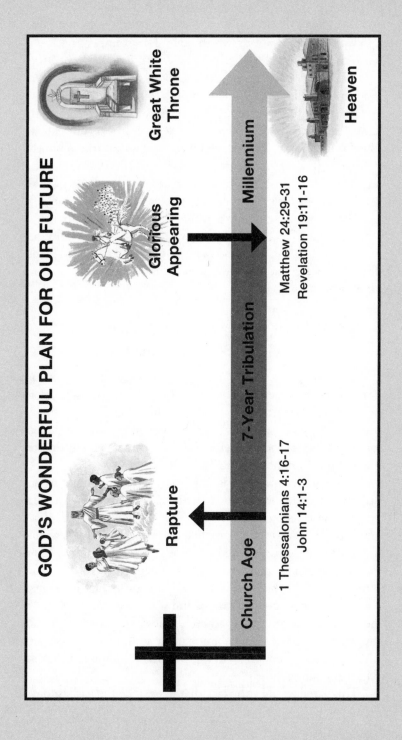

GOD'S WONDERFUL PLAN FOR OUR FUTURE

Rapture

Glorious Appearing

Great White Throne

Heaven

Church Age

7-Year Tribulation

Millennium

1 Thessalonians 4:16-17
John 14:1-3

Matthew 24:29-31
Revelation 19:11-16

Now, the chart is not drawn to scale. For example, the 2000-year church age is longer than the 7-year Tribulation period (the Tribulation occupies a tremendous amount of space in Scripture and is second in length only to our Lord's life).

The unveiling of this plan will begin with the rapture of all believers, just as our Lord predicted, followed by seven years in the Father's house, after which Christ will return triumphantly to set up His kingdm on earth. Then comes 1000 years of peace and blessing, during which Christ Himself will rule this world. And then our future gets even better! The Lord will make a new heaven and a new earth, where righteousness and blessing awaits us (see Revelation chapters 21–22). Our merciful God will be in charge forever and ever. The heaven that God plans for us is far beyond anything we can ask for or think of. You don't want to miss it!

Fulfilled Prophecy Guarantees Jesus' Second Coming

Everything Scripture teaches about God and His plans for our future depends on Christ's second coming. We recognize that His return is the start of it all. What God originally intended when He placed Adam and Eve in the idyllic Garden of Eden was for God Himself to reign on this earth. But sin prevented this from happening.

Now, the second coming of Christ is not an obscure teaching in the Bible—it is one of the most frequently mentioned future events recorded. In the *Tim LaHaye Prophecy Study Bible* are listed 329 such future prophecies. Some prophecy scholars have said they've discovered more. We tried to eliminate duplicate passages and count only each unique mention of a specific prophecy, which brought us to 329. Given the fact Jesus' *first* coming was predicted 109 times and it is one of the most certified facts in ancient history, then it follows that the 329 predictions of our Lord's *second* coming make it all the more certain that His second coming will know a literal fulfillment, just as His first coming did.

This is reflected by the fact that ever since the earliest days of Christianity, the return of Christ has always been mentioned in every doctrinal statement or church council on record. Regardless of how the many divergent groups of Christianity have differing doctrinal views, they are all in agreement on the fact of the second coming of Christ. Admittedly they do not all agree on the *timing* of His coming, but all agree He is coming back to this earth. That is why the future return of Christ is included in the cardinal doctrines of the Christian faith.

The deity of Jesus is verified when one considers that He existed before He was born of a virgin, that He lived a sinless life, that He died a sacrificial death on the cross, that He rose again three days later, and that He is coming again to take His church to heaven. And Bible prophecy proves that without doubt, His return could very well take place soon. It also indicates there is no question that Jesus *is* coming again. The only question is *when?*

2

The Second Coming in Scripture

Tim LaHaye

The classic statement "These are the times that try men's souls" has never been more appropriate than it is today. Everywhere you look there is political chaos, danger, and disaster. With each passing day it is more and more likely that madmen who are bent on conquering the world could gain access to weapons of mass destruction. And we've seen first-hand the tragic results of those who have proven they are willing to sacrifice their own lives and the lives of others in order to impose their will on the general populace.

It is no wonder that even secular-minded people who have little or no time for God and His Bible are growing increasingly pessimistic about the future. Some suggest that with the continuing growth and proliferation of previously unimaginable means of human destruction—including poisonous gases and biological warfare—there is little hope for this world beyond the next few decades. However, those who know their Bible are confident that the next major event on God's prophetic calendar is not world annihilation, but the second coming of His Son Jesus Christ.

One of the most heavily documented series of events in all of ancient history is the birth, life, death, and resurrection of

Jesus Christ. No one before or since has influenced this world for good more than Jesus. Countless volumes have been written about this man who changed this world more than any of the estimated 13 billion people who have lived on the earth since the dawn of recorded history. Jesus Himself prophesied that the church He founded would survive the onslaught of kings, dictators, prelates, and heretics, and it has done exactly that, to the point that today, Christianity has spread far and wide.

Today, over two billion people claim to be Christian, which is almost twice as many people as are found in the closest rival—Islam. This is due to one factor that distinguishes Christianity from all the other faiths in the world. Christianity is the only faith whose founder died for His followers in order to enable them to escape the consequences of their sins. And God Himself proved that such a sacrifice was acceptable to Him by raising Jesus from the dead (Romans 1:4). While there are many logical reasons for one to believe that Jesus rose supernaturally from the dead three days after His crucifixion (just as He prophesied six times during His lifetime that He would), none is more powerful than the very existence of Christianity itself after 2000 years! Does anyone think we would still be discussing Christianity today if Jesus had not risen on that first Easter morning?

Think about it. Two thousand years after the fact, the world remains fascinated by a 30-year-old carpenter from an obscure town called Nazareth who hung up His tools and began a three-year itinerate teaching ministry in an equally obscure province known as Galilee. Why the interest? Because of His empty tomb. For without the resurrection of Jesus, there would be no Christianity. And without Christianity there is no hope for the future. But as Jesus stated, "Because I live [after death], you [His followers] will live also" (John 14:19).

Because Christianity is based entirely on the fact of Jesus' resurrection, it is important that we understand how He triumphed over death. On the morning of the third day following His crucifixion, some grieving women came to the tomb to anoint His lifeless body with oil. They wondered how they were going to roll away the heavy stone that blocked the tomb's entrance (estimated by scholars to weigh about two-and-a-half tons). When they arrived at the tomb, to their amazement, they found that the stone had already been rolled back. Note what Scripture says:

> Behold, there was a great earthquake; for an angel of the Lord descended from heaven, and came and rolled back the stone from the door, and sat on it. His countenance was like lightning, and his clothing as white as snow. And the guards shook for fear of him, and became like dead men. But the angel answered and said to the women, "Do not be afraid, for I know that you seek Jesus who was crucified. He is not here; for He is risen, as He said. Come, see the place where the Lord lay. And go quickly and tell His disciples that He is risen from the dead, and indeed He is going before you into Galilee; there you will see Him. Behold, I have told you." So they went out quickly from the tomb with fear and great joy, and ran to bring His disciples word (Matthew 28:2-8).

Jesus had prophesied at least six times that He would be killed and would rise again—not after two days or four, or even a week, but on the third day. In fact, He said, "As Jonah was three days and three nights in the belly of the great fish, so will the Son of Man be three days and three nights in the heart of the earth" (Matthew 12:40). Why is that important? Because it is Jesus Himself who predicted He would rise again on the third day. Note carefully what the angel told the women in Matthew 28:5-6: "Do not be afraid...He is not here; for He is risen, *as He said.*" The miracle of the resurrection occurred right on schedule, fulfilling yet another prophecy about Jesus Christ. Likewise, we can trust that one day He will return, "as He said."

The Promise of His Second Coming

The event that will save this world from self-destruction will be the second coming of Jesus Christ. As He and the prophets taught us, "holy men of God spoke as they were moved by the Holy Spirit" (2 Peter 1:21). But Jesus was more than a prophet. Certainly He was that, for He prophesied more than anyone else in the Bible. Yet He was also God in human flesh (Philippians 2:5-11). That is why we call Him the greatest of all the prophets, for He was more than a prophet. He was God incarnate.

Four days before Jesus died and rose again, He gave what is acknowledged to be the first prediction of the *first* stage of His second coming, at which time He will rapture His church to heaven. He had already predicted He would come in power and glory to set up His millennial kingdom on earth. But His statement here introduces the fact there are two phases to His coming—first He will come to rapture His church, then He will return to the earth. We will substantiate the biblical support for these two phases in a future chapter. For now, let's focus on our Savior's promise to come for all believers of the church age:

> Let not your heart be troubled; you believe in God, believe also in Me. In My Father's house are many mansions; if it were not so, I would have told you. I go to prepare a place for you. And if I go and prepare a place for you, I will come again and receive you to Myself; that where I am, there you may be also (John 14:1-3).

The Certainty of His Second Coming

The most significant truth in all of biblical prophecy is the certainty of the second coming of Jesus Christ. That event is the prophetic key that unlocks all other future events. It fulfills both the Old and New Testament prophecies, including many of Christ's own; it completes His work of salvation begun during His first coming; and it starts God's prophetic end-time clock for the future. In fact, His second coming will kick off a chain of more than 15 events (these are detailed in chapter 4), and it is possible to predict the sequence leading up to and including the end of this world once the rapture has occurred.

However, the date and time of the rapture itself is unknown to us, for Jesus said of it, "Of that day and hour no one knows, not even the angels of heaven, but my Father only" (Matthew 24:36). Although we may speculate on the general time when our Lord will reappear, there is absolutely no question that He *will* indeed come again!

That fact is the primary reason no Christian should be anxious about the end of this age or the chaotic times in which we live. At prophecy conferences, people often ask me, "Will the world be destroyed by an atomic holocaust?" Naturally this question is motivated by fear for one's personal safety and that of their loved ones. Let me put you at ease immediately. Although this world will be destroyed someday (see 2 Peter 3:10-16), that will not be accomplished by man, but by God Himself. Furthermore, the earth will not be destroyed until after Jesus comes back to this earth. In fact, the complete destruction of this world won't take place until more than 1000 years after the rapture of the church—at the end of Christ's millennial kingdom (see Revelation 19:11–20:10).

If the value of a certain doctrine were to be judged by the frequency of its mention, then the second coming of Christ would easily rank as one of the most important in the Bible. Only the subject of salvation is referred to more. Given that the 216 chapters of the New Testament contain 318 references to Christ's second coming, that means 1 out of every 30 verses provides us with assurance this event will take place.

To help you appreciate the extent of the New Testament's emphasis on the second coming of Christ, I would like to give you a quick survey of some key mentions of Christ's return:

Matthew. Two entire chapters, 24 and 25, are devoted to this subject. This message is often called "The Olivet Discourse." It was delivered by our Lord just prior to His death. This passage contains the most important and complete chronology of future events found in Scripture, with the exception of the book of Revelation. Consider this description of the glorious-appearing phase of Christ's second coming, which came from Jesus Himself:

Immediately after the tribulation of those days the sun will be darkened, and the moon will not give its light; the stars will fall from heaven, and the powers of the heavens will be shaken. Then the sign of the Son of Man will appear in heaven, and then all the tribes of the earth will mourn, and they will see the Son of Man coming on the clouds of heaven with power and great glory. And He will send His angels with a great sound of a trumpet, and they will gather together His elect from the four winds, from one end of heaven to the other (Revelation 24:29-31).

Mark. This author compresses the entire life of Christ into just 16 chapters, and he devotes one of them, chapter 13, to end-time prophecies, including the second coming of Jesus (13:19-37).

Luke. The great first-century historian, Dr. Luke, included second-coming prophecies in two chapters of his book, chapters 17 and 21. He quotes Jesus as saying, "They will see the Son of Man coming in a cloud with power and great glory" (21:27).

John. The "beloved disciple," who outlived all the other apostles, penned his version of the life of Christ about 50 years after the Lord ascended into heaven. Although he does not repeat the Olivet prophecy covered by the other three Gospel writers, he quotes one of the clearest promises to come from the Savior's own lips on this subject: "Let not your heart be troubled; you believe in God, believe also in Me. In My Father's house are many mansions; if it were not so, I would have told you. I go to prepare a place for you. And if I go and prepare a place for you, I will come again and receive you to Myself; that where I am, there you may be also" (14:1-3).

Acts. Dr. Luke's excellent record of the work of the Holy Spirit through the lives of the apostles contains several promises of Christ's second coming. The first act of the ascended Christ was to dispatch two angelic messengers who announced to his disciples, "Men of Galilee, why do you stand gazing up into heaven? This same Jesus, who was taken up from you into heaven, will so come in like manner as you saw Him go into heaven" (1:11). And the first sermon Peter preached after the day of Pentecost records this promise given to the Jews of Jerusalem, many of whom had doubtless participated in calling for the death of Christ: "Repent therefore and be converted, that your sins may be blotted out, so that times of refreshing may come from the presence of the Lord, and that He may send Jesus Christ, who was preached to you before" (3:19-20).

Thirteen Epistles of Paul. The writings of the apostle Paul probably had a greater impact on the early church than those of any other human being. These epistles, read and reread in the churches, were accepted on the same level as the Old Testament Scriptures (2 Peter 3:15-16). Paul imparted deep doctrinal teaching, practical exhortation, correction, and instruction on many aspects of the Christian life. Thirteen times he mentioned baptism, and only twice did he touch on communion. Yet he mentioned the second coming of our Lord *50 times*. As we will note later, some of these passages refer to Jesus' appearing only to rapture His church to heaven (John 14:1-3), while other passages reference His later appearance before all mankind.

First Thessalonians is historically considered to be the first letter Paul wrote. In it he mentioned the second coming of Christ in every chapter (see 1:10; 2:19; 3:13; 4:13-18; 5:2,23). He repeated that emphasis in even greater detail in 2 Thessalonians (see 1:7-10; 2:1-12; 3:5). These epistles demonstrate how quickly and insistently Paul taught new converts the doctrine of Christ's return, for he was in Thessalonica for only three weeks before angry Jews drove him out.

The apostle's love of the second coming is seen in his rather stern words at the conclusion of 1 Corinthians: "If anyone does not love the Lord Jesus Christ, let him be accursed. O Lord, come!" (16:22). In the King James Version, this verse concluded with the word *Maranatha*, which means, "The Lord is coming." That expression gained popularity during the first century and became a common mode of greeting and parting. Christians often included it in letters, and in some cases even soldiers used it as a slogan when they went off to war.

The first-century church was populated by the most fervent

and evangelistic generation of believers that twenty-plus centuries of church history have yet produced. By the third century, Christianity had established such a foothold in the pagan world that it was acknowledged as the state religion of the Roman Empire. By contrast, even with all our sophisticated means of communication at our disposal today, the twenty-first-century church's program of evangelization lags behind the world's birth rate. If we possessed the same confident expectation as the "Maranatha" Christians, we could doubtless reach more people for Christ. But strangely, the closer we get to the coming of Christ, the less confident the church seems to be about His coming.

As a teacher of Bible prophecy for over 50 years, I can recall many "sleeping" Christians who were suddenly "turned on" spiritually when the truth of Christ's imminent coming gripped them. Church-ianity doesn't motivate anyone, but the Maranatha concept does. It makes carnal, cold, and indifferent believers fervent in spirit. I suggest that each night before you go to bed you read some of the Bible passages about the Lord's coming and then go to sleep thinking about them. Before a month has gone by you will gain a new fervency in your heart. Maranatha!

The story is told of an old Scottish minister who passed the home of a parishioner on his way to church one Sunday morning. Obviously, the parishioner, who was chopping wood, was not going to church. Their eyes met and the pastor felt he should say something, so he simply called out, "The Lord is coming!" and went on to church. About five minutes after he began his message, the wood-chopping parishioner entered. After the service he admitted, "Pastor, the more I thought about the Lord coming, the more I realized I didn't want Him to find me cutting wood during church." No wonder John said, "Everyone who has this hope in Him purifies himself, just as He is pure" (1 John 3:3).

All but two of Paul's epistles contain one or more references to the second coming. It is obliquely cited in the book of Romans (11:26), clearly presented in 1 Corinthians 15 (where Paul expounds upon the resurrection), and mentioned in 2 Corinthians 1:14 and 5:10. Galatians, which offers a thorough discussion of the finished work of Christ on the cross, does not contain a clear reference to the second coming, although an allusion to the event appears in 1:4. Ephesians presents the Christian "in the heavenly places" and "the day of redemption" (1:3 and 4:30), which can only mean deliverance through Christ's return. Philippians contains several references to the Lord's coming, the most important found in chapter 3:

> Our citizenship is in heaven, from which we also eagerly wait for the Savior, the Lord Jesus Christ, who will transform our lowly body that it may be conformed to His glorious body, according to the working by which He is able even to subdue all things to Himself (Philippians 3:20-21).

Colossians. This epistle contains the thrilling promise, "When Christ who is our life appears, then you also will appear with Him in glory" (3:4).

1 and 2 Timothy. Like 1 and 2 Thessalonians, the epistles to Timothy provide many references to the coming of Christ. In fact, they contain two of the signs being fulfilled today, which show that we are already in the last days. We will study those in a later chapter. In addition, 2 Timothy 1:10 and 4:1-8 both refer to the appearing of Jesus Christ.

Titus. This book contains the advice of a veteran servant of God to a young preacher on how to conduct the work of the Lord in the church. Paul challenges Titus to teach the people to deny themselves their "ungodliness and worldly lusts...[and] live soberly, righteously and godly in the present age, looking for the blessed hope and glorious appearing of our great God and Savior Jesus Christ" (2:12-13).

Hebrews. This is a magnificent presentation of Christ as the fulfillment of Old Testament types and symbols. One of the promises of our Lord's return states that "Christ was offered once to bear the sins of many. To those who eagerly wait for Him He will appear a second time, apart from sin, for salvation" (9:28).

When all of Paul's writings are considered, we find that only two omit mention of the second coming, and one of these is Philemon, a personal letter of only one chapter. There is no question that the certainty of Christ's return dominated in the mind of the apostle Paul.

James. This little book, which challenges Christians to show their faith by their works, culminates with a strong appeal relative to the coming of Christ: "You also be patient. Establish your hearts, for the coming of the Lord is at hand" (5:8).

Peter. Writing to the church while it was undergoing trials of persecution, the apostle Peter challenged the elders to remain faithful leaders on the basis of the Lord's coming: "When the Chief Shepherd appears, you will receive the crown of glory that does not fade away" (1 Peter 5:4). Peter's second epistle contains a lengthy prophecy concerning the rise of scoffers in the days just preceding Christ's return. He promises in spite of their ridicule that "the day of the Lord will come as a thief in the night" (2 Peter 3:10).

1 John. The beautiful epistle that brings assurance and confidence to the believer also challenges him to holy living on the basis of Christ's coming. One example: "Abide in him, that when He appears, we may have confidence and not be ashamed before Him at His coming" (2:28).

Jude. This one-chapter book contains a quotation from the patriarch Enoch, who walked in intimate fellowship with God during the chaotic days preceding the flood and was suddenly caught up to be with God. Genesis 5:24 says, "And Enoch walked with God; and he was not, for God took him." Some prophecy scholars suggest that what happened to Enoch is a picture of what will happen to Christians just before the chaotic days of the Tribulation, when the Lord suddenly removes them from this earth to be with Himself. This is the rapture of the church (see 1 Thessalonians 4:13-18 and 1 Corinthians 15:51-52). Before Enoch's "rapture" or sudden departure, he gave this inspired prophecy: "Now Enoch, the seventh from Adam, prophesied about these men also, saying, 'Behold, the Lord comes with ten thousands of His saints, to execute judgment on all, to convict all who are ungodly among them of all their ungodly deeds which they have committed in an ungodly way, and of all the harsh things which ungodly sinners have spoken against Him'" (Jude 14-15). This, of course, is Enoch's reference to the Lord's coming in power and great glory.

Revelation. The Bible ends with an entire book of prophecy. It directs us to a study of events foretold, from the first century after Christ's ascension until the end of the world. Some people erroneously call it the Revelation of Saint John, but he was just the penman. Its prophecies are far too complex for a mere Galilean fisherman to come up with. It is really the revelation of Jesus Christ, for it shows His future unveiling as the glorious King of all creation, including heaven. The following summary denotes the main time periods covered in the book:

> Chapter 1: Christ's present heavenly glory.
>
> Chapters 2–3: Christ's relationships with the church's seven ages from AD 30 to the rapture.
>
> Chapters 4–18: Christ's role in the seven-year Tribulation.
>
> Chapters 19–20: Christ's majestic return to the earth and the establishment of his 1000-year kingdom.
>
> Chapters 21–22: Christ's destruction of the earth and establishment of His everlasting kingdom.

There are so many references to Christ's coming in this book that space does not permit tabulation. And the last chapter gives Christ's specific endorsement of the book itself. It is as though He put His personal signature beneath its contents by saying, "I, Jesus, have sent My angel to testify to you these things in the churches. I am the Root and the Offspring of David, the Bright and Morning Star" (22:16).

The final challenge to believers throughout all the ages is, "He who testifies to these things says, 'Surely I am coming quickly.' Amen. Even so, come, Lord Jesus!" (22:20). The word "quickly" does not mean His coming would occur in John's day; rather it refers to Jesus' coming as a "sudden" event. Christians in every generation should expect the Lord to come suddenly.

This overview of key references to the Lord's second coming found all through the New Testament is by no means comprehensive. Through the rest of this book, we'll look at additional passages that establish the absolute certainty of Christ's future return to this earth.

Further Proof of the Certainty of Christ's Coming

In summary, 23 of the 27 books of the New Testament refer to the Lord's return to the earth. Of the four books that include no mention, three are single-chapter letters written to a specific person about a non-second-coming issue. And the fourth book, Galatians, does not refer to the second coming, although, as noted, an implied reference appears in 1:4.

The sheer weight of evidence leads to the conclusion that if one believes the Bible, he must believe in the second coming of Christ. Not only was belief in this event a universal conviction and motivating factor of the early church, but all nine authors of the New Testament mentioned it. After they universally accepted so literally our Lord's promise, "I will come again," can we do less?

If the frequency of a prophecy determines the certainty of its eventual fulfillment, then there is nothing more certain than the second coming of Jesus. For it is mentioned at least 329 times in Scripture. What is so significant about this is that there are at least 109 prophecies recorded in the Old Testament concerning Jesus' first coming. The fact that He fulfilled literally all those messianic prophecies down to the letter is what makes it so certain that He is the one and only Messiah who "came to seek and to save that which was lost" (Luke 19:10), and who will return again. That Jesus fulfilled every one of the 109 prophecies about His first coming tells us we can be all the more certain He will fulfill the prophecies of His second coming, which are three times greater in number.

Christ's Coming Is a Doctrinal Necessity

The New Testament teaches the return of Christ both

directly and indirectly. Several major doctrines are absolutely dependent on the second coming of Christ. For example, the doctrine of the resurrection of the human body cannot be fulfilled until Christ comes again (1 Corinthians 15:23). The promised victory of Christ over Satan, which is first mentioned in Genesis 3:15, will not be completed until He comes again. Even the recognition of loved ones in eternity, and the physical proof of our being born into the family of God, will not be evidenced until His second coming:

> Beloved, now we are children of God; and it has not yet been revealed what we shall be, but we know that when He is revealed, we shall be like Him, for we shall see Him as He is. And everyone who has this hope in Him purifies himself, just as He is pure (1 John 3:2-3).

The most important doctrine in all of the Scriptures, the one upon which all others depend, is the deity of Jesus Christ. He promised so many times to return that there is simply no way to vindicate His divine nature if He does not come again. God cannot lie or deceive. If Jesus does not come again, He will be guilty of fraud, to say the least. But since that possibility is so incompatible with His earthly life, His promises, and His divine nature, we need not concern ourselves with it. The fact remains that He said, "I will come again" (John 14:3).

A man once asked me, "Don't you have anything better than Christ's own words to prove He is coming again?" I replied, "What could possibly be better than the word of the one who, by the power of His word, created all things?" (compare Genesis 1 with John 1:3 and Colossians 1:15-18). Besides, there is nothing so absolute as His Word. Jesus said, "Heaven and earth will pass away, but My words will by no means pass away" (Matthew 24:35).

In the final analysis, it all comes down to what you believe about Jesus Christ, who demanded from Peter's lips the most important response in life: "Who do you say that I am?" (Matthew 16:15). If you believe He is the Son of God, then you will have no difficulty accepting what Scripture says about

His return. If you don't know Him yet as the eternal Son of God, then I suggest you concentrate on Him, not his second coming. There is ample reason for believing in Christ's deity based on His resurrection alone. Scripture, history, and human logic cry out to men to accept Jesus Christ as the Son of God, who died for our sins, was buried, and rose again the third day (1 Corinthians 15:3-4).

One evening, after I spoke on the resurrection of Jesus Christ, I was confronted with an amazing proposition by a brilliant young physicist with a master's degree from Stanford University. "I am an atheist," he confessed, "an unscientific atheist." He went on to explain: "I have been taught to thoroughly investigate all sides of a matter before I accept it. So far I have never done that with Christianity. This year I am working as an engineer at General Dynamics to earn enough money so I can begin working on my PhD program at Brandeis University. Since I am not engaged in academic pursuits this year, I have decided to investigate Christianity to see if there is anything credible to it." He added, "I plan to be a college professor and have found that my atheism offers no real philosophy of life to impart to the students. Although I cannot accept Christian beliefs, I have observed that the Christian way of life offers a meaningful philosophy to pass on to others."

Then he handed me a ten-page analysis of his atheistic doubts and invited me to tutor him in his study of Christianity. As we met regularly that year, I soon found him so methodical that we didn't have time for research on the credibility of the Bible, fulfilled prophecy, or even the full concept of the deity of Christ. After praying about it, I suggested, "Let's concentrate on the bodily resurrection of Jesus Christ." That concept is so basic that its logical proof offers an easy transition to all other biblical doctrines. The young man began to study diligently. Frankly, I was amazed to discover so many books written about the resurrection. He very carefully made two lists, one marked "reasons for accepting the resurrection of Christ," and the other marked "reasons against Christ's resurrection."

To my dismay, September came and he had not yet completed his research. When he left for Brandeis University, I thought we had lost him. But to my amazement he came into my office during the Christmas holidays and informed me that, lo and behold, he had become a Christian! He then related this story: During the Thanksgiving holiday he culminated his research and discovered that he had amassed five reasons for accepting the resurrection of Christ for every one he had thought he found against accepting it. "I was forced by the sheer weight of evidence to accept the bodily resurrection of Christ as a historical fact." Then he added, "But that didn't make me a Christian. Suddenly it dawned on me that I had to ask this Christ, in whom I now believed, to come into my life and save me from my sins." Needless to say, after that happened, it wasn't long before he accepted the teaching that Christ would return one day.

As you read through this book, if you have any doubt as to whether or not you have received Christ as your Lord and Savior, I suggest that you drop to your knees and ask Christ to come into your heart. The Bible promises that "whoever calls on the name of the LORD shall be saved" (Romans 10:13).

3

WHAT IS
THE RAPTURE?

Tim LaHaye

Recently, I have been amazed at the number of nonreligious people who are asking questions about the rapture. What is it? When will it happen? Will I be included? When I started preaching the Bible over 60 years ago, it wasn't enough to just mention the rapture; I had to take the time to explain it. But not anymore. Today, large numbers of people have heard the term and many are aware it involves Jesus shouting from heaven and calling His church up to be with Him in His Father's house.

I have had many well-known TV hosts, radio commentators, and all types of journalists request interviews on the subject. Many of them ask if the rise of terrorism, the chaos in the Middle East, and the increase in radical natural disasters—including earthquakes and tsunamis—may somehow be related to biblical prophecy. Much of today's awareness can be attributed to the plethora of authors, publishers, movie producers, songwriters, and knowledgeable preachers who have been faithfully heralding Christ's coming for the last few decades.

In recent years, God has chosen to bless the LEFT BEHIND® series of novels that I cowrote with Jerry B. Jenkins. This series has not only broken all previous publishing records for adult fiction, but has been used to win tens of thousands of readers to Christ. It's no accident that we placed a "believable conversion" in every book so that the Holy Spirit could speak privately to each reader, encouraging him or her to receive Christ as Savior. In the more than 60 years I have been in the ministry, I have never been involved in anything that was so spiritually successful in reaching people for Christ. Praise the Lord! As an added blessing, the series helped to awaken the world to the divine prediction that Jesus Christ is coming soon to rapture His church.

Paul Taught New Christians About the Rapture

I have long wondered why so many ministers, seminary professors, and veteran Bible teachers rarely, if ever, mention the second coming of Christ. It's one of the most prominent topics in the New Testament. The apostle Paul certainly wasn't quiet about the second coming. All you have to do is read his first letter written to the church at Thessalonica. Keep in mind that he was in that pagan Greek city for only three weeks before he was driven out of town. So Paul didn't have much time to teach about the second coming, but he gave it prominent attention. In fact, Paul wrote to this infant church about the second coming *in all five chapters* of 1 Thessalonians. Then about six months later, he addressed the Lord's return again in the first two chapters of 2 Thessalonians. Obviously Paul was passionate about the second coming of Jesus and saw this as an important subject worth sharing with new believers.

Clearly, Paul believed that even baby Christians were spiritually mature enough to be taught Bible prophecy, particularly as it related to the Lord's return. And as you read these chapters, pay special attention to the depth of his teaching. First Thessalonians 4, for example, reveals the people were well aware that Jesus would one day return and take all Christians with Him back to heaven.

The Eight Events of the Rapture

Let's take a closer look at 1 Thessalonians 4. As Paul taught about the rapture, the Christians in Thessalonica became concerned. What about their already-dead relatives who had died recently? Would they miss the rapture? Paul responded, "I do not want you to be ignorant, brethren, concerning those who had fallen asleep, lest they sorrow as do those who have no hope" (verse 13). During my 37 years as a pastor, I conducted hundreds of funerals. It is easy to tell the difference between those who had confidence they would meet their loved ones again in the next life, and those who did not. Now, while Christians do sorrow over the temporary separation from their loved ones, they don't grieve as the hopeless do. And in 1 Thessalonians 4, Paul assures us that we will indeed be reunited in heaven. This is "the blessed hope" of all believers (Titus 2:13).

I witnessed a graphic example of this at a funeral in which the beloved wife of a Christian husband was forced to say a temporary goodbye to him. After shedding some tears at the loss of her companion, she thanked the Lord that she would one day see him again. But her unsaved sister, who had come to town for the service, supposedly to comfort her sister, suddenly came unglued and wailed openly. In a reversal of roles, the widow put her arm around her sister and said, "Don't worry Esther, I will see him again." And that is the difference between someone who has faith in the resurrected Christ and someone who doesn't. The unsaved have no hope beyond the grave. It's no wonder that those of us who share "the blessed hope"—or as I like to call it, the blessed confidence—know beyond a shadow of a doubt that we will see our loved ones in the next life. We can face even the unexpected deaths of our saved friends or family members differently than those who have no faith. For we have the promise of our Lord that He will come again and take us to be with Him in heaven (John 14:1-3).

In 1 Thessalonians 4, Paul makes it clear that all who believe in the death, burial, and resurrection of Jesus will be taken to heaven by Christ. More specifically, verse 15 states that those who are alive on earth when Christ comes to rapture His church will not precede those "who are asleep" (those who are already dead) in Jesus.

Before Paul goes into detail in his teaching on the rapture, he makes an important point that accentuates his authority for laying out this teaching. He states, "This we say to you by the word of the Lord" (1 Thessalonians 4:15). In other words, "This truth I am about to share comes not from me, but by divine revelation." Remember, there was no New Testament in those early days of the Christian church. Consequently, God gave the gift of prophecy to certain apostles and prophets for the edification of the saints. This is one such truth, and it was included within the New Testament Scriptures so that Christians of all ages could benefit and be comforted by it.

So what are the specific details we can know about the rapture?

The Resurrection Shout Heard Around the World

"The Lord Himself will descend from heaven with a shout" (1 Thessalonians 4:16). This is obviously the shout of resurrection. Jesus will descend from heaven to an area above the earth but below heaven. It should be comforting to realize this resurrection shout is an "experienced" shout, for while the Lord was on the earth, He called at least three people back to life: a small girl, the daughter of Jairus; a widow's son in the city of Nain; and the most astounding miracle of all—the raising of His friend Lazarus after he had been dead for four days and was already decaying. All responded to the Lord's call, demonstrating that His resurrection voice indeed has the power to raise the dead—a fact witnessed by many people (John 11:1-45). There is no question that Jesus Christ's resurrection shout will be more than sufficient to raise all believers from throughout all the ages and to transform those who are alive on earth at the time of His coming.

With the Voice of the Archangel

Michael the archangel will once again help lead the children of Israel, as he did in the Old Testament. But this time He will lead them through the seven-year Tribulation. The events of this time period are described in both Daniel and Revelation.

The Trumpet of God

"The trumpet of God" (verse 16) refers to the judgments that are about to come upon the world (there are at least 21 of them). These are described in Revelation chapters 6–19.

The Dead in Christ Will Rise First

Not only will the dead in Christ be remembered in the rapture, their resurrection will precede that of the believers who are alive on earth at the time.

Living Believers Will Be Transformed and Receive Glorified Bodies

This is the resurrection Paul talked about in 1 Corinthians 15:50-57, when our corruptible bodies (those inherited from Adam which are in a constant state of dying) will be changed and made incorruptible, just like Christ's resurrected body, which is immortal and eternal, thus giving us victory over sin and death.

Both Groups Will Be Caught Up Together in the Clouds

It is in the original text of 1 Thessalonians 4:17 that we find the Greek word *harpadzo*, which means "caught up," or as some translate it, "snatched up together in the clouds." Some opponents of the doctrine of the rapture love to point out that the word *rapture* does not appear in the original Greek text. What they fail to realize is the true meaning of the Greek word *harpadzo* is indeed "rapture." Proof is found in the fact that Jerome, in the fourth century, when constructing his translation of the Bible, used the word *rapturo*. From that point on it became the favorite word used to describe the event in which Jesus snatches up both dead and living believers into the clouds. How long that meeting will be, we are not told. I would think that our merciful Lord will give us sufficient time to reconnect with our loved ones prior to moving on to the most exciting event in all of history...

We Will Meet the Lord in the Air

Our scheduled meeting with Jesus will be above the clouds,

but not in heaven as such—that will come later. We will meet in the heavenlies, or what we know as the atmospheric heavens above the earth. Have you ever wondered what that first meeting with the resurrected Christ will be like? Have you ever contemplated what you would say to Him in that moment? This won't be the Judgment Seat of Christ, where we hope to hear Him say, "Well done, good and faithful servant." That comes later, when He takes us to heaven. At this first meeting, we may have only a moment to greet Him. Now think—what would you say? I think I know what I would say: "Thank you, Lord, for saving my soul and letting me be part of your incredible rapture and eternal future!" And then it gets even better...

We Will Always Be with the Lord

Paul wrote that "we shall always be with the Lord" (1 Thessalonians 4:17). What's more, Jesus revealed to His servant John, at the beginning of the book of Revelation, that we believers have no cause to worry about the future. He said, "Do not be afraid; I am the First and the Last. I am He who lives, and was dead, and behold, I am alive forevermore...And I have the keys of Hades [the place of all departing souls] and of Death." What better guarantee could we have about the future—our eternal future—than the personal guarantee of the Son of God, who died for our sins and rose again? And remember, He said, "Heaven and earth will pass away, but My words will by no means pass away" (Matthew 24:35).

Rapture: The Supreme Word of Comfort

The apostle Paul then admonished the Thessalonian Christians to "comfort one another with these words" (1 Thessalonians 4:18). This "comfort of the rapture," which it has often been called, reveals itself every time we attend a believer's funeral. No other religious faith has anything similar to offer grieving believers who remain here on earth. Not only have I shared this comfort at hundreds of funerals myself, as nearly all Bible-believing pastors do, I have noticed that some liberal Christians and even amillennialists use it also. The reason is because their poems and pious platitudes of unbelief won't cut it when you enter into the chapel of death.

I experienced that comfort personally when my father died suddenly from a heart attack three weeks before my tenth birthday. I was devastated. I wept until I had no more tears, and could not be comforted until we arrived at the cemetery. The minister who conducted the service had led my parents to Christ six years earlier. I will never forget the moment when he put his hand on the casket and said, based on Paul's great passage above, "The world has not heard the last of Frank LaHaye." Then pointing to heaven, the minister said, "The day is coming when Jesus will shout from heaven and the dead will rise from their graves, and will be transformed and resurrected. And together we will be taken up to be with Jesus in the rapture."

As the pastor was speaking he pointed upward, and suddenly some sunlight burst through an opening in that overcast Michigan sky and entered my young heart. That was the first time I realized that one day I would see my father again! On that day, the "blessed hope" of Christ's return for His children was born into me and has never left. I want everyone to accept Him as the Lord and Savior of their life and to enjoy the blessed confidence of knowing that when He shouts from heaven to rapture His own, that they will not be left behind.

4

THE SECOND COMING: A TWO-PHASED EVENT

Tim LaHaye

Two thousand years ago, Jesus Christ promised to take His church to His Father's house (John 14:1-3). This event is known as the second coming or second advent. However, there are some who hold to the confusing and erroneous belief that the rapture and the glorious appearing of Jesus are the same event or occur simultaneously. Those who make a practice of taking the Bible literally (which should be the norm except when the context clearly indicates otherwise) recognize that it's impossible for the rapture and glorious appearing to happen at the same time. If one were to take all of the biblical accounts of the second coming into consideration, it becomes clear that the second coming has two distinct phases: first the rapture, when Christ comes in the air to take His church to His Father's house; then the glorious appearing, when Christ returns visibly to earth to destroy the followers of Antichrist and to establish His 1000-year millennial kingdom. The apostle Paul seems to make that distinction when teaching about the second coming in Titus 2.

The Blessed Hope and the Glorious Appearing

In Titus 2:12-13, Paul wrote that "we should live soberly, righteously, and godly in the present age, looking for the

blessed hope and glorious appearing of our great God and Savior Jesus Christ." Note his references to "the blessed hope" and
"glorious appearing." These two very different events will be
separated by the seven-year Tribulation, as the prophet Daniel
foretold in Daniel 9. Those who believe the rapture will occur
before the Tribulation and the glorious appearing will occur
afterward are often accused by critics of advocating two second
comings. But that isn't correct. At the rapture, Christ comes in
the air above the earth and calls His church up to the heavens.
By contrast, at the glorious appearing, Christ will come physically to the earth.

There are at least 15 distinct differences between Christ's
coming in the air for His church and His appearing on earth
for the whole world to see. Each event has a different purpose.
The rapture, of course, will take place in the air and sets the
stage for the Tribulation. The glorious appearing, however,
will bring the Tribulation to a close and begin Jesus' 1000-year
reign upon earth. The following chart lists the various elements of the rapture and the glorious appearing and demonstrates they are clearly two different events.

I am persuaded the apostle Paul had these two separate
phases of the Lord's second coming in mind when he wrote to
his young friend Titus, whom tradition suggests was the lead
pastor to the Christian churches on the isle of Cyprus. The
"blessed hope" is an apt description of Christ coming for His
church at the rapture ("hope" in Titus 2:13 really means "confidence," for Paul is not speaking of something merely wished
for, but a confident expectation of Jesus' future return for His
church).

In 1 Thessalonians 4, Paul's description of the rapture was
designed to bring comfort to those who had lost loved ones
prior to Christ's return. The glorious appearing, on the other
hand, features Jesus coming to the earth as King of kings and
Lord of lords to end the Tribulation and to set up His 1000-
year kingdom. Both events are part of the second coming of
Jesus, yet neither encompasses the event in its totality.

The first phase of the second coming is the rapture. That's
when believers "who are asleep" in Jesus (those who have died)

THE 15 DIFFERENCES BETWEEN THE RAPTURE AND THE GLORIOUS APPEARING

Rapture / Blessed Hope	Glorious Appearing
1. Christ comes in the air for His own *1 Thessalonians 4:14-17*	1. Christ comes with His own to earth *Revelation 19:11-16*
2. Rapture/translation of all Christians *1 Thessalonians 4:16-17; 1 Corinthians 15:50-54*	2. No one raptured
3. Christians taken to the Father's house *John 14:1-3*	3. Resurrected saints do not see Father's house
4. No judgment on earth	4. Christ judges inhabitants of earth *Matthew 25:31-46*
5. Church taken to heaven *1 Thessalonians 4:16-17*	5. Christ sets up His kingdom on earth *Revelation 19–20*
6. Imminent—could happen any moment *Matthew 24:42-44*	6. Cannot occur for at least 7 years *Daniel 9:26-29*
7. No signs	7. Many signs for Christ's physical coming *Matthew 24:3-36*
8. For believers only *1 Thessalonians 4:14*	8. Affects all humanity *Revelation 1:7*
9. A time of joy *Titus 2:13; 1 Thessalonians 2:19-20; 4:18*	9. Time of mourning *Revelation 1:7*
10. Before the "day of wrath" (Tribulation) *Revelation 3:10; 1 Thessalonians 5:8-9*	10. Immediately after Tribulation *Matthew 24:29-36*
11. No mention of Satan	11. Satan bound in abyss for 1000 years *Revelation 19:20–20:3*
12. The judgment seat of Christ *1 Corinthians 4:5; 2 Corinthians 5:9-10*	12. No time or place for judgment seat of Christ
13. Marriage of the Lamb *Revelation 19:7-10*	13. His bride as an army descends with Him *Revelation 19:11-14; Jude 14*
14. Only His own see Him *1 Thessalonians 4:14-17*	14. Every eye will see Him *Revelation 1:7*
15. Tribulation begins *Matthew 24:9-32; 2 Thessalonians 2:3-12*	15. 1000-year kingdom of Christ begins (Great White Throne) *Revelation 19:11-15; 20:4-6*

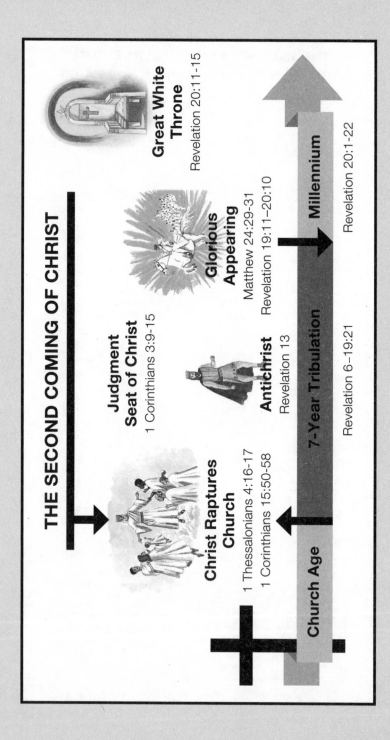

THE SECOND COMING OF CHRIST

Christ Raptures Church
1 Thessalonians 4:16-17
1 Corinthians 15:50-58

Judgment Seat of Christ
1 Corinthians 3:9-15

Antichrist
Revelation 13

Glorious Appearing
Matthew 24:29-31
Revelation 19:11—20:10

Great White Throne
Revelation 20:11-15

Church Age

7-Year Tribulation
Revelation 6—19:21

Millennium
Revelation 20:1-22

will be taken up in the air and then joined by believers who are alive at that moment. They will all be transformed and given new, glorified bodies (1 Corinthians 15:50-58). Then Jesus will take these believers to the Father's house to be with Him forever. Meanwhile, those who are left behind on the earth will experience what the prophets and the Lord Himself describe as the worst seven-year period in the history of the world. "There will be great tribulation, such as has not been since the beginning of the world until this time, no, nor ever shall be" (Matthew 24:21).

This horrific period will culminate with the return of Jesus to the earth, or the second phase of the second coming, which Paul labels the "glorious appearing." It's obvious these two phases are not the same and cannot occur at the same time. The blessed hope, or rapture, is for believers only and occurs prior to the Tribulation, whereas the glorious appearing occurs at the end of that seven-year period and includes unbelievers who will be judged for rejecting Christ.

Two Distinctly Separate Phases

When we carefully examine the 15 differences between the rapture of the church and the glorious appearing, it becomes very clear that the two cannot possibly occur simultaneously. They are two distinctly different events. First is the second coming of Christ for His church. Then seven or so years later will come the glorious appearing, in which Christ defeats the rebellious armies of the world, casts the Antichrist and false prophet into the lake of fire, and binds Satan for 1000 years so the world can enjoy peace, prosperity, and blessing. All this is made possible for believers by Jesus Christ, who made salvation from sin possible for us through the sacrificial gift of Himself on the cross.

In several of my books I have included this list of 15 differences, and to date I have not received a single letter that attempts to explain away these clear-cut distinctions. Of all the differences on the chart, I believe number six is the most telling. That's because the rapture could take place at any moment, for it is imminent. Not so for the glorious appearing. It cannot occur till after Israel and the Antichrist sign their covenant and, three-and-a-half years later, the Antichrist desecrates the temple in Jerusalem (Daniel 9:27). What could be more different than a rapture that could occur at any time, and a glorious appearing that cannot happen until the end of the seven-year Tribulation?

That is why we share Christ with as many people as possible—so they will be ready at any time for the rapture, when the "last trumpet" for the church is sounded (see 1 Corinthians 15:51-58). While no one knows "that day and hour" (Matthew 24:36), we certainly can recognize the "season" in which we are now living.

A HISTORY OF THE RAPTURE TEACHING

Thomas Ice

Critics of the pretribulation view of the last days frequently state that belief in the rapture is a doctrinal development of recent origin. They argue that the doctrine of the rapture or any semblance of it was completely unknown before the early 1800s and the writings of John Nelson Darby. While it is clear that pretribulationism was not widely known since the days of the New Testament writers, there have been clear examples of some form of pretribulationism sprinkled throughout church history.

We need to deal with the history of the rapture not because it is the basis for determining truth, which can only be found in Scripture alone, but because these issues are often at the heart of the criticisms brought against the pretribulation view. Dr. Charles Ryrie has rightly said, "The fact that the church taught something in the first century does not make it true, and likewise if the church did not teach something until the twentieth century, it is not necessarily false."[1] Norman Geisler notes that "heresies can be early, even in apostolic times (cf. 1 Timothy 4 and 1 John 4), and [re]discovery of some truths can be later [like pretrib]."[2] With this in mind, a careful study of church history shows that the pretribulation rapture position has historical precedent well before Darby.

Finding the Rapture in History

What do we look for as we examine the historical record of the church in regard to pretribulationism? Pretrib rapture critic William Bell has formulated four criteria for establishing the validity of a historical citation regarding pretribulationism. If any of his four criteria are met, then he acknowledges such a reference is "of crucial importance, if found, whether by direct statement or clear inference." The criteria are as follows:

1. Any mention that Christ's second coming was to consist of more than one phase, separated by an interval of years

2. Any mention that Christ was to remove the church from the earth before the tribulation period

3. Any reference to the resurrection of the just as being in two stages

4. Any indication that Israel and the church were to be clearly distinguished, thus providing some rationale for a removal of Christians before God "again deals with Israel."[3]

Bell's criteria will be used to evaluate proposed pre-Darby rapture statements.

The Shepherd of Hermas

An ancient writing known as *The Shepherd of Hermas* (ca. AD 140) speaks of a possible pretribulational concept of escaping the tribulation:

> You have escaped from great tribulation on account of your faith, and because you did not doubt in the presence of such a beast. Go, therefore, and tell the elect of the Lord His mighty deeds, and say to them that this beast is a type of the great tribulation that is coming. If then ye prepare yourselves, and repent with all your heart, and turn to the Lord, it will be

possible for you to escape it, if your heart be pure
and spotless, and ye spend the rest of the days of
your life in serving the Lord blamelessly.[4]

While Hermas clearly speaks of escaping the tribulation, pretribulationists and non-pretribulationists tend to agree that he does not articulate a clear message similar to modern pretribulationism. Pretrib scholar John Walvoord argued that the central feature of pretribulationism is the doctrine of imminency, and that it is "a prominent feature of the doctrine of the early church."[5]

Irenaeus

Some have thought the following words from Irenaeus (c. 180) could be taken as a pretrib rapture statement because he actually speaks of the rapture: "the church shall be suddenly caught up from this [the tribulation]," as noted below:

And therefore, when in the end the church shall be
suddenly caught up from this, it is said, "There shall
be tribulation such as has not been since the beginning, neither shall be." For this is the last contest of
the righteous, in which, when they overcome they
are crowned with incorruption.[6]

However, the very next statement speaks of believers in the Tribulation. When taken within the context of all of Irenaeus' writings on these subjects, it appears that he was not teaching pretribulationism even though he held to imminency.

Imminency in the Early Church

Pretribulationists such as Charles Ryrie define imminency as something that is "'impending, hanging over one's head, ready to take place.' An imminent event is one that is always ready to take place."[7] Some have recognized that it is common for ante-Nicene writers to speak of an imminent return of Christ, especially during the first century after the apostles.[8] Patristic scholar Larry Crutchfield argues that the early church fathers believed in what he calls "imminent intratribulationism." He summarizes the views of pretribulational scholars on this issue as follows:

> In sum, with few exceptions, the premillennial fathers of the early church believed that they were living in the last times. Thus they looked daily for the Lord's return. Even most of those who looked for Antichrist's appearance prior to the second advent, saw that event as occurring suddenly and just as suddenly being followed by the rescue and rapture of the saints by Christ...This belief in the imminent return of Christ within the context of ongoing persecution has prompted us to broadly label the views of the earliest fathers, imminent intratribulationism...
>
> It should be noted that dispensationalists have neither said that the early church was clearly pretribulational nor that there are even clear individual statements of pretribulationism in the fathers. As Walvoord says, "The historical fact is that the early church fathers' view on prophecy did not correspond to what is advanced by pretribulationists today except for the one important point that both subscribe to the imminency of the rapture." This view of the fathers on imminency and in some the references to escaping the time of the tribulation constitute what may be termed, to borrow a phrase from Erickson, "seeds from which the doctrine of the pretribulational rapture could be developed..." Had it not been for the drought brought by Alexandrian allegorism and later by Augustine, one wonders what kind of crop those seeds might have yielded—before Darby and the nineteenth century.[9]

Historian Kurt Aland also sees in the early church an imminent expectation of the Lord's return:

> Up until the middle of the second century, and even later, Christians did not live in and for the present, but they lived in and for the future; and

this was in such a way that the future flowed into the present, that future and present became one—a future which obviously stood under the Lord's presence. It was the confident expectation of the first generations that the end of the world was not only near, but that it had really already come. It was the definite conviction not only of Paul, but of all Christians of that time, that they themselves would experience the return of the Lord.[10]

Aland sees the decline of a true imminence that began around AD 150:

> As soon as the thought of a postponement of the Parousia was uttered once—and indeed not only incidentally, but thoroughly presented in an entire writing—it developed its own life and power. At first, people looked at it as only a brief postponement, as the Shepherd of Hermas clearly expresses. But soon, as the end of the world did not occur, it was conceived of as a longer and longer period, until finally—this is today's situation—nothing but the thought of a postponement exists in people's consciousness. Hardly any longer is there the thought of the possibility of an imminent Parousia. Today we live with the presumption—I would almost say *from* the presumption—that this world is going to continue; it dominates our consciousness. Practically, we no longer speak about a postponement, but only seldom does the idea of the end of the world and the Lord's return for judgment even occur to us; rather, it is pushed aside as annoying and disturbing—in contrast to the times when faith was alive. It is very characteristic that in ages when the church flourishes, the expectation of the end revives—we think of Luther; we think of Pietism, if we judge our present time by its expectation of the future.[11]

Posttribulationists like J. Barton Payne also admit that the early fathers held to an imminency viewpoint. He surmises:

It must therefore be concluded that the denial of the imminence of the Lord's coming on the part of post-tribulationists who have reacted against dispensationalism is not legitimate...

Belief in the imminency of the return of Jesus was the uniform hope of the early church; and it was only with the rise of a detailed application of Bible prophecy, at the close of the second century, to yet future history that its truth was questioned.[12]

An Ancient End-times Sermon

A clear statement of the pretrib rapture position can be found as early as the fourth through seventh centuries AD. A sermon preached by Pseudo-Ephraem, entitled *On the Last Times, the Antichrist, and the End of the World* or *Sermon on the End of the World*, includes a concept very similar to that found in the pretrib rapture view more than 1000 years before the writings of Darby. The sermon is considered to be "one of the most interesting apocalyptic texts of the early Middle Ages."[13] The sermon contains just under 1500 words.

Concerning the timing of the rapture the sermon reads:

> We ought to understand thoroughly therefore, my brothers, what is imminent or overhanging...Why therefore do we not reject every care of earthly actions and prepare ourselves for the meeting of the Lord Jesus Christ, so that he may *draw us from* the confusion, which overwhelms all the world?... For all the saints and elect of God are gathered together *before the tribulation*, which is to come, and are taken to the Lord, in order that they may not see at any time the confusion which overwhelms the world because of our sins (emphasis added).[14]

Pseudo-Ephraem clearly presents at least three important features found in modern pretribulationism:

- there are two distinct comings: the return of Christ to rapture the saints, followed later by Christ's second advent to the earth,

- a defined interval between the two comings, in this case three-and-a-half years, and

- a clear statement that Christ will remove the church from the world before the Tribulation.[15]

The fact that Pseudo-Ephraem placed the rapture three-and-a-half years before the Tribulation is not an argument for midtribulationism because it appears that for him the whole Tribulation was only three-and-a-half years in duration. (Even Darby first believed that the rapture would occur three-and-a-half years before the second coming).[16] Therefore, we can assuredly say that the pretrib rapture position is not a recent view. It was held and preached possibly as early as AD 373.

Posttribulational scholar Bob Gundry wrote an objection to Pseudo-Ephraem's sermon as a pretrib statement. He concluded, "Pseudo-Ephraem urges Christians to forsake worldliness in preparation for meeting Christ when he returns after the great tribulation. Meanwhile Christian evangelism is taking people to the Lord and gathering them into the Church... This interpretation...[puts] the resurrection of Christians and their meeting Christ at his coming after the tribulation to destroy the Antichrist, making imminent the advent of Antichrist rather than that of Christ."[17]

In a rejoinder to Gundry's critique, I have noted that Gundry did not establish that Pseudo-Ephraem ever used "gather" in an evangelistic way as he contends. Further, the late Paul Alexander, the Byzantine scholar who first published this statement in one of his books,[18] "understood this disputed passage as a pretribulational transportation."[19]

Brother Dolcino

In AD 1260 a man named Gerard Sagarello (d. 1300) founded a group known as the Apostolic Brethren in northern Italy. He founded this order after he was turned down for membership by the Franciscan order.

At that time it was against church law to form a new ecclesiastical order, so the Apostolic Brethren were subjected to severe persecution. In 1300, Gerard was burned at the stake, and a man named Brother Dolcino[20] took over leadership of the movement. Under his guidance, the order grew and eventually numbered in the thousands. End-time prophecy evidently held an important place in the study and teachings of the Apostolic Brethren.

Brother Dolcino died in 1307, and in 1316 an anonymous notary of the diocese of Vercelli in northern Italy wrote a brief treatise in Latin that set forth the deeds and beliefs of the Apostolic Brethren. This treatise was called *The History of Brother Dolcino*. Francis Gumerlock, a non-pretribulationist, recently discovered Brother Dolcino's teaching on the rapture.

At one point in the treatise the following paragraph appears:

> Again, [Dolcino believed and preached and taught] that within those three years Dolcino himself and his followers will preach the coming of the Antichrist. And that the Antichrist was coming into this world within the bounds of the said three and a half years; and after he had come, then *he [Dolcino] and his followers would be transferred into Paradise*, in which are Enoch and Elijah. And in this way they will be *preserved unharmed from the persecution of Antichrist*. And that then Enoch and Elijah themselves would descend on the earth for the purpose of preaching [against] Antichrist. Then they would be killed by him or by his servants, and thus *Antichrist would reign for a long time*. But when the Antichrist is dead, Dolcino himself, who then would be the holy pope, and his preserved followers, will descend on the earth, and will preach the right faith of Christ to all, and will convert those who will be living then to the true faith of Jesus Christ."[21]

Several of the points in this statement are similar to concepts taught in modern pretribulationism:

- The Latin word *transferrentur*, meaning "they would be transferred," is the same word used by medieval Christians to describe the rapture of Enoch to heaven.

- The subjects of this rapture were to be Brother Dolcino and his followers. This was not a partial rapture theory because Brother Dolcino considered the Apostolic Brethren to be the true church in contrast to the Roman Catholic Church.

- The purpose of the rapture was to preserve the people from the persecution of the Antichrist.

- The text presents the "transference" of believers to heaven and the "descent" of believers from heaven as two separate events.

- The text shows that a long gap of time must intervene between the rapture of the saints to heaven and the return of the saints from heaven. [22]

Gumerlock clearly believes that this is a pretrib rapture statement. He concludes:

> This paragraph from *The History of Brother Dolcino* indicates that in northern Italy in the early fourteenth century a teaching very similar to modern pretribulationalism was being preached. Responding to distressing political and ecclesiastical conditions, Dolcino engaged in detailed speculations about eschatology and believed that the coming of the Antichrist was imminent. He also believed that the means by which God would protect His people from the persecution of the Antichrist would be through a translation of the saints to paradise. [23]

It appears that Joachimist scholar Marjorie Reeves also saw a rapture associated with Dolcino. She says of the Apostolic Brethren, "They would preach the immediate advent of Antichrist, and when he appeared Dolcino and his followers would be removed to Paradise, while Elijah and Enoch descended to combat. When Antichrist was disposed of, they would descend again to convert all nations." [24] The Dolcino statement very well appears to have presented some form of a two-stage coming, a rapture followed by a time of tribulation, then a return of those saints at the second coming. However, such a view falls short of Darby's developed form of a rapture within a dispensational, futurist framework.

Thomas Collier

Frank Marotta, a Brethren researcher, believes that Thomas Collier (d. 1691) in 1674 makes reference to a pretribulational rapture, but rejects the view,[25] thus showing his awareness that such a view was being taught in the late seventeenth century. Collier, in *The Body of Divinity*,[26] said the following:

> 7. *Quest.* At what time may we suppose the Saints shall be raised? at his first appearing in the Clouds of Heaven? or at the entrance of the thousand years? or after the thousand years are finished?
>
> *Ans.* Very probably at the entrance of the 1000 years, and that for these reasons.
>
> 1. Because it is not likely that they should be raised before the Nations are subdued and the new Heavens and new Earth prepared.
>
> 2. The Scripture saith, that it shall be at the sound of the last Trump...We may groundedly suppose that after Christ's appearing in the work, he may ascend and descend often.[27]

"Collier certainly *considered* the idea of a pretribulation rapture. If the saints were raised when Christ appears and this is prior to the fulfillment of the bulk of Revelation, it is pretribulational," explains Marotta. "Whether anyone actually held to the pretribulational view contemporary to Collier, or this was just an exercise of the mind, we cannot say."[28]

If Collier was making a pretrib rapture statement, it was hardly recognized as such at the time. It is true that Collier had a futurist view of Revelation, which was rare to nonexistent in his day. As Marotta says, "Collier was clearly posttribulational." Even if this were a pretrib statement, it had no known impact as such at the time.

John Asgill

There is the interesting case of John Asgill (1659–1738), who wrote a book in 1700 about the possibility of translation (i.e., rapture) without seeing death.[29] As a result, Asgill was removed from the Irish parliament in 1703 and then from the English parliament in 1707. "His book had been examined and pronounced blasphemous, and had been burnt by order of the House without his having been heard in its defense."[30] Asgill spent the last 30 years of his life in prison because of what he wrote. This would have thrown cold water on anyone else desiring to make known their thoughts on the rapture.

Asgill did not relate this possible any-moment translation to the Tribulation or any other prophetic event. Thus, his view could hardly be called any form of pretribulationism. William Bramley-Moore said, "He did not hold the truth in its relation to other truths. He was looking for an *individual* translation, on which he expressed himself somewhat strongly, and to which he did not attain; for he failed to understand that the promised change or translation of the saints is not to be that of solitary individuals, but of a corporate body."[31]

Morgan Edwards

One of the clearest references to a pretribulation rapture before the time of Darby came from a Welsh Baptist named Morgan Edwards (1722–1795). Edwards was born in Trevethin parish, Pontypool, Wales,[32] and likely heard George Whitfield preach as a young student at Trosnant Academy in Trevethin parish, Wales.[33] He graduated from Bristol Baptist College or Bristol Academy in Bristol, England, in 1744.[34] He served several small Baptist congregations in England for seven years before moving to Cork, Ireland, where he pastored for nine years. Edwards emigrated to America and in May 1761 became pastor of the Baptist Church in Philadelphia[35] upon the recommendation of the famous hyper-Calvinist John Gill (1697–1771).[36] After the Revolutionary War (he was the only known Baptist clergy of Tory persuasion), Edwards became an educator and the premier Baptist historian of his day. He was awarded an honorary MA degree in 1762 by the College of Philadel-phia.[37] His major text *Materials Toward a History of the Baptists* is an important seminal work outlining American Baptist history of the era.[38] Edwards cofounded the first Baptist college in the colonies, Rhode Island College, which we know today as Brown University.[39]

As was typical of early American colonists, Edwards experienced significant tragedy in his life. He outlived two wives and most of his children. During a dark period in his life, he ceased attending church, took to drinking, and was excommunicated from his church. "After making repeated efforts to be restored, he was received into the church on October 6, 1788, and thereafter lived an exemplary life."[40] Baptist historian Robert Torbet described Edwards as "a man of versatility, being both a capable leader for many years and a historian of some importance. In temperament he was eccentric and choleric...With all of his varied gifts, he was always evangelistic in spirit."[41] Another historian similarly says of Edwards:

> Scholarly, laborious, warm-hearted, eccentric, choleric Morgan Edwards, one of the most interesting of the early Baptist ministers of our country and one of those most deserving of honor. His very faults had a leaning toward virtues side, and in good works he was exceeded by none of his day, if indeed by any of any day...He was an able preacher and a good man, but not always an easy man to get on with.[42]

Edwards first wrote about his pretrib beliefs in 1742[43] as a student at Bristol College in order to fulfill an assignment. "I will do my possible: and in the attempt will work by a rule you have often recommended, viz. 'to take the scriptures in a literal sense, except when that leads to contradiction or absurdity.'... Very able men have already handled the subject in a mystical, or allegorical, or spiritual way."[44] Edwards' work was first written in Latin during his student days (1742), so years later when it was published (1788) he must have translated it into English verbatim, thus reflecting his thoughts from 1742.

Historian John Moore, quoting from Rev. William Rogers' sermon at Edwards' funeral, said, "There was nothing uncommon in Mr. Edwards' person; but he possessed an original genius."[45] So Edwards was an original thinker, and his views flowed from a literal reading of the Bible.

Almost a century before Darby developed and popularized a view of the second coming of Christ known as pretribulationism, or the view that Christian believers will be raptured or translated to heaven with Christ before the events of the Tribulation, Edwards taught an amazingly similar view. Like Darby, his views on this matter were developed during an early phase of his life.[46]

Edwards saw a distinct rapture three-and-a-half years before the start of the millennium. He taught the following about the rapture:

> II. *The distance between the first and second resurrection will be somewhat more than a thousand years.*
>
> I say, *somewhat more*—because the dead saints will be raised, and the living changed at Christ's "appearing in the air" (I Thes. iv. 17); and this will be about three years and a half before the millennium, as we shall see hereafter: but will he and they abide in the air all that time? No: they will ascend to paradise, or to some one of those many "mansions in the father's house" (John xiv. 2), and disappear during the foresaid period of time. The design of this retreat and disappearing will be to judge the risen and changed saints; for "now the time is come that judgment must begin," and that will be "at the house of God" (I Pet. iv. 17).[47]

Edwards made three key points that are consistent with modern pretribulationism. First, he clearly separated the rapture from the second coming by an interval of three-and-a-half years. Second, he used modern pretrib rapture verses (1 Thessalonians 4:17 and John 14:2) to describe the rapture and support his view. Third, he believed the judgment seat of Christ for believers' rewards will occur in heaven while the

Tribulation is raging on earth, as is commonly held in contemporary pretribulationism.

The main difference between Edwards and modern pretribulationism is Edwards' time interval of three-and-a-half years between the rapture and the second coming, instead of seven. As was noted earlier,[48] Jonathan Burnham pointed out that Darby held to a three-and-a-half year Tribulation until 1845. However, this does not mean Edwards was a midtribulationist. Rather, it appears he believed the total length of the Tribulation was three-and-a-half years.

Edwards reiterated his pretribulational stance when he said:

> 5. Another event previous to the *Millennium* will be the appearing of the son of man in the clouds, coming to raise the dead saints and change the living, and to catch them up to himself, and then withdraw with them, as observed before.[49] This event will come to pass when Antichrist be arrived at Jerusalem in his conquest of the world; and about three years and a half before his killing the witnesses and assumption of godhead.[50]

It is clear that Edwards separated the rapture and the second coming:

> 8. The last event, and the event that will usher in the *millennium*, will be, the coming of Christ from paradise to earth, with all the saints he had taken up thither (about three years and a half before) to justify, against the accuser of the brethren; and to settle their future businesses and rewards.[51]

> ...millions and millions of saints will have been on earth from the days of the first Adam, to the coming of the second Adam. All these will Christ bring with him. The place where they will alight is the "mount of Olives, which is before Jerusalem on the east" Zech. xiv, 4.[52]

Of interest is the fact Edwards penned 140 handwritten sermons that were never published.[53] Other than his historical writings and ecclesiastical helps, his essay on Bible prophecy was his only other published work. It is significant that this essay, written as a young man, was published and did not come from his later years of ministry. This evidences that as an older man he was still interested in the importance of the Lord's return. Thomas McKibbens and Kenneth Smith tell us that during 1788 (the same year that Edwards' book mentioning the rapture was published) "he began to lecture again throughout the Middle Colonies...The lectures were probably based upon subjects contained in two books published in 1788, *Res Sacrae: An Academical Exercise Composed in Latin in the Year 1742; and Now Translated into English* and *Two Academical Exercises on the Subjects Bearing the Following Titles; Millennium and Last-Novelties.*"[54]

Such a preaching tour would indicate that Edwards' pre-tribulationism was likely spread to some extent throughout Baptist circles, at least in the Middle Colonies. However, Baptists were not numerous in the earliest days of America,[55] so this likely had a limited impact. Also, the book had only one printing, demonstrating that there was not great demand for it. Nevertheless, Edwards' work on Bible prophecy did have some circulation and exposed some early Americans to ideas that would come to dominate evangelicalism a century later.

Edwards' book on the rapture was essentially lost for a time as far as any popular, public knowledge of it. It came to light in the 1990s in order to satisfy a challenge made by pretrib opponent John Bray, who promised to pay $500 to anyone "who will furnish me with a documented statement by anybody (in a sermon, article or commentary) in any country, published BEFORE LACUNZA'S TIME," which would be 1812.[56] Bray acknowledged that the Edwards material satisfied his challenge and on March 21, 1995 he mailed a $500 check to an individual who showed him Edwards' book.[57]

Edwards' pre-Darby rapture statements are receiving increased recognition in the scholarly world. Burnham, in his Oxford University PhD thesis, said, "Darby was certainly not the first theologian to advance pretribulational premillennialism. As a recent study has revealed, Morgan Edwards, the founder of Brown University in Rhode Island, has articulated the concept during the eighteenth century, well before Darby and contemporaries."[58]

I searched about a dozen of the leading libraries in the United Kingdom in person and could not find a single copy of Edwards' book.[59] Not even the British Library had a copy. Further, I searched the online catalogues of every library in the United Kingdom that had an electronic catalog and did not find a single copy listed. However, a copy was easily found in the United States, where the book was published. I was able to get a photocopy of it at the Library of Congress in Washington, DC.[60] Even though Edwards' view of the rapture is similar at many points to what Darby developed, there does not appear to be any reliance by Darby on American sources. It is interesting that Edwards developed his view in Britain, but he does not appear to have left any traces of it behind.[61]

Interesting New Research on Rapture History

Ever since the discovery of Edwards' teaching on the pretrib rapture in 1742—which effectively put to death the false charge that John Darby was the inventor and teacher of the concept beginning around 1827—additional writers and researchers have found further evidence of other earlier Bible teachers who shared this view.

For example, Dr. William Watson, PhD, a well-trained, careful researcher and writer, has discovered that others throughout church history have also found rapture teachings in Scripture. He has consented to allow us to publish this interesting chart of some of his discoveries, which indicates this was not an unknown body of thought to scholars of the Middle Ages. We are confident that future research will reveal more of such findings.

A Right Understanding of the Origins of Rapture Teaching

The idea that the pretrib rapture is a recent invention is

English Words Usage / Concept of Rapture

"Rapt"		"Rapture"		"Left Behind"	
Vernon Manuscript	1320s?	Joseph Mede	1627	Robert Maton	1642
John Lydgate	1420	Nathaniel Homes	1653	Thomas Vincent	1667
William Bond	1531	Capt. John Browne	1654	author of *Theopolis*	1672
Thomas Draxe	1613	William Sherwin	1665–1700	Oliver Heywood	1700
Barton Holyday	1626	Cotton Mather	1726		
George Walker	1638	John Gill	1748		

Separate appearance in clouds well before Earth		Saints to heaven for safety, escaping troubles	
Epraim Huit	1643	Elizabeth Avery	1647
Samuel Hutchinson	1646	Peter Sterry	1648
		Nathaniel Homes	1653
		John Aspinwall	1653
		John Brown	1654
		Timothy Rogers	1702

Note: Although "rapt" and "rapture" can refer to a spiritual or emotional experience of being "swept up into heaven," those listed here are only those instances of a physical, corporeal "sweeping up" within the context of Matthew 24 or 1 Thessalonians 4–5.

Use of the words "Left Behind" is within the context of the rapture mentioned in Matthew 24 or 1 Thessalonians 4–5.

Chart created by William C. Watson, PhD, Colorado Christian University, 2011. Used with permission.

a well-worn straw-man argument. It's incorrect, and pretrib opponents should stop using it. Francis Gumerlock, a Latin scholar, has said via e-mail that he has three file drawers full of ancient antecedents to the pretrib rapture, mainly from the Middle Ages. He simply has not had time to translate all of them yet. Norman Geisler says, "...heresies can be early, even in apostolic times (cf. 1 Tim. 4 and 1 Jn, 4), and [re]discovery of some truths can be later [like pretrib]. The final question is not whether the early Fathers held it but whether the New Testament taught it."[62] A person may choose to reject the pretrib rapture position on other grounds, but no rejection of this view should be based on the faulty, mistaken argument that pretribulationism was invented in the 1830s by Darby.

6

THE DOCTRINE OF AN IMMINENT RAPTURE

Wayne A. Brindle

C hristians of the Apostolic period (AD 33–100) expected Jesus to return imminently, which means that Jesus can return for His church at any moment, and no predicted event must necessarily precede His return.[1] As Renald Showers notes, "Other things *may* happen before the imminent event, but nothing else *must* take place before it happens. If something else must take place before an event can happen, that event is not imminent."[2] Showers also points out three other significant things about an imminent event: (1) Since we do not know how much time will elapse before the imminent event, we should be ready for it to happen at any moment; (2) we cannot set a date for it to occur; and (3) we cannot say that it has to happen soon (implying a short period of time). The rapture was "just as imminent when the New Testament was written as it is today."[3]

A few posttribulationists have claimed that the Tribulation, with its accompanying signs (see Matthew 24), has already occurred, and so the second coming can indeed occur at any time. Others say that the Bible does not teach imminency in any sense. Most try to redefine the concept, saying imminency does not mean "any moment," but only that Christ's return "*could* take place within any limited period of time."[4] This, of course, is not the way the New Testament describes the rapture.

Does the Bible Teach Imminency?

How would we know whether a Bible passage teaches that the rapture will occur imminently, or whether it is simply saying that Jesus will return someday? There are four criteria that could be used, any of which may indicate imminency:

1. Christ's return is said to be able to occur "at any moment" or that we can expect it to occur "at any moment."

2. Christ's return is described as giving believers hope or encouragement, without any mention that they will suffer tribulation before it occurs.

3. Christ's return is depicted as giving hope to believers without being specifically related to God's judgment.

4. Christ's return is said to be "near," with no signs necessarily preceding His coming.

On the contrary, when Matthew 24–25 says the return of Christ will rescue the "elect" from tribulation and certain death, it does not specifically prove imminency, since the tribulation might have to precede the "rescue." Revelation 6–19 predicts signs that will precede Christ's physical return to this earth, and thus also does not depict imminency. In this chapter we will look at biblical teaching that clearly shows Christ can return at any moment without the need for any preceding signs to be fulfilled.[5]

What Did Jesus Say About Imminency?

JOHN 14:1-3

> Let not your heart be troubled; you believe in God, believe also in Me. In My Father's house are many

mansions; if it were not so, I would have told you. I
go to prepare a place for you. And if I go and prepare a place for you, I will come again and receive
you to Myself; that where I am, there you may be
also.

Most scholars interpret Jesus' statement as referring to the
same event described later by the apostle Paul in 1 Thessalonians 4, which today is known as the rapture. When Jesus
said, "I go" and "if I go," He was not speaking metaphorically
of His coming death or even His resurrection, but rather to a
literal departure in which he would bodily ascend to heaven
(Acts 1:11). The statement that follows—"I will come again to
receive you to Myself"—similarly refers to a bodily and literal
return from heaven to earth (not a mystical coming by Christ
to believers at the time of their death[6] or as the Holy Spirit).

Jesus made it clear that when He returns, He will take
believers to be with Him forever in His "Father's house," which
is surely a reference (ultimately) to heaven. The "many mansions" are located in the Father's house, and thus in heaven.
And in verses 2-3, Jesus said He will "prepare a place" for
believers in His "Father's house."[7] Then, sometime after that
He will "come again" and "receive" them "to Myself." Where
will He take them? "Where I am." And where is that?

This question can be answered by looking at the clues Jesus
gave in His statement. Jesus referred twice to "prepar[ing] a
place" in heaven. This statement would be irrelevant if He was
not planning to take believers there when He receives them to
Himself. The context forces us to conclude He is planning to
take them to heaven—the same place where He will be.

In verse 4 Jesus said, "Where I go you know, and the way
you know." Was Jesus being intentionally misleading here? If
not, then we have to assume He is still referring to heaven. In
fact, when Thomas asked a question about "the way" (verse 5),
Jesus answered that no one is able to go "to the Father except
through Me" (verse 6).

So Jesus said He would go to heaven (at His ascension),
later return to earth (bodily and literally) for His people, and

then (at the rapture) take them (literally) to heaven to be with Him.

Now we can relate this to the preceding chapter, John 13. The disciples had reacted in fear to Jesus' teaching about His coming departure. When Jesus said, "Where I am going you cannot follow Me now, but you shall follow Me afterward," Peter replied, "Lord, why can I not follow You now?" (verses 36-37). This induced Jesus to introduce His statements about the rapture with "Let not your heart be troubled." Jesus presented the rapture as an antidote to their fears. The truth about the coming rapture would be a great encouragement (a "blessed hope," Titus 2:13) to them as they contemplated His soon departure back to the Father.[8] There is no reference here to any trials or tribulation from which this rapture would rescue them. No signs are mentioned that would precede Christ's return. The disciples would be reunited with their Lord, culminating in their being eternally at home with Jesus and the Father.

This passage "cannot refer to Christ's second [glorious appearing] coming to the earth, since at that time Christ will rule on earth rather than return to heaven with His people."[9] At the second coming (glorious appearing), no one is said to go from earth to heaven.[10] The tribulational and millennial events related in Matthew 24–25 and Revelation 19–20 cannot be connected to John 14:1-3, and there is no suggestion in John 14 of an intervening event.

REVELATION 22:7,12,20

"Behold, I am coming quickly! Blessed is he who keeps the words of the prophecy of this book."... "And behold, I am coming quickly, and My reward is with Me, to give to every one according to his work."...He who testifies to these things says, "Surely I am coming quickly." Amen. Even so, come, Lord Jesus!

In Revelation 22 the apostle John quoted Jesus three times as saying that He is "coming quickly."[11] After describing the grand sweep of the Tribulation and Christ's glorious return to conquer His enemies, followed by a glorious kingdom and the final defeat of Satan and all rebels for all time, Jesus finished off His revelation with repeated exhortations to be ready because He is coming to give everyone a reward according to His work.

The Greek word *tachus* is an adjective meaning "quick" or "swift." The adverbial form, *tachu*, used here, carries two major meanings: (1) "quickly, without delay," and (2) "in a short time, soon."[12] This has created a problem of interpretation since, if we take Christ's promises literally, it appears to some that He was mistaken when He said He was coming back "quickly."[13] Commentators differ on how to solve this problem,[14] but most likely Jesus was describing the rapture as imminent and ready to occur "at any moment." The word "quickly" refers to the *suddenness* of Christ's coming whenever it happens to occur.

There is a related promise in Revelation 16:15: "I am coming as a thief." G.K. Beale has suggested this includes the idea of a "swift, unexpected appearance," describing the "possibility that Jesus could come at any time."[15] That these promises refer to an imminent rapture is made even more certain by the reference in 22:12 to Christ bringing rewards based on works, as at the Judgment Seat of Christ (2 Corinthians 5:10-11).

What Did Paul Say About Imminency?

1 Corinthians 1:7

> ...so that you come short in no gift, eagerly waiting
> for the revelation of our Lord Jesus Christ.

At the beginning of some of his epistles, Paul thanked God for the good things he had heard about the churches to whom he was writing (see Ephesians 1:15-16; Colossians 1:3-4; 1 Thessalonians 1:2-4; 2 Thessalonians 1:3). In 1 Corinthians, in the midst of such a thanksgiving focusing on the believers' wealth of spiritual gifts (they "come short in no gift"), he reminded them that they were "eagerly waiting" for the revelation or "unveiling" (*apokalypsis*) of Jesus Christ. The verb "await eagerly"[16] (*apekde-chomai*) always refers to Christian hope in the New Testament,[17] and Paul used it only in connection with prophecy.[18]

Why the reminder? Paul wanted to refocus their expectation on Christ, rather than on themselves. They were "eagerly expecting" Christ at any moment, in an imminent rapture. The Greek word *apokalypsis* ("revelation") refers at different times in the New Testament to either the rapture (1 Peter 1:7,13; 4:13) or the second coming (Romans 8:19; 2 Thessalonians 1:7). Where no intervening signs are mentioned (as here), an imminent rapture is most likely. The statement that they were watching to see an unveiled Christ as He really is echoes 1 John 3:2, a clear rapture passage, where John wrote that the church will "see Him as He is."

1 THESSALONIANS 1:9-10

> They themselves declare concerning us what manner of entry we had to you, and how you turned to God from idols to serve the living and true God, and to wait for His Son from heaven, whom He raised from the dead, even Jesus who delivers us from the wrath to come.

When Paul first visited Thessalonica, many of his hearers "turned to God from idols"—that is, they responded by faith to the gospel of Christ and became born-again Christians. Now they were serving "the living and true God" as they waited for Christ to return from heaven. One day, Jesus would appear out of heaven and deliver them "from the wrath to come."

Since Christ's appearance "out of heaven" is described in 4:15-17 as the rapture (being "caught up" with Christ in the air), this "wrath to come" must be the same wrath depicted in 5:3,9, the wrath of the prophesied Tribulation.[19] The prophetic issue that Paul discussed in both Thessalonian epistles is the Day of the Lord, which will precede and lead up to Christ's second coming.

In what way will believers be rescued from this wrath? Paul said they would be delivered "from," "out of," or "away from" the coming wrath,[20] pointing to a deliverance *before* the wrath began. The preposition "emphasizes the completeness of the deliverance."[21] This passage thus argues strongly that Paul believed in an imminent rapture.

Some scholars object that because the participle translated "Jesus who delivers us" is present tense, this must be interpreted as a progressive, current deliverance from God's present wrath. However, this type of substantival participle can be considered timeless.[22]

F.F. Bruce said "the participle plays the part of a *nomen agentis*, 'our deliverer'" (see the same expression in Romans 11:26—"The Deliverer will come out of Zion").[23] It could also be taken as futuristic—"Jesus who will deliver us." Interpreting it this way would correspond well to the final phrase, "the wrath to come," which is also a participle—literally, "the coming wrath," which is clearly futuristic. This highlights a close connection between the future deliverance and the fact that the object of the deliverance is itself a wrath that is still coming.

This passage seems to be a summary of the eschatological teaching that Paul had given the infant Thessalonian church shortly after its founding. He further explained it in chapters 4 and 5.

1 THESSALONIANS 5:1-9

> Concerning the times and the seasons, brethren, you have no need that I should write to you. For you yourselves know perfectly that the day of the Lord so comes as a thief in the night. For when they say, "Peace and safety!" then sudden destruction comes upon them, as labor pains upon a pregnant woman. And they shall not escape. But you, brethren, are not in darkness, so that this Day should overtake you as a thief. You are all sons of light and sons of the day. We are not of the night nor of darkness. Therefore let us not sleep, as others do, but let us watch and be sober. For those who sleep, sleep at night, and those who get drunk are drunk at night. But let us who are of the day be sober, putting on the breastplate of faith and love, and as a helmet

the hope of salvation. For God did not appoint us to wrath, but to obtain salvation through our Lord Jesus Christ.

Before discussing the Day of the Lord, Paul assured the Thessalonian believers that they knew "the times and the seasons" (5:1) and did not need him to give them any new information on this subject. For example, they knew "perfectly" well (accurately) that "the day of the Lord so comes [will come] as a thief in the night" (5:2). It will be a day of wrath—the "wrath to come" of 1:10—coming as suddenly and unexpectedly as "labor pains upon a pregnant woman" (5:3). Unbelievers will not escape.

The "destruction" of verse 3 speaks of the Tribulation as a whole, not the "vengeance" related specifically to Christ's second coming (2 Thessalonians 1:7-9) or the later Great White Throne judgment (Revelation 20:11-15). This is clear from the fact that the ones who suffer this destruction are quoted as saying, "Peace and safety!" just before it falls on them. It is hard to imagine that those who are living through the horrors of the last part of the Tribulation or are standing at God's last judgment would say anything like "peace and safety."[24] Jesus said that men's hearts will faint from fear during the Tribulation (Luke 21:25-27).

In 1 Thessalonians 5:4 Paul contrasted believers with those who will not escape. The Day of the Lord will overtake unbelievers because they are like the night (darkness—see John 3:19, "men loved darkness rather than light, because their deeds were evil"). On the other hand, believers will not be surprised, as they are "sons of light and sons of the day" (verse 5).[25] Paul makes it clear that the church *will* escape, given the strong contrast between the "you" (believers) in verses 1-2, 4-5, and the "they" (unbelievers) of verse 3 ("they shall not escape").

As they awaited that day, the Thessalonians were to be spiritually alert and self-controlled (verses 6-8), growing in faith and love, assured of salvation. This is the kind of life that is proper for the day (see Romans 13:12-13). People get drunk and sleep at night, but daytime should be characterized by alertness and soberness (see 1 Peter 5:8).[26] A key verse in support of the pretrib rapture is 1 Thessalonians 5:9, in which Paul clearly affirmed God did not appoint believers to suffer this eschatological wrath (the "wrath to come" of 1:10), but has instead destined them to "obtain salvation" through Christ. This salvation is defined in verse 10—that "we should live together" with Christ. The parallel to the deliverance of 1:10 and the "catching up" (rapture) of 4:17 ("thus we shall always be with the Lord") is so clear that it is astonishing anyone could miss it!

The Day of the Lord is a literal period of time that will stretch from the Tribulation through the millennial kingdom to the new heavens and earth (2 Peter 3:7-13). It will begin in the night, like a thief. Paul said the church is not of the night, but the day (1 Thessalonians 5:4-5,8). The church is always of the day, and unbelievers are of the night, destined to suffer God's wrath.[27]

In contrast to tribulational wrath, the church is appointed to receive God's salvation, whose purpose is that believers will "live together with Christ." The result is the same as the rapture (4:17), and even the exhortation ("therefore comfort each other"—5:11) is the same ("therefore comfort one another"—4:18). The rapture will include all living believers (4:17; 1 Corinthians 15:51), and Paul emphasized that it is the means of saving the church from the wrath of the Day of the Lord.

Some interpreters attempt to explain the deliverance in 1 Thessalonians as the martyrdom of believers during the Tribulation, in that they will be "set free" from earthly wrath. According to Matthew 24 and Revelation 6 and 13, many who come to faith during the Tribulation will indeed experience suffering and martyrdom before Christ returns. But this martyrdom will come from the hands of God's enemies—not from God Himself. Martyrdom cannot be thought of as delivery from God's wrath.

Indeed, if the church were to find itself in the Tribulation, then at least some of the church would not be delivered, since many believers would likely be martyred. This seems contrary to the teaching of 1 Thessalonians 1:10 and 5:9, where no exceptions to the deliverance are indicated. The promise of deliverance by rapture is for the entire church. A faithful Christian may be delivered during the Tribulation from his own weakness or from God's enemies, but not from God's "wrath to come." It would be too late for that. Given Paul's assurance that the church will be literally and truly delivered from the coming wrath, we must conclude that his exhortation to "watch and be sober" (5:6) and his promise that the church is not appointed to wrath (5:9) necessitate a rapture that can occur at any moment.

TITUS 2:13

> ...looking for the blessed hope and glorious appearing of our great God and Savior Jesus Christ.

Why does Paul describe Christ's return as "the blessed hope"? The term "blessed" (Greek, *makarios*) has a possible meaning of "happy"[28] (it is translated this way twice in the NKJV—Acts 26:2; Romans 14:22). Paul's par excellence terminology here presents the rapture, the Christian's ultimate hope, as a totally joyful expectation.

Because this passage also uses the word "appearing" (Greek, *epiphaneia*), some scholars think it refers to the glorious appearing phase of the second coming of Christ rather than the rapture. But in Paul's pastoral epistles, when the term refers to a future appearance of Christ (1 Timothy 6:14; 2 Timothy 4:1,8; Titus 2:13), it always presents the event as a happy and joyous expectation apart from signs or tribulation and thus should be interpreted as the rapture.

It is likewise argued by some that the phrase "glorious appearing" needs to be restricted to the second coming, since it must mean that Christ will present Himself as a glorious and exalted ruler to the entire world (Matthew 16:27; 19:28; 24:30; 25:31). However, although the world will not see Christ's glory until His physical appearing, the church will experience His glory (and be glorified) when it meets Him in the air (Romans

5:2; 8:18,30; 1 Corinthians 15:43; Philippians 3:21; Colossians 1:27; 3:4; 1 Peter 5:1; 1 John 3:2; Jude 24). For clarity's sake, nothing about the words "glorious appearing" should restrict this to the second phase of Christ's second coming.

In Titus 2:13, Paul exhorted believers to look for the rapture as the blessed, "happy" hope (expectation) for the church. The absence of any mention of signs or tribulation strongly implies its imminence. The rapture can occur at any time.[29]

What Did James and John Say About Imminency?

JAMES 5:7-9

> Be patient, brethren, until the coming of the Lord. See how the farmer waits for the precious fruit of the earth, waiting patiently for it until it receives the early and latter rain. You also be patient. Establish your hearts, for the coming of the Lord is at hand. Do not grumble against one another, brethren, lest you be condemned. Behold, the Judge is standing at the door!

In this passage the "coming of the Lord" is clearly the return of Christ. Even though experiencing trials can make us long for Christ to come back, such troubles can also lead us to be impatient toward others. So James commanded his readers to be patient as they looked for Christ's return. They were going through ordinary problems experienced by many Christians (not the prophesied Tribulation). James warned them that the coming of Christ was "at hand" (verse 8). Because this is the perfect tense of the verb to "approach" or "draw near," it can suitably be translated "the coming of the Lord has drawn near." If something must happen someday, and could happen today, then it can be described as "at hand" and imminent. This event is therefore the rapture, and as such, James reminds us that "we are not separated from it by any known event at all."[30]

James then told his readers to quit grumbling (groaning or sighing) against each other, because the Judge (Christ) is "standing at the door" (literally "before the doors"). Christ is pictured as a Judge who is already standing at the doors of the judgment hall, ready to push them open and begin rendering judgment.[31] Zane Hodges illustrated the scene as follows:

> The readers are thereby likened to a group of litigants, or defendants, standing within a courtroom. Total silence is required out of respect for the judge who is just outside the courtroom door and about to step inside to take his place on the judgment seat. Like a Roman lictor announcing a judge's impending entry, as it were, James cries "Quiet!" His Christian readers must fully silence their complaints against one another in the realization that their Lord and Judge can at any moment appear and sit down on the Bema (Judgment Seat) in order to assess their lives (cf. 2:12-13; see also 2 Cor 5:10; Rom 14:10-12).[32]

There can be no doubt that James pictures this return of Christ as imminent. He assumed it will be followed by Christ's judgment of the church, taught by Paul as the Judgment Seat of Christ.

1 John 2:28; 3:2-3

> Little children, abide in Him, that when He appears, we may have confidence and not be ashamed before Him at His coming...Beloved, now we are children of God; and it has not yet been revealed what we shall be, but we know that when He is revealed, we shall be like Him, for we shall see Him as He is. And everyone who has this hope in Him purifies himself, just as He is pure.

Five times in 1 John 2, the author wrote about the importance of abiding in Christ. In verse 28 he said that if a Christian is abiding in Christ "when He appears" ("at His coming"), he will be able to have confidence before him. But John also implies that if a Christian is not abiding in Christ, he will want to shrink away from Christ in shame (literally, "be ashamed away from him"). Clearly this refers to the rapture, and John said Christians must continually abide in Christ *now* because Christ's coming (appearance) can occur at any moment (imminently).

This point is made even more clearly in the next paragraph. In order to motivate Christians to purify themselves from sin (see 3:4-11), John reminded them that when Jesus appears, they will become like Him. He then said that everyone who has this hope in Christ and His return will begin purifying himself now. Obviously this assumes that a Christian who believes that Christ can return imminently (at any moment) will pay more attention to becoming pure than one who does not.

Why does a belief in an imminent return make such a difference? If someone expects an important guest to arrive at his home imminently, he may energetically clean his house and eagerly prepare for his guest. This would assumedly result in a strong focus on "purifying" the house and getting it ready. If the potential guest were to suddenly cancel the visit, the busy preparations would probably end and the motivation for house-cleaning would dissipate. An expectation or "hope" motivates people in proportion to its imminence.[33] Of course Christians have other motivations for obedience and purification beyond simply an imminent rapture, but the exhortation in 1 John 3:3 is most urgent and significant if Christ's coming is imminent.[34]

In 3:2 John puts forth a threefold sequence of events: (1) Christ will appear, (2) believers will see Him just as He is, and (3) they will be like Him. This sequence describes the essential elements of the rapture. The phrase "when He is revealed" repeats (in the Greek text) "when He appears" from 2:28. At that moment all true believers will become "like Him"—conformed to the likeness of Christ (Romans 8:29). "The complete transformation of the Christian into the likeness of Jesus awaits the moment of seeing Him 'as He really is.'"[35]

A true hope for the future provides a strong motivation to live in purity in the present. The rest of 1 John 3 presents the importance of rejecting sin. Keeping pure involves continually staying away from sin. The hope of becoming like Christ when He returns promotes conformity to Christ's character now, especially if that hope truly remains imminent.

Living in Expectation of the Lord's Return

Living the Christian life can be likened to driving a car. As we drive on the highway, we keep two viewpoints in balance: looking ahead at the upcoming road, and looking behind through the rearview mirror. As we move toward heaven, we also need to maintain a balance between two biblical viewpoints: looking for the blessed return of Christ that will bring eternal glorification and reward, and looking back to the atoning death of Jesus that provided everything we have received in redemption, are experiencing in sanctification, and will receive in the inheritance reserved for us in heaven (1 Peter 1:4).

The Bible provides many motivations for us to grow in Christ and persevere in our spiritual walk. Many of them are directly connected to the imminent return of Christ for the church. In Titus 2:12, Paul said the grace of God teaches us to "live soberly, righteously, and godly in the present age" as we look for the "blessed hope" of the return of Christ (verse 13). In 1 John 2:28, John urged us to abide in Christ, living expectant lives of fellowship and obedience, so that when Christ returns we will have confidence and not want to shrink away in shame. In 1 Thessalonians 5:23, Paul asked God Himself to sanctify us (a progressive "setting apart" by the Holy Spirit) and preserve our soul, spirit, and body "blameless at the coming of our Lord Jesus Christ."

The biblical passages that promise the rapture of the church teach imminence as an event that can occur at any moment. In these passages, there are no events or signs that must precede the rapture. They either encourage believers to continue to look forward to the hope that awaits them, or they motivate believers to pursue holiness in anticipation of seeing Christ soon. And until the rapture, believers are "to look, not for some sign," but for the Lord Himself.[36]

THREE FOUNDATIONAL RAPTURE PASSAGES

Robert Dean, Jr.

I n the New Testament, there are three Scripture passages that irrefutably prove the pretribulation rapture. Together these verses answer the who, what, when, where, and how questions concerning the rapture of the church. The central passage, 1 Thessalonians 4:13-18, details the sequence of events at the rapture and the correlation between the resurrection of the bodies of dead church-age believers and the rapture of living saints. Paul borrowed language from Jesus' statement in John 14:1-3 that designates the destination of the resurrected and raptured church. First Corinthians 15:50-58 reveals details of the duration and purpose of our transformation at the rapture and confirms the sequence of events between the resurrection of dead and living church-age believers. These three passages form not only a scriptural basis for the pretribulational rapture, but together they provide a confident foundation that our future blessed hope precedes the Tribulation, Daniel's seventieth week.[1]

What Happens When the Lord Returns (1 Thessalonians 4:13-18)

The apostle Paul penned two short epistles to the persecuted congregation in Thessalonica to answer their questions concerning loved ones who had died before the return of Jesus. His purpose was to comfort and encourage rather than to warn or alarm (1 Thessalonians 4:18; 5:11). Paul stated he had already taught them about future events in God's plan, and thus they had no need to know more about the "times and the seasons" (5:1). Jesus had used this exact phrase when He responded to the disciples' inquiry about when He would restore the kingdom (Acts 1:6), and He said they were *not* to know the times and seasons. Such a difference, from not being informed to being informed, can be explained only by realizing that at the time of Acts 1 certain prophetic details were yet to be revealed.[2]

Paul wrote 1 Thessalonians some 20 years later, and evidently some prophetic details had been divinely disclosed by then. The Thessalonian Christians had been taught about the future return of the Lord and understood Christ's coming to be imminent, and were concerned when some of their loved ones died before the Lord's arrival. They feared these dead believers would not participate in the Lord's coming, and they may have also received erroneous teaching indicating the Day of the Lord had already arrived, which might mean they were already in the Tribulation.[3]

The Purpose of Paul's Explanation (4:13)

Paul did not write this discourse as some abstract explanation of eschatology. The apostle provided confident answers that offered comfort to believers whose Christian loved ones had died. Paul's words would enable the bereaved to not grieve, but to have confident expectation of a future reunion with their beloved dead. This hope is not a wishful optimism, but an objective eschatological certainty.[4]

The Basis for Our Confident Hope (4:14)

The resurrection of our Lord Jesus Christ was the clarion call of the future victory over death for all who trust in Him (1 Corinthians 15:54-57). Our Lord's resurrection from the dead was "the firstfruits of those who have fallen asleep"

(1 Corinthians 15:20). If we believe He died and rose again, and Paul assumes we do, there is a significant implication. Because Christ rose from the dead, we should also believe that all church-age believers who die physically will undergo bodily resurrection. Thus, when He returns, we will be reunited with Jesus as well as other church age believers who died in the past.

Paul informs us that when the Lord returns He will be accompanied by those who "sleep in Jesus" (1 Thessalonians 4:14). The euphemism "sleep" describes the temporary state of a believer's physical body between physical death and resurrection (Matthew 27:52; John 11:11; Acts 13:36; 1 Corinthians 11:30; 1 Thessalonians 4:13-15).[5] Since the dead in Christ return with Jesus before these saints receive their incorruptible resurrection bodies (cf., 1 Corinthians 15:52) this indicates some sort of interim body that allows the individual to have a conscious presence before the Lord at death (2 Corinthians 5:8).

The Events at the Coming of the Lord (1 Thessalonians 4:15-17)

To reinforce the divine authority of his comments, Paul asserted that the information regarding these events originated directly from Jesus. This was part of the "mystery" revelation given to Paul by the Lord Jesus for the edification of church-age believers (1 Corinthians 15:51). This was new information, not previously revealed in the Old Testament or the Gospels. No specific revelation on the relation between the resurrection of living and dead believers had yet been given. Paul summarized his comforting answer in 1 Thessalonians 4:15: Those believers alive at the coming of the Lord would be raptured immediately following the bodily resurrection of those believers in Christ who had already died. Paul's inclusion of himself as part of the group that would still be alive at the Lord's coming reinforced his sense of the Lord's imminent return. Paul then described the sequence of events.

First, the Lord Himself will descend from heaven (4:16a). In light of John 14:3, this confirms that the place to which Jesus said He was going and from which He would return must be heaven (more below at John 14:3; cf. 1 Thessalonians 1:10). Since His ascension, the glorified resurrection body of the Lord Jesus Christ has been seated at the right hand of God the Father (Psalm 110:1 cf. Acts 2:33; 5:31; Colossians 3:1; Hebrews 8:1; 10:12; 12:2; Revelation 3:21). The emphatic use of "Himself" reinforces that this will be the same Jesus who ascended through the clouds to return to heaven (Acts 1:11; Hebrews 4:14) and not an angel or other divine representative. Just as Jesus ascended *through* the heavens to God, so too He will descend or come down *from* heaven (Greek, *katabaino*). And He will be accompanied by those church-age believers who have already died and are in their interim state (1 Thessalonians 4:14).

Second, the Lord's descent will be heralded by three simultaneous announcements (4:16b). First, there is a shout. "Shout" (Greek, *keleusma*) was a common word for a verbal directive or command issued by someone in authority to those under him. *Keleusma* is used in the Apocrypha for a military comand, a royal directive, a prophet's mandate, or God's directive. The New Testament uses the word in the same way—commands from human authorities as well as divine mandates. The usage is too broad and general to claim that this is the shout of triumph of the Lord returning to the earth in conquest, which would indicate the return at the end of the Tribulation period. The shout alerts the church to our Lord's return and commands them to "form up" on Him. Nothing informs the reader who shouts the command. Some have suggested it is the archangel, but John 5:25 indicates that at the "voice of the Son of God" the dead will live (see John 11:25).

The shout is accompanied by the voice of "*an* archangel."[6] Only one archangel is mentioned in Scripture, Michael (Jude 9). At the same time there is a blast of the "trumpet of God." Trumpets are used many times in Scripture to herald some new event in God's plan for the future. In the book of Revelation the middle series of judgments are each announced by a sounding trumpet. In 1 Corinthians 15:52 the dead are raised by the blast of the "last trumpet." Identification of this trumpet will be discussed more later, but here this is the last trumpet of the church age and it's identical to the trumpet mentioned in 1 Thessalonians 4:17. Though these three events may indeed describe only one combined sound, the repetition of the preposition with each clause suggests three distinct but simultaneous events to signal the assembly of the church with her Lord.

The third event is the resurrection of the physical bodies of the dead believers. Paul comforts his readers that those who have died "in Christ" participate first, immediately followed by those still alive at the time of His coming. He strongly emphasizes the timing: the living "will by *no* means precede" the dead.[7] This is extremely significant, for both here and in 1 Corinthians 15 we see that the resurrection of the dead precedes the translation of the living. This is also clear from the use of the Greek terms for "first" (*proton*), and "then" (*epeita*). These express a temporal or chronological sequence.[8]

The dynamics of this transformation is described in more detail in the section below on 1 Corinthians 15:50-58. That this does not refer to a general resurrection of the dead saints from all history is clear as they are described as the dead "in Christ." Old Testament saints are never described as being "in Christ." Only those who believe in Christ subsequent to His death are united with His death, burial, and resurrection through the baptism of the Holy Spirit (Romans 6:3; 2 Corinthians 5:17) and are entered into the body of Christ (1 Corinthians 12:13).

The fourth event follows immediately after the resurrection of the dead church-age believers. All living believers will subsequently be caught up to meet the Lord in the air. "Caught up" translates the Greek verb *harpazo*, "to snatch, seize, to suddenly grab or take something away." The translation of this verb in the Latin Vulgate, *rapio*, is the basis for the English term *rapture*.[9] Thus, the claim that *rapture* is not found in the Bible is spurious. The word rapture *is* biblical.

The destination of both those resurrected and raptured is the clouds in the air. There, those alive and translated are reunited with departed loved ones and with our Lord. Paul comforts with the truth that from the moment of this reunion we will always be with the Lord (4:17c).

The emphasis in these verses is of a movement upward, to meet Christ, who has completed His descent and awaits in the clouds. No indication of a further downward movement is present (the posttribulational interpretation). However, this alone is not sufficient evidence on which to base the timing of the rapture.

The Message of the Rapture Is One of Comfort (4:18)

The conclusion from this description is that rather than being frightened by events preceding the coming of the Lord, such as the period of intense judgments during the time of Daniel's seventieth week, we are to be comforted as we anticipate the coming of the Lord for His own. Church-age believers are not looking for the Antichrist, but for the Lord Jesus; we are not looking for the signs of judgment, but for the appearance of our Blessed Hope.

The Rapture Precedes the Day of the Lord (1 Thessalonians 5:1-10)

Paul answered the Thessalonian believers' worries by reminding them that they would not go through the Day of the Lord, a time of "sudden destruction," a time of divine wrath. The Old Testament refers to this Day of the Lord's wrath (Psalm 110:5; Ezekiel 7:12,19) as well as the time of "Jacob's trouble" (Jeremiah 30:7). The Thessalonians were comforted by the truth God had not appointed them ("us" in the text refers to believers) to wrath, but to deliverance. Throughout 1 Thessalonians Paul reminded them that Jesus would deliver them and the rest of the church from the "wrath to come."

Some attempt to restrict the Day of the Lord to the latter half of Daniel's seventieth week to the period following the abomination of desolation, but this has two problems. First, it voids the imminent expectation of Christ's return for the church. Second, it misconstrues the timing of the first two series of judgments (the seal and trumpet judgments) which must precede the abomination of desolation and must occur during the first half of the Tribulation.[10]

Where Do We Go with the Lord
When He Returns? (John 14:1-3)

John 14:1-3 may not appear to be a strong rapture passage. However, the late Mennonite commentator on Revelation, J.B. Smith, noted eight striking vocabulary parallels occur between these verses and 1 Thessalonians 4:13-18.[11] Smith also compared the vocabulary in these two passages to the second coming passage of Revelation 19:11-12 and found no significant similarities.[12] It is also striking that these eight words or phrases occur in the same order in both passages.[13]

Both John 14:1-3 and 1 Thessalonians 4:13-18 were designed to ease the mind of distressed believers. In John 14:1 Jesus comforted believers who were confused and disturbed by the announcement of His departure; in 1 Thessalonians 4:13 Paul comforted those who were grieving. Both passages emphasize belief in Christ as a central discriminating factor (John 14:1; 1 Thessalonians 4:14). Both passages focus on God and Jesus—"God...Me" (John 14:1), "Jesus...God," (1 Thessalonians 4:14). Both passages instruct their audience, "told you" (John 14:2), "say to you" (1 Thessalonians 4:15). The return of Jesus is mentioned next in both (John 14:3; 1 Thessalonians 4:15). John recorded Jesus then saying He would receive them (John 14:3) and Paul said believers would be caught up to Him (1 Thessalonians 4:17). Their destiny is "to Myself" (John 14:3) and "to meet the Lord" (1 Thessalonians 4:17). And finally, in both passages, believers will continue to be with the Lord (John 14:3; 1 Thessalonians 4:17). Together, these eight phrases, common to both passages, reinforce their connection.

The night before our Lord went to the cross He celebrated the Passover seder with His disciples. Following the seder, Jesus announced his impending departure. Confused, Thomas inquired where He was going and why they couldn't follow Him. Jesus answered that He was going to His Father's house to prepare places for them and that He would come again to receive all believers to Himself that they may be with Him. The announcement that He "will come again" places His instruction within the realm of eschatology.

There are four phrases that demonstrate Jesus was indeed speaking of what would transpire at the rapture and where church-age believers would go after the return mentioned in John 14:3: the meaning and location of the "Father's house" (John 14:2a), the meaning of "mansions" (John 14:2b), the location of these mansions (John 14:2c), and Jesus' destiny with those He returns for at that time (John 14:3).

What and Where Is the "Father's House"? (John 14:2a)

The phrase "My Father's house" has only one other similar use. In John 2:16, Jesus used a similar phrase to refer to the temple. The important distinction between the two phrases is that in John 2:16 Jesus used the masculine noun *oikos*, but in John 14:2 He used the feminine noun *oikia*. Though these terms are cognates, there does appear to be a subtle distinction in their use. *Oikos* is typically used with "of God" as a designation for the temple in the Septuagint, as well as in John 2:16, but *oikia* never is.[14] *Oikia* is used of a standard house or dwelling, and never for the temple of God. This indicates an important distinction, showing that Jesus was not speaking of the temple in John 14:2. By the analogy of Scripture we discover that the place to which Jesus was going is the right hand of the Father's throne (Psalm 110:1; cf. Acts 2:33-35; Revelation 3:21). Jesus' destiny was not earthly, but the heavenly abode of the Father.[15] There He would sit until the Father gave Him the kingdom (Daniel 7:14).

Mansions or Dwelling Places? (John 14:2b)

The image of mansions in heaven has unfortunately been firmly ingrained in the hymnology and idiom of Christianity due to Tyndale's use of the English word "mansion," based on the Latin Vulgate "*mansiones*," which translated the Greek term *mone*. However, *mone* has little to do with an expansive, impressive dwelling. The word *mone* is best understood as a dwelling place, perhaps an apartment or flat, or a temporary dwelling such as an inn.[16] *Mone* is used only one other time in the New Testament (John 14:23), where it describes the indwelling abode of the Father and the Son in the individual believer, a nuance quite different from that in 14:2, the abode of the Father. In John 14:2 Jesus spoke of an abode the believer will have in heaven while awaiting the conclusion to the events of Daniel's seventieth week, after which he will return to earth with the Lord.

Where Is Jesus Preparing These Places? (14:2c)

When we join the conclusions reached from the previous two questions, we realize Jesus does not speak of preparing dwelling places on earth, but in heaven. Here, Jesus answered Peter's question in 13:36-37. Peter had not asked a question in view of the crucifixion, for that event was still not clear to the disciples. Peter desired to know Jesus' ultimate destiny.

The idea of preparation is also important to understand. Jesus was not talking about a construction project, but providing a temporary residence for the arrival of His bride, the church, until the wedding feast that will occur just prior to His second coming (Revelation 19:7-10).

Jesus Promised to Return to Receive Us to Where He Is (John 14:3)

Though some commentators attempt to interpret this to mean Jesus coming for the believer at death, this has no support in Scripture, which instead speaks of angels coming for the believer (Luke 16:22) and of Jesus awaiting the arrival of the believer (Acts 7:56). Jesus' use of the present tense—"I am coming"—has a future nuance, for His future coming is so certain that it was expressed as a present reality.[17] The present tense may describe an event that is *wholly* subsequent to the time of speaking, expressed as if in the present. Such confidence comforts those confused or anxious about a current situation. This same phrase, also in the present tense, was used seven times by Jesus in His Revelation to John. Though the events of Revelation are revealed to John over 60 years after the statement in John 14:3, the meaning is the same. Jesus' future coming is certain. It is not to be confused with the coming of the Holy Spirit or the events of the AD 70 judgment on Israel.

Two more observations secure our understanding of this passage. First, Jesus said He was going to the domain of the Father in heaven. It is to that location He promises to take the believers for whom He comes. Since Jesus' destiny was heaven, this must also be the location to which He will take the church. Second, in subsequent verses (14:6-7) Jesus answered Thomas' question by saying He was going to the Father.

Thus, John 14:1-3 clearly speaks of Jesus' departure from the earthly realm to the heavenly abode of the Father. There He will prepare for the arrival of the church and the marriage of the bride. Following Jewish wedding customs, He will return to take His bride to the location He has prepared, which is not on the earth but in heaven. Once the bride is gathered, then comes the purification, which occurs at the judgment seat of Christ, and the wedding feast, which occurs before the second coming.

This means Christ's future return cannot be at the same time as the coming to the earth described in Revelation 19:7-9. In that case, Jesus would simply be catching up the bride to Himself on His way down to the earth with no time for either the judgment seat of Christ or the wedding feast. The destiny of the church then would be the earth rather than heaven. Yet John 14:1-3 clearly states the Lord will take us to heaven at His return at the rapture.

How Christians Are Resurrected and Raptured (1 Corinthians 15:50-58)

First Corinthians 15 provides an in-depth apologia for physical bodily resurrection from the dead. The first 11 verses list the evidence and witnesses for the physical bodily resurrection of the Lord Jesus Christ. Then verses 12-34 explain that without Christ's resurrection from the dead, Christianity has no foundation. Here Paul provided a general order of events: The resurrection of Jesus is first, next is the resurrection of all who are Christ's, then the end. The phrase "those who are Christ's" (verse 23) has one clear parallel and one similar statement; both indicate church-age believers only, *not* inclusive of Old Testament believers (Galatians 5:24; cf. 1 Corinthians 6:15).[18] Because Paul was addressing the concerns of church-age believers he did not focus on other future resurrections (i.e., Old Testament saints, Tribulation martyrs, or the unsaved).[19] The certainty of Christ's past resurrection makes certain the future resurrection of the Corinthian believers.

Christ's resurrection is further described through an Old Testament analogy, firstfruits, which depicts the initial production of the field, and the term implies that more production will follow. Consistent with what our Lord already promised in John 14:2-3, Jesus will return for those who comprise the church, "those who are Christ's at His coming" (1 Corinthians 15:23). This coming, however, will not include Old Testament saints, who are not resurrected until just prior to the millennial kingdom. It will include only church-age believers, both those asleep in Christ and those alive (1 Thessalonians 4:16).

Evidence of different stages of resurrection comes from 1 Corinthians 15:23-25. First, distinct groups are resurrected.[20] Second, lengthy time periods separate some of these resurrections. The resurrection of Christ precedes the next group to be resurrected by at least 2000 years. Then comes Christ's reign over His kingdom before He delivers it to God the Father (1 Corinthians 15:24). The phrase "the end" describes the final victory of God and Christ over all opposing "rule and all authority and power." The time frame preceding "the end" must certainly include both the seven-year Tribulation and the 1000-year kingdom.

It is during Daniel's seventieth week (the Tribulation) that the Lamb brings judgment upon the earth through the seal, trumpet, and bowl judgments. But at that point not all His enemies have been vanquished. Even during His millennial reign, Christ will still be subduing His opponents. Death, the final enemy (1 Corinthians 15:26), will not be defeated until after the annihilation of those who follow Satan in his last revolt against God, the last battle of Gog and Magog (Revelation

20:7-9). Death will not be fully conquered until Satan is finally defeated (Hebrews 2:14). From this we see the firstfruits resurrection of Christ, followed by at least 2000 years and another resurrection. Though amillennialism and postmillennialism see only one resurrection here, when this is compared with Revelation 20 we know that at least 1000 years must come between the resurrection of Revelation 20:4 and the resurrection of the dead (Revelation 20:12-14).

Paul then explained what will happen to those who have died as well as their relationship to those who have not passed through death at the time of the resurrection (1 Corinthians 15:35). As in 1 Thessalonians 4:16-18, first the dead receive their resurrection bodies, then the living. In 1 Corinthians 15:50-58 Paul provided never-before revealed information about what transpires for those who are not dead at the time of Christ's coming.

The previous verses established the truth that mortal, corruptible bodies must first be transformed into immortal, incorruptible bodies before they can participate in Christ's kingdom.

The term "mystery" (verse 51) is critical to the significance of this passage for its bearing on the timing of the rapture. "Mystery" is most often a Pauline term for never-before disclosed divine revelation. The significance of this is often ignored or overlooked.[21] The Old Testament clearly revealed a future resurrection of the dead (Daniel 12:2), but revealed nothing about the event or the timing of the rapture. Furthermore, as John Walvoord emphasized, nothing is said in the Old Testament about the church, the church age, or the translation of the church, although Christ's second coming is clearly described as subsequent to the Tribulation.[22]

The rapture of church-age believers could not be revealed in the Old Testament because nothing is said of a future church. To have revealed the existence of another people of God in the future, and the intercalation between the cross and the crown, would have prejudiced the real offer of the kingdom by hinting of a future rejection by Israel. Thus nothing about the church could have been revealed in the Old Testament without affecting the legitimacy of the offer of the kingdom. So the mention of the direct translation of living believers into resurrection bodies is unknown in Old Testament revelation because it is not associated with the second coming.

Paul explained that not all church-age believers will undergo physical death, euphemistically called "sleep." Those still alive (cf. 1 Thessalonians 4:16) will be changed or altered in "the twinkling of an eye" (1 Corinthians 15:52). The speed at which this occurs is described by the Greek word *atomos,* "a moment," a unit of time so small it cannot be subdivided—a nanosecond.

This event will occur "at the last trumpet" (verse 52). The attempt to equate this "last trumpet" with that of the seventh or last trumpet of Revelation 11:15-18 is a stretch. Trumpets were used in Old Testament times to summon God's people to Himself (Exodus 20:18; Leviticus 25:9; Psalm 98:6). Many trumpets are described in reference to the end times. This trumpet blast signals the end of the church age. The use of the "we" here indicates Paul expected to be alive at this time. If the Tribulation were to intervene before this transformation, then he would not have been able to make this assumption.

In both 1 Thessalonians 4:16 and in 1 Corinthians 15:52 the resurrection of the dead into their immortal bodies immediately precedes the instantaneous translation of the living saints into their immortal bodies. Both occur within the twinkling of an eye. By contrast, in Revelation 20:4, the resurrection of the dead at the time of the Tribulation *follows* the arrival of Christ on the earth. If there is no pretribulation rapture, then church-age believers would not be distinguished from Tribulation believers and both would become martyrs during the Tribulation since the church would continue through the full seven years of Daniel's seventieth week. The sequence of events at the return of Christ does not mention the translation of the living. The physical resurrection of the Tribulation martyrs occurs only after the return of Christ and His victory of the Armageddon campaign, the casting of the Antichrist and False Prophet into the Lake of Fire, and the incarceration of Satan in the abyss. This sequence of events does not at all resemble the sequence in 1 Thessalonians 4 or in 1 Corinthians 15.

Thus the resurrection and translation of church-age believers cannot be placed at the end of the Tribulation.

A Consistent Affirmation of Imminency

From these passages we learn that a specific order of events occurs at Christ's return for the church. He returns in the clouds; in a nanosecond the dead in Christ receive their resurrection bodies immediately before the living believers are translated into their resurrection bodies and snatched up to be with the Lord in the clouds. From there the Lord will return to the Father's house, where He has prepared temporary dwelling places for His bride. Immediately following this the purification of the bride occurs at the judgment seat of Christ and then Jesus will take the seven-sealed scroll and open it to begin the process of defeating His enemies on the earth. This will take seven years, at the conclusion of which He will return with His bride to the earth, defeat the armies of the Antichrist and the kings of the earth, and then raise the Tribulation martyrs from the dead and give them their resurrection bodies. At that time He will then establish His kingdom.

One common thread connects these three passages, that of imminency. Nothing is said to indicate some intervening event must occur before our Lord returns. In all these passages, the assumption is that Jesus could return for us today. No Antichrist, no Tribulation, no Day of the Lord will indicate its proximity.

THE PRETRIBULATION RAPTURE TEACHING IN THE EARLY CHURCH

Grant R. Jeffrey

An ancient manuscript attributed by some scholars to Ephraem the Syrian (AD 373) or possibly derived from his teaching during the next two centuries (Pseudo-Ephraem) clearly taught the pretribulation rapture. Regardless of which date is accepted, this ancient manuscript provides proof that the pretribulation rapture teaching was well known before AD 630 in the early church, especially in the Middle East.

> All the saints and elect of God are gathered together before the tribulation, which is to come, and are taken to the Lord, in order that they may not see at any time the confusion which overwhelms the world because of our sins.
>
> —EPHRAEM THE SYRIAN (AD 373) or Pseudo-Ephraem
> (an early seventh-century text based on Ephraem the Syrian)

Many of those critics in our generation who reject the pretribulation rapture have dogmatically asserted this doctrine was never taught before AD 1830. Obviously, the truth or error of the pretribulation rapture can only be determined by an appeal to the authority of Scripture. However, those critics who condemn the teaching of the pretribulation rapture have confused many Christians with their assertion that it cannot possibly be biblically valid because they claim no one ever taught this doctrine during the first 18 centuries of the church until 1830.

As an example, George E. Ladd wrote in his book, *The Blessed Hope*, "We can find no trace of pre-tribulationism in the early church; and no modern pre-tribulationist has successfully proved that this particular doctrine was held by any of the church fathers or students of the Word before the nineteenth century."[1] A prominent critic of the pre-tribulation rapture, Dave MacPherson, claimed in his book *The Great Rapture Hoax*, "during the first 18 centuries of the Christian era, believers were never 'Rapture separaters' [sic]; they never separated the minor Rapture aspect of the Second Coming of Christ from the Second Coming itself."[2]

In his book *The Incredible Cover-Up*, MacPherson claimed that no one ever taught the pretribulation rapture until a woman named Margaret Macdonald proclaimed it during a trance vision in AD 1830. He claimed this was the origin of the theory of the rapture as widely taught by John Darby and the Plymouth Brethren. However, this claim is false. Darby himself declared that he developed this doctrine from the clear teaching of the New Testament and no one has ever proven his statement to be false.

Research has proven that the doctrine of the pretribulation rapture, as derived from the Scriptures, was in fact taught by a number of people living more than 1000 years before 1830. Most significantly, new evidence proves that the pretribulation rapture was taught by a prominent orthodox theologian in the early days of the Byzantine church over 16 centuries ago.

A Key Manuscript from the Early Church

After ten years of careful searching, I discovered a fascinating manuscript that proves the doctrine of the pretribulation rapture was taught in the early church. Ephraem the Syrian (AD 306–373) was a major theologian of the early Eastern church who taught in Asia (Turkey-Syrian border). His hymns are still used in the liturgy of the Eastern Orthodox church and his writings appear in the Post-Nicene Library (a collection of major theological writings following the AD 325 Council of Nicea) but most of his commentaries were never translated from the original Syriac, Greek, or Latin.

Ephraem's fascinating teaching on the pretribulation rapture had never before been published in English until my discovery of his manuscript in the early 1990s and my quotation of it in my 1995 book *Final Warning*.[3] This important manuscript reveals that he used a literal principle of biblical interpretation and taught the premillennial return of Christ. However, Ephraem's most important statement clearly described the pretribulational return of Christ to take His elect saints to heaven to escape the coming Tribulation. In addition, Ephraem described a Jewish Antichrist who will rule a revived Roman Empire and a literal Great Tribulation of 1260 days with a rebuilt temple in Jerusalem and the two witnesses.

Details Regarding Ephraem's Text

While the text is attributed to Ephraem the Syrian (AD 373), his teaching was so popular in the early Byzantine church in Syria that numerous authors later wrote commentaries on his works and incorrectly attributed their later manuscripts to Ephraem the Syrian. These attributed works are designated as *pseudo* (false) if scholars are not totally convinced the books were actually written by the attributed authors. Some scholars have suggested that this text should be called Pseudo-Ephraem, while others conclude that Ephraem is the original author.

The author of *On the Last Times, the Antichrist, and the End of the World* states this text was written by Ephraem of Nisibis (306–373), who was recognized as a prolific author and the greatest teacher of the ancient Syrian church. He was honored for his numerous defenses of the biblical faith in his confrontations with the heresies of Marcion and the Arians. Professor Paul J. Alexander, in his article "The Diffusion of Byzantine

Apocalypses in the Medieval West and the Beginnings of Joachimism," demonstrated that Pseudo-Ephraem was "heavily influenced by the genuine works of Ephraem."[4]

The vocabulary and style of the manuscript are consistent with the known writings of Ephraem and that period of history. Professor Wilhelm Bousset's book *The Antichrist Legend* (1895) accepted the authorship of Ephraem and the probable date of writing of 373.[5] The majority of scholars believe the present text would have been created at some time prior to the rise of the Islamic Arab conquest in the early years of the seventh century.

Ephraem's text was titled *On the Last Times, the Antichrist, and the End of the World.* Ephraem's ten-section manuscript described the events of the last days in chronological sequence beginning with the rapture, followed by the seven-year Tribulation, which includes the three-and-a-half-year Great Tribulation as the last part of the Tribulation and the tyranny of the Antichrist followed by Christ's return at the Battle of Armageddon. Significantly, in Section 2, Ephraem wrote about the rapture as an "imminent" event that will occur without warning: "We ought to understand thoroughly therefore, my brothers what is imminent or overhanging."

Ephraem then described the pretribulation rapture as follows: "All saints and the Elect of the Lord are gathered together before the tribulation which is about to come and are taken to the Lord in order that they may not see at any time the confusion which overwhelms the world because of our sins." Ephraem reminded his Christian readers that we need not fear the coming tribulation—"we neither become very much afraid of the report nor of the appearance" because the rapture will occur prior to the Tribulation. Further, Ephraem called on Christians to spiritual watchfulness, to "prepare ourselves for the meeting of the Lord Christ, so that He may draw us from the confusion, which overwhelms the world."

Ephraem described the "great tribulation" as lasting "three and a half years," precisely "1260 days." He summarized: "there will be a great tribulation, as there has not been since people began to be upon the earth." In Section 10 he wrote: "When the three and a half years have been completed, the time of the Antichrist, through which he will have seduced the world, after the resurrection of the two prophets...will come the sign of the Son of Man, and coming forward the Lord shall appear with great power and much majesty." It's also fascinating to note he taught that the War of Gog and Magog would precede the Tribulation.

In another book, *The Book of the Cave of Treasures*, Ephraem revealed that the whole Tribulation period encompassed "that sore affliction" lasting "one week" of seven years. He wrote that the sixty-ninth week of Daniel 9:24-27 ended with the crucifixion of Jesus. Although there are curious elements in Ephraem's manuscript, he clearly taught that the seventieth week of Daniel's seventy weeks will be fulfilled in the final seven years of this age. "At the end of the world and at the final consummation...After one week of that sore affliction (Tribulation), they will all be destroyed in the plain of Joppa... Then will the son of perdition appear, of the seed and of the tribe of Dan."[6]

This discovery of the 1600-year-old Ephraem manuscript *On the Last Times, the Antichrist, and the End of the World* reveals that the doctrine of the blessed hope and deliverance of the saints was clearly held by some of the faithful early in the church age. The full text of this vital manuscript can be read in my book *Final Warning*. The promise of God remains our hope today: "For the Lord Himself will descend from heaven with a shout, with the voice of an archangel, and with the trumpet of God. And the dead in Christ will rise first. Then we who are alive and remain shall be caught up together with them in the clouds, to meet the Lord in the air. And thus we shall always be with the Lord" (1 Thessalonians 4:16-17).

Specifics of Ephraem's Teaching on the Pretribulation Rapture

For all the saints and Elect of God are gathered, prior to the tribulation that is to come, and are taken to the Lord lest they see the confusion that is to overwhelm the world because of our sins.

On the Last Times, the Antichrist, and the End of the World,
EPHRAEM THE SYRIAN (between 373 and 630)

The early Christian writer and poet Ephraem the Syrian (who lived from AD 306–373) was a very important theologian of the early Byzantine Eastern church. He was born near Nisibis, in the Roman province of Syria, near present-day Edessa, Turkey. Ephraem displayed a profound love of the Scriptures in his writings, as illustrated by several of his written comments quoted in the works of Nathaniel Lardner. "I esteem no man more happy than him, who diligently reads the Scriptures delivered to us by the Spirit of God, and thinks how he may order his conversation by the precepts of them."[7]

To this day, his hymns and homilies are used in the liturgy of the Greek Orthodox and Middle Eastern Nestorian church. While the 16-volume Post-Nicene Library includes a number of homilies and psalms by Ephraem the Syrian, the editors noted that he also wrote a large number of commentaries that have never been translated into English.

The following section includes key passages from Ephraem's important text (1500 words), written about AD 373 or, at the latest, before 630. Ephraem's Latin text was translated into English at my request by Dr. Cameron Rhoades, professor of Latin at Tyndale Theological Seminary.

On the Last Times, the Antichrist,
and the End of the World

1. Most dearly beloved brothers, believe the Holy Spirit who speaks in us. Now we have spoken before, because the end of the world is very near, and the consummation remains. Has not the first faith withered away in men?

2. We ought to understand thoroughly therefore, my brothers what is imminent or overhanging. Already there have been hunger and plagues, violent movements of nations and signs, which have

been predicted by the Lord, they have already been fulfilled, and there is not other [another] which remains, except the advent of the wicked one in the completion of the Roman kingdom. Why therefore are we occupied with worldly business, and why is our mind held fixed on the lusts of the world or the anxieties of the ages? Why therefore do we not reject every care of earthly actions and prepare ourselves for the meeting of the Lord Christ, so that He may draw us from the confusion, which overwhelms the world? Believe you me, dearest brothers, because the coming of the Lord is nigh, believe you me, because the end of the world is at hand, believe me, because it is the very last time.

Because all saints and the Elect of the Lord are gathered together before the tribulation which is about to come and are taken to the Lord, in order that they may not see at any time the confusion which overwhelms the world because of our sins. And so, brothers, most dear to me, it is the eleventh hour, and the end of this world comes to the harvest, and angels, armed and prepared, hold sickles in their hands, awaiting the empire of the Lord.

3. When therefore the end of the world comes, there arise diverse wars, commotions on all sides, horrible earthquakes, perturbations of nations, tempests throughout the lands, plagues, famine, drought throughout the thoroughfares, great danger throughout the sea and dry land, constant persecutions, slaughters and massacres everywhere.

4. When therefore the end of the world comes, that abominable, lying and murderous one is born from the tribe of Dan. He is conceived from the seed of a man and from a most vile virgin, mixed with an evil or worthless spirit.

5. But when the time of the abomination of his desolation begins to approach, having been made legal,
   he takes the empire…Therefore, when he receives
   the kingdom, he orders the temple of God to be
   rebuilt for himself, which is in Jerusalem; who,
   after coming into it, he shall sit as God and order
   that he be adored by all nations…then all people
   from everywhere shall flock together to him at the
   city of Jerusalem, and the holy city shall be tram-
   pled on by the nations for forty-two months just
   as the holy apostle says in the Apocalypse, which
   become three and a half years, 1260 days.

6. In these three years and a half the heaven shall
   suspend its dew; because there will be no rain
   upon the earth…and there will be a great tribulation, as there has not been, since people began to
   be upon the earth…and no one is able to sell or
   to buy of the grain of the fall harvest, unless he is
   one who has the serpentine sign on the forehead
   or the hand…

7. And when the three and a half years have been
   completed, the time of the Antichrist, through
   which he will have seduced the world, after the
   resurrection of the two prophets, in the hour
   which the world does not know, and on the
   day which the enemy or son of perdition does
   not know, will come the sign of the Son of Man,
   and coming forward the Lord shall appear with
   great power and much majesty, with the sign of
   the word of salvation going before him, and also
   even with all the powers of the heavens with the
   whole chorus of the saints…Then Christ shall
   come and the enemy shall be thrown into confusion, and the Lord shall destroy him by the Spirit
   of his mouth. And he shall be bound and shall
   be plunged into the abyss of everlasting fire alive
   with his father Satan; and all people, who do his

wishes, shall perish with him forever; but the righteous ones shall inherit everlasting life with the Lord for ever and ever.

Summary of the Key Points in Ephraem's Text

1. Ephraem's manuscript lays out the events of the last days in chronological sequence. Significantly he began with the rapture, using the word *imminent,* then he described the Great Tribulation of three-and-a-half years' duration under the Antichrist's tyranny, followed by the second coming of Christ to earth with His saints to defeat the Antichrist.

2. Significantly, at the beginning of his treatise in Section 2, Ephraem used the word *imminent* to describe the rapture occurring before the Tribulation and the coming of the Antichrist. "We ought to understand thoroughly therefore, my brothers what is imminent or overhanging."

3. He clearly described the pretribulation rapture: "Because all saints and the Elect of the Lord are gathered together before the tribulation which is about to come and are taken to the Lord, in order that they may not see at any time the confusion which overwhelms the world because of our sins."

4. He then gave the purpose of God in resurrecting the church "before the tribulation"—so that "they may not see at any time the confusion which overwhelms the world because of our sins." Ephraem used the word *confusion* as a synonym for the Tribulation period.

5. Ephraem described the duration of the "great tribulation" (the last half of the seven-year tribulation) in sections 7, 8, and 10 as follows: "forty-two months" and "three and a half years" and "1260 days."

6. He summarized: "There will be a great tribulation, as there has not been since people began to be upon the earth," and described the mark of the beast system.

7. He declared that Christ will come to the earth after the "three and a half years" Tribulation period in Section 10: "And when the three and a half years have been completed, the time of the Antichrist, through which he will have seduced the world, after the resurrection of the two prophets...will come the sign of the Son of Man, and coming forward the Lord shall appear with great power and much majesty."

The late Dr. Paul J. Alexander, perhaps the most authoritative scholar on the writings of the early Byzantine church, concluded that in *The Last Times, the Antichrist, and the End of the World*, Ephraem taught that the Lord would supernaturally remove the saints of the church from the earth "prior to the tribulation that is to come." Ephraem wrote that the saints will be "taken to the Lord lest they see the confusion that is to overwhelm the world because of our sins." Dr. Alexander believed this text was written by some unknown writer in the sixth century, but he concluded it was derived from an original Ephraem manuscript (AD 373).[8]

Other scholars, including the German editor Professor Caspari, who wrote a German commentary on this Latin manuscript in 1890, believed that Ephraem's manuscript was written by Ephraem himself in AD 373.[9]

Ephraem on Daniel's Seventieth Week—The Tribulation

Daniel prophesied that Jerusalem would be rebuilt "even in troublesome times" during the initial period of "seven weeks" of years (49 years). He foretold that this initial period of 7 "weeks" of years would be immediately followed by a further period of 62 "weeks" of years, ending with the cutting off of the Messiah (483 years). The combined total of 69 weeks of years

(7 weeks plus 62 weeks) was to conclude with the rejection of Christ. Ephraem taught that Jesus Christ was slain at the end of the combined 69 weeks of years.

However, in his book *The Book of the Cave of Treasures,* which deals with the future war of Gog and Magog, Ephraem wrote about a substantial parenthesis or gap between the ending of the 69 weeks and the beginning of the final (seventieth) week of Daniel as follows:

> At the end of the world and at the final consummation...suddenly the gates of the north shall be opened...They will destroy the earth, and there will be none able to stand before them. After one week of that sore affliction [Tribulation], they will all be destroyed in the plain of Joppa...Then will the son of perdition appear, of the seed and of the tribe of Dan...He will go into Jerusalem and will sit upon a throne in the Temple saying, "I am the Christ," and he will be borne aloft by legions of devils like a king and a lawgiver, naming himself God...The time of the error of the Anti-Christ will last two years and a half, but others say three years and six months.

Clear Evidence of Pretribulation Rapture Teaching in the Early Church

Although there are some curious elements in his description of prophetic events, it is clear that Ephraem believed that the seventieth week of Daniel's prophecy of the 70 weeks would be fulfilled during the final seven years of this age when the Antichrist will appear. That this clear evidence of a belief in a "gap" or "parenthesis" between the sixty-ninth and seventieth week of Daniel 9:24-27 came from an important fourth-century Christian writer is significant. This teaching that there would be a gap between Daniel's sixty-ninth and seventieth week of years was also taught by others in the early church, including the Epistle of Barnabas (AD 110) and the writings of Hippolytus (AD 220).

We now have clear evidence of a definitive pretribulation rapture teaching by a prominent Christian theologian written sometime between 373 (if Ephraem is the author) or at the latest around 632 (if it was wrongly attributed to Ephraem). Regardless, this discovery confirms that the pretribulation rapture was taught in the early Byzantine church some 12 centuries before John Darby's "rediscovery" in 1830.

THE PURPOSE AND
ROLE OF THE TRIBULATION

Ed Hindson

The rapture of the church will bring the bride of Christ to heaven. Those left behind will face the difficult and dreadful times known in the Bible as "the great tribulation" (Revelation 7:14). This will be a terrible time of war, conflict, suffering, and death. While many will become Christians during this time, doing so will generally cost them their lives.

After the rapture, God's judgments will be unleashed upon the world as the seven-sealed scroll is opened (Revelation 6, 8). These result in a series of catastrophic events that express the "wrath of the Lamb." Each opening of a seal hurtles the world further along a course of ultimate disaster. Eventually, the opening of the seventh seal results in the sounding of seven trumpets, which herald even more severe judgments.[1]

The trumpet judgments (Revelation 8–11) and the bowl judgments (Revelation 15–16) have several obvious similarities. Merrill Tenney observed, "The seven bowls are a closely knit series following each other in rapid succession. They parallel the trumpets in their spheres of action, but they are more intense."[2]

While there are some differences in the two accounts (wormwood, locusts, kings of the East, Armageddon), there are far more similarities. Both accounts describe a succession of events that result from catastrophic wars:

1. Vegetation destroyed
2. Sea waters polluted
3. Fresh waters polluted
4. Air pollution
5. Demonic plagues
6. Armies of millions
7. Final victory of God

One of the key interpretive issues in the book of Revelation has to do with the issues of divine sovereignty and human agency. In other words, who is doing what? Are these judgments directly from the hand of God (cosmic destruction)? Or are they the result of human conflict (nuclear war)? While it is easy to speculate one way or the other, we must let the text of Scripture speak for itself.

The seal judgments result when Christ Himself breaks the seven seals. Yet those involve people killing one another (6:4-8). They also involve geological forces such as earthquakes (6:12) and cosmic disturbances involving the sun, moon, stars, and heavens (6:12-14). The trumpet judgments result from angelic pronouncements (8:7) and include cosmic and geological upheavals (8:7-12). They also seem to include demonic forces (locusts from the bottomless pit) and human armies and modern weapons (9:16-19). The bowl judgments follow the same pattern and include the same elements.

All of these judgments in Revelation (seals, trumpets, bowls) involve divine, demonic, human, and natural forces. Satan is pictured as spewing out his wrath on the earth (12:12). The beast and the False Prophet are pictured as his human agents (13:1-18; 19:19-21). At times the forces of evil are an individual (beast, or the Antichrist). At times they are an entire system of human government (Babylon). In other passages, the evil forces seem to come from hell itself (9:1-11). But time and time again our attention is refocused on the immediate factor: human armies bent on mass destruction. Thus we read of swords, weapons, armies, horsemen, kings, battles, and finally, Armageddon.

The grand overview of the apocalypse presents every possible perspective on the catastrophic destruction that will come in the future. Nothing in previous human history compares to the intensity or extent of these disasters. The whole world is pictured as being at war, and the entire planet is descending into horrific chaos.

The overarching theology of the apocalypse touches every possible element of the coming conflict:

> Divine—God is in control of all forces
>
> Satanic—Satan tries to destroy mankind
>
> Demonic—Demons assist Satan's attempt
>
> Angelic—Angels announce the judgments of God
>
> Human—Armies are at war
>
> Geologic—The planet is reeling from destruction
>
> Cosmic—The heavens are shaken and depart

The World at War

The destruction described in the first four seals is a preview of what is to come in the trumpet and bowl judgments. First we have the wide-angle panorama; then the detailed snapshots follow. When the final seal is opened (Revelation 6:12-17), the planet is shaken to its very core. Disorder reigns supreme; the powers of nature and human government collapse. Chaos ensues, and people call upon the rock and mountains to "fall on us." In this awful moment of divine retribution, there is no repentance by the ungodly. They call upon the powers of nature to deliver them, and refuse to call upon God.

A "great earthquake" will rock the planet, the sun will darken, stars will fall, and the heavens (atmosphere) will depart "as a scroll." These passages describe some sort of nuclear or cosmic disaster that causes the entire planet to be shaken so that the sun, moon, and stars appear to be moving and the atmosphere recedes. John's description is very similar to what we read in 2 Peter 3:10. In both passages, the "heavens" refer to earth's atmosphere, not the dwelling place of God (which, of course, remains undamaged). But the planet is totally dev-astated, and universal terror reigns supreme in the hearts of unregenerate men.

What is all of this? The text says it is "the wrath of the Lamb! For the great day of His wrath has come, and who is able to stand?" (Revelation 6:16-17). With the opening of each seal we see the divine judgment become more intense, culminat-ing in international wars, planetary devastation, and what cer-tainly sounds like the consequences of nuclear holocaust. The prophet Amos predicted this day "will be darkness" (5:18). Isa-iah said it will "shake terribly the earth" (Isaiah 2:19,21 KJV), turning it "upside down" and scattering the inhabitants of the earth (Isaiah 24:1).

With the opening of the first six seals, the process of judg-ment begins. The world is at war, and the future of the planet is in jeopardy. But behind the scenes, one thing remains clear: God is still in control. Jesus Christ is in charge of the open-ing of the seals, and the sovereign will of heaven shall prevail despite the inhumanity of a depraved and corrupt society.

A World Gone Mad

Ever since the atomic bomb was dropped on Hiroshima, Japan, in 1945, mankind has lived with the threat of nuclear annihilation. Those born in the population explosion after World War II could easily be called the generation of the bomb. Many psychologists believe that the people in this genera-tion do not think like any generation that has preceded them because they have to live with the reality of their own vulner-ability every day.

Educator Arthur Levine has described the current mental-ity as "going first class on the Titanic."[3] In his study sponsored by the Carnegie Foundation for the Advancement of Teach-ing, Levine found that today's students are self-centered, indi-vidualistic "escapists" who want little responsibility for solving society's problems, yet want society to provide them with the opportunity to fulfill their pleasures. They have given up noble causes because they have given up any real hope of solving the world's problems. They see themselves as being on a hopeless voyage destined for disaster. Unable to turn the ship around, they simply clamor for the first class seats so they can enjoy the ride until the inevitable strikes.

It should not surprise us, then, that people today will spare almost no expense for elaborate and expensive pleasures. They pretend everything is all right, even though they know it isn't. While the desire for peace clings to the deepest crevice of the human heart, the prospects for global destruction are far greater than they are for global peace. Undoubtedly, people will continue to strive for peaceful solutions. But there is nothing they can do to avoid the coming final holocaust.

The Final Blast

The Bible predicts the final devastation in "one hour" (Revelation 18:10) of the prophetic "Babylon," the symbolic name for the kingdom of the Antichrist. Scripture says, "All your riches and splendor have vanished, never to be recovered" (Revelation 18:14). Merchants and sailors will "stand afar off for the fear of her torment" and cry out, "In one hour so great riches is come to nought!" (Revelation 18:15,17).

The apostle Peter provides an even more vivid description of the final blast that shall devastate this planet when he warns, "The day of the Lord will come as a thief in the night; in which the heavens shall pass away with a great noise, and the elements shall melt with fervent heat, the earth also and the works that are therein shall be burned up" (2 Peter 3:10).

John Phillips notes that Peter's prophecy of a great end-times conflagration of the earth and its atmosphere uses terminology that accurately describes a nuclear explosion. The "elements" (Greek, *stoicheia*) are defined by Liddell and Scott's *Lexicon* as "the components into which matter is divided" (or atoms), and the term "dissolved" in the KJV (Greek, *luo*) comes from the basic Greek word meaning "to loose" that which is bound (as in nuclear fission). The term "great noise" (Greek, *rhoizedon*) is found nowhere else in the New Testament and signifies "a rushing sound as of roaring flames." The term "fervent heat" is derived from the Greek medical term *kausoo*, denoting a fever. But Peter's use of it in application to inanimate objects is the only known such usage anywhere in Greek literature. Thus, Phillips concludes, "Peter described in accurate terms the untying of the atom and the resulting rushing, fiery destruction which follows it."[4]

The Seven Trumpets

During the trumpet judgments (Revelation 8:2–11:19) the entire planet will be affected by massive destruction, loss of life, and human suffering. The chaos that results will destabilize both the global economy and the world government predicted in Revelation 13.

The seventh seal of the scroll is opened in Revelation 8:1, and the imagery that follows, including the half-hour of silence, follows the liturgy of the Jewish temple services.[5] After the sacrificial lamb was slain, the altar of incense was prepared. Two of the priests would go into the holy place and take burnt coals and ashes from the golden altar and relight the lamps of the golden candlestick. One priest filled the golden censer with incense, while the other placed burning coals from the altar into a golden bowl. Complete silence fell over the temple during this solemn ceremony.

The scene here in Revelation is very similar. There is silence for one half-hour after the opening of the seventh seal. It is the silence of solemn worship, and it is also a holy hush before the oncoming storm—one last gasp before all hell breaks loose.

The angel offers the "prayers of all saints [believers]" from the golden censer (8:3). Then he fills the censer with fire from the golden altar and "cast[s] it into the earth" (8:5). This initiates the conflagration that is about to engulf the planet. Bruce Metzger writes, "Then—bang! Catastrophic consequences follow. Seven angels, one after another, blow their trumpets, announcing hail-storm with fire and blood descending, volca-nic eruption, blood in the sea, blight in the land...climaxed by an enormous plague of demonic locusts."[6]

These trumpets may involve divine cosmic judgments or they may be associated with nuclear or chemical warfare. The devastation they predict was beyond anything known to the people of John's day, which makes the apocalypse all the more fascinating. There is no way John could have merely imagined these great catastrophes had he not seen them by divine per-mission in these visions. The destruction he describes certainly sounds like the devastating effects of nuclear warfare.

For example, a *limited* nuclear exchange between two mod-ern superpowers would kill an estimated one billion people and seriously injure another 500 million. The immediate results would include:

- radiation poisoning
- environmental destruction
- uncontrollable fires
- massive food shortages
- air and water pollution
- soil contamination
- unparalleled human suffering

The long-term effects could lead to the decivilization of the earth. Human culture would be thrown back into primitive liv-ing conditions. Roving bands of lawless raiders would become the only means of survival in contaminated areas. Whole population centers would likely be wiped out, with people in remote regions being the primary survivors left on the planet.

John Phillips writes, "Truly the dawning of the atomic age is of great prophetic significance...We have lived on the edge of a potential holocaust for so long we find it difficult to believe that we are on the brink of the Rapture of the Church and the subsequent unleashing of apocalyptic doom."[7] Ironically, even the seer's description of "hail and fire" fits the nuclear descrip-tion of an explosion of fire and ice.

The first four trumpets will herald human devastation brought about by war and the forces of nature. And the last three trumpets have to do with supernatural forces—angels and demons. They take us behind the scenes of the human conflict to see the underlying spiritual warfare being fought for control of the earth.

These judgments will affect the whole world. If the church were still on the earth during this time, she would be caught right in the middle of this great global disaster. Even nondispensationalist Leon Morris admits, "The trumpet judgments do not concern the church as such. They are God's judgments on the world."[8] But if the church were still in the world, she could hardly escape such horrific devastation. But there is no mention of the church in these chapters because she has already gone home to glory in the rapture.

Can Anyone Be Saved After the Rapture?

John Walvoord wrote, "The question has often been asked, 'Will anyone be saved after the rapture?' The Scriptures clearly indicate that a great multitude of both Jews and Gentiles will trust in the Lord after the church is caught up to glory."[9] Later, two "witnesses" are introduced who are instrumental in the conversion of the Jews (Revelation 11:3-12).

Premillennialists believe Christ will return at the end of the church age and judge the world in order to set up His kingdom on earth for a literal 1000 years. Most also believe there will be a period of great devastation on earth prior to the return of Christ. Among premillennialists are those who believe the church will go through the Tribulation (postribulationists), and those who believe the church will be raptured prior to the Tribulation (pretribulationists) and even a few who believe the church will be raptured in the middle of the Tribulation (midtribulationists). Despite these differences over the timing of the rapture of the church, premillennialists generally believe in the future restoration of the state of Israel and the eventual conversion of the Jews to Christianity.

The Jewish people who will be saved during the Tribulation

are called the 144,000 "servants of our God" from "all the tribes of the children of Israel" (Revelation 7:4). The number seems to be literal, but it could also be symbolic of totality (i.e., national conversion of the Jews). There is no indication in the text that they are to be viewed as the New Testament church or Gentile Christians. They are on earth during the Tribulation and are given a seal to protect them from the judgments coming upon the earth. When we consider the symbolism of the "woman" (Israel) and the "remnant of her seed" (converted Jews) in Revelation 12:1-17, it is clear that the 144,000 are literal Israelites. In fact, Revelation 7:5-8 specifically states there are 12,000 people from each of the 12 tribes of Israel.

If the 144,000 didn't represent specific people of Israel, the listing of the 12 tribes would be irrelevant. The specification of the tribes is consistent only with a literal interpretation of those tribes. John Walvoord wrote: "The fact that the twelve tribes of Israel are singled out for special reference in the tribulation time is another evidence that the term 'Israel' as used in the Bible is invariably a reference to the descendants of Jacob who was first given the name Israel."[10]

The apostle John then says, "After this..." (7:9; Greek, *meta tauta*). This literary expression moves the reader on to the next event, or in this case, the next group of people. The "great multitude" in 7:9 isn't made up of Jews from the 12 tribes of Israel. Rather, they comprise people from every nation (Gentiles and Jews) and are so great in number they cannot humanly be counted.

John specifically identifies this group as coming from every nation (Greek, *ethnos*, "ethnic" group), kindreds (Greek, *phylon*, "family" groups), people (Greek, *laon*, "people" groups), and tongue (Greek, *glosson*, "language" group). The partitive *ek* ("from") means only some from every one of these groups will be represented. That this is a body of redeemed people is obvious from the fact that they stand before the Lamb in white robes (righteousness) waving palm branches (victory).

The text says, "These are they which came out of the great tribulation" (Revelation 7:14 KJV). They are pictured as already standing before the throne of God, serving Him day and night in the heavenly temple (Revelation 7:15). This multitude of saved people, mostly Gentiles, are in heaven praising God. There is no reference to their having been martyred to get there. The fact that one of the elders (representing the church) asked who they are (Revelation 7:13) implies they are not church-age saints.

This multitude represents the believers who will come to faith in Christ during the Tribulation. Non-pretribulationalists say this is the church of Jesus Christ, persecuted, martyred, and betrayed down through the centuries of church history. To hold this position, they must view the entire church age as being the Great Tribulation.

Pretribulationalists believe, as the text says, that these people will be saved on earth during the Tribulation (first six seals) and "came out of" (Greek, *ek*, "from") the Great Tribulation (seventh seal and following). In other words, they will have died during the first half of the Tribulation and been taken from the earth prior to the Great Tribulation.[11]

Divine Wrath and Great Tribulation

The Great Tribulation (Greek, *tes thlipseōs tēs megalēs*) refers to that eschatological period of God's wrath. It is not merely the persecution or "troubles" of John's own time but a time of future global retribution, called in Revelation 3:10 the "hour of temptation" (KJV) and in 6:16 "the wrath of the Lamb."

Understanding the nature of these judgments is crucial to one's interpretation of the apocalypse. If the judgments of the Tribulation period are something less than divine wrath, one might better argue for the church's remaining on earth during the Tribulation. But there are two glaring contradictions present to that viewpoint: (1) This is divine wrath; and (2) the multitude is already in heaven, but the Tribulation judgments are not yet finished.

The church is pictured in Revelation 19:7-10 as the bride of Christ. She is in heaven at the marriage supper of the Lamb. She is also preparing to return to earth with Christ in His ultimate triumph (19:11-16). She is the object of His love, not

His wrath. She may be disciplined, corrected, or rebuked in the days of her earthly sojourn (Revelation 3:19). But she is *never* the object of the Lord's wrath! He cannot pour out divine wrath on the church because that wrath was already poured out on Jesus Christ at the cross. Jesus already took the punishment of divine wrath for believers (see Isaiah 53:1-12; 2 Corinthians 5:17-21; Hebrews 9:24-28; 10:5-25). He is our perfect substitute. He paid the price in full. "There is therefore now no condemnation to those who are in Christ Jesus" (Romans 8:1).

There is no logical way to explain how these judgments—the wrath of the Lamb—could be allowed to fall on Christ's bride. He wouldn't be much of a husband if He beat her up *then* took her to the wedding reception. That is one reason why many believe the church will already have been raptured.

People will become saved during the Tribulation. While the witness of the church and its restraining force upon society will be missing, the omnipresent Holy Spirit will still convict men of sin, righteousness, and judgment (John 16:7-11). It is true that many will believe a lie and be deceived by "strong delusion" (2 Thessalonians 2:10-12). Nevertheless, in Revelation 7 we see both Jewish and Gentile converts believing in Jesus as their Savior. It's no wonder they "cried out" (literally, "keep on crying"), "Salvation belongs to our God" (Revelation 7:10).

Revelation 7 ends with all of heaven on its face before God. His sovereignty is extolled in His redemption of Israel and the Gentiles alike, just as it was extolled in His divine act of creation (Revelation 4:11). What a powerful and beautiful picture! It is God who saves people...

1. Before the Law (Abraham and the patriarchs)

2. Under the Law (Old Testament believers)

3. During the church age (New Testament church)

4. During the Tribulation (Tribulation saints)

5. During the millennial kingdom (kingdom saints)

Salvation is a free gift of God's grace. It is secured for all believers by the sacrificial and substitutionary death of Christ on the cross. It was there that He bore our sins and endured the wrath of God against us. In those awful moments, suspended between heaven and earth, the cup of divine judgment fell upon Him. He who knew no sin was made sin for us, that we might receive the righteousness of God as a free gift (2 Corinthians 5:17-21). In His death on the cross, He triumphed over sin, death, and hell. No wonder He said, "It is finished!" (John 19:30).

Salvation is possible after the rapture. Many Jews and Gentiles will be saved during the Tribulation. And most of them will lose their lives for the cause of Christ. The vast majority of people who are left behind after the rapture will be deceived by the Antichrist and False Prophet, and that delusion will condemn them forever (2 Thessalonians 2:10-12). Don't take any chances with your eternal destiny. Make sure you are ready to go when Jesus comes to call His people home to heaven.

10

THE WRATH TO COME IS NOT FOR BELIEVERS

Tim LaHaye

Anyone who has read the book of Revelation and is of the understanding that the Bible should always be interpreted literally whenever possible would certainly be troubled by the apostle John's description of God's wrath poured out upon a rebellious and unbelieving world. So great is this coming wrath that unbelievers will seek a rather unusual deliverance from it:

> The kings of the earth, the great men, the rich men, the commanders, the mighty men, every slave and every free man, hid themselves in the caves and in the rocks of the mountains, and said to the mountains and rocks, "Fall on us and hide us from the face of Him who sits on the throne and from the wrath of the Lamb! For the great day of His wrath has come, and who is able to stand?" (Revelation 6:15-17; see also Revelation 6:8; 9:18; 14:20; 19:21; Matthew 24:4-29).

The Day of the Lord

Both the Old and New Testaments outline a seven-year

period of unparalleled devastation that will be unlike anything that has come before, or will ever come again. It is referred to as the Day of the Lord and is referenced throughout the Bible. In fact, it is one of the most important prophetic subjects detailed in Scripture. The "day" in this instance is not just a 24-hour period, but a period of seven years known as the Tribulation:

> Wail, for the day of the LORD is at hand! It will come as destruction from the Almighty. Therefore all hands will be limp, every man's heart will melt... Behold, the day of the LORD comes, cruel, with both wrath and fierce anger, to lay the land desolate; and He will destroy its sinners from it (Isaiah 13:6-7,9).

> Let all the inhabitants of the land tremble; for the day of the LORD is coming, for it is at hand: A day of darkness and gloominess, a day of clouds and thick darkness...For the day of the LORD is great and very terrible; who can endure it? (Joel 2:1-2,11).

> The great day of the LORD is near; it is near and hastens quickly. The noise of the day of the LORD is bitter; there the mighty men shall cry out. That day is a day of wrath, a day of trouble and distress, a day of devastation and desolation (Zephaniah 1:14-15).

> I will show wonders in heaven above and signs in the earth beneath: Blood and fire and vapor of smoke. The sun shall be turned into darkness, and the moon into blood, before the coming of the great and awesome day of the LORD (Acts 2:19-20).

> The day of the Lord will come as a thief in the night, in which the heavens will pass away with a great noise, and the elements will melt with fervent heat; both the earth and the works that are in it will be burned up (2 Peter 3:10).

The Great Tribulation will consist of a series of cataclysmic disasters, including famines, droughts, earthquakes, and mass executions. A global dictator will rule the land and will demand that all men and women take his mark in order to buy and sell. Deception will be at an all-time high. There will be warfare on an unprecedented scale. Hail and fire mixed with blood will rain down from the sky. The earth's vegetation will be burned. Swarms of locust-like creatures will torment men with their scorpion-like sting. Rivers and springs will be poisoned and sea life will be destroyed. Light from the sun, moon, and stars will be darkened, yet heat from the sun will continue to scorch the earth. Mountains and islands will be shaken out of their places. And 100-pound hailstones will slam into the earth, decimating everything in their path.

Mercifully, God will see to it that this horrific period should not linger:

> There will be great tribulation, such as has not been since the beginning of the world until this time, no, nor ever shall be. And unless those days were shortened, no flesh would be saved; but for the elect's sake those days will be shortened (Matthew 24:21-22).

In fact, Jesus Christ Himself will return visibly to earth at the conclusion of the Tribulation in what will be the most dramatic event in all of history—His glorious appearing—in order to bring the Antichrist's reign of terror to a close and to set up His own 1000-year-long millennial kingdom of peace.

Kept from the Wrath of God

When a person comes to realize the horrors that await those who will experience the Tribulation, he often asks, "Will true believers in Christ have to endure these judgments?" The answer, based on a literal interpretation of all of the end-times passages found in the Bible, is an unequivocal *no*. The Tribulation marks the unleashing of God's wrath upon a vicious, unrepentant world—upon those who have rejected the love of God's Son and His gracious gift of salvation. The Christian has, of course, already embraced God's salvation and therefore is not in line to experience such wrath:

> [We] wait for His Son from heaven, whom He raised from the dead, even Jesus who delivers us from the wrath to come (1 Thessalonians 1:10).

> God did not appoint us to wrath, but to obtain salvation through our Lord Jesus Christ (1 Thessalonians 5:9).

> Because you have kept My command to persevere, I also will keep you from the hour of trial which shall come upon the whole world, to test those who dwell on the earth (Revelation 3:10).

Through the ages, Christians have had to endure various trials and persecutions that are a result of being "not of the world" and belonging to Christ. John Foxe's *Book of Martyrs*, for example, vividly depicts such sufferings that have been part and parcel of the Christian life ever since the first century. Scripture tells us,

> If you were of the world, the world would love its own. Yet because you are not of the world, but I chose you out of the world, therefore the world hates you. Remember the word that I said to you, "A servant is not greater than his master." If they persecuted Me, they will also persecute you (John 15:19-20).

> To you it has been granted on behalf of Christ, not only to believe in Him, but also to suffer for His sake (Philippians 1:29).

> All who desire to live godly in Christ Jesus will suffer persecution (2 Timothy 3:12).

Now, there is a great difference between these everyday kinds of trials and those that will occur during the Tribulation. The "tribulations" experienced in the daily life of the Christian come from the world and from Satan, whereas the trials experienced during the Tribulation are primarily judgments on those who have rejected God's offer of grace through the acceptance of His Son, Jesus Christ, as Savior. In fact, God has a dual purpose for the Tribulation—to judge the Christ-rejecting Gentile nations of the earth and to purify Israel. But what about the church? Because God has not "appointed us to wrath" (that is, the church), how and where does it fit into the Tribulation scenario? The judgments that will take place during the Tribulation are documented in Revelation chapters 4–18. While we can find evidence of wicked men, godless nations, and persecution against Israel in these chapters, there is no mention at all of the church. Why not? Where is the church during the Tribulation?

Comfort One Another with These Words

Ever since the truth of the rapture was first presented to the Thessalonian Christians by the apostle Paul, it has proven to be a source of tremendous comfort to believers throughout the ages. Clearly, the rapture is God's merciful way of removing the church from the earth prior to His judgments being poured out on the wicked. During the first century, believers living in the city of Thessalonica were concerned that they may have missed the rapture and were about to enter the Tribulation. Paul wrote to them about the sequence of both the rapture and the glorious appearing, which are separated by a seven-year Tribulation.

> This we say to you by the word of the Lord, that we who are alive and remain until the coming of the Lord will by no means precede those who are asleep. For the Lord Himself will descend from heaven with a shout, with the voice of an archangel, and with the trumpet of God. And the dead in Christ will rise first. Then we who are alive and remain shall be caught up together with them in the clouds to meet the Lord in the air. And thus we shall always be with the Lord. Therefore comfort one another with these words (1 Thessalonians 4:15-18).

If the rapture were to occur midway through or at the end

of the Tribulation, as those who adhere to a mid- or posttribulation position believe, then how could a discussion involving the rapture bring about any comfort? Who in their right mind could possibly take comfort in facing plagues, disease, executions, earthquakes, and death? Relegating the rapture to among the many end-time events diminishes its meaning and nullifies its purpose. By contrast, a pretribulation rapture fits with the fact believers are asked to watch and be ready for the rapture itself, and not for the events of the Tribulation which follow:

> Watch therefore, and pray always that you may be counted worthy to escape all these things that will come to pass, and to stand before the Son of Man (Luke 21:36).

> You, brethren, are not in darkness, so that this Day should overtake you as a thief...Let us watch and be sober...For God did not appoint us to wrath, but to obtain salvation through our Lord Jesus Christ, who died for us, that whether we wake or sleep, we should live together with Him. Therefore comfort each other and edify one another (1 Thessalonians 5:4,6,9-11).

By taking all the end-times scriptures at face value and examining them within their context, it is obvious that the church will be spared the judgments of the Day of the Lord and be taken to heaven prior to the start of the Tribulation.

The Restrainer

Within today's world, there is a restraining influence which keeps unrighteousness in check: "The mystery of lawlessness is already at work; only He who now restrains will do so until He is taken out of the way. And then the lawless one will be revealed, whom the Lord will consume with the breath of His mouth and destroy with the brightness of His coming" (2 Thessalonians 2:7-8).

In addition, the Antichrist ("the lawless one") who is to come apparently cannot be revealed nor can his satanic work be unleashed upon the earth until this "restraining influence" is somehow taken out of the way. Again, basing our understanding on a literal interpretation of the complete prophetic scriptures, it is clear that this restrainer is the Holy Spirit.

The church age represents the age of grace, and the Holy Spirit's indwelling of believers began at Pentecost. This phase of God's plan will come to an end at the moment the rapture occurs. Spirit-filled Christians must be removed from the earth before God's judgment upon the earth can move forward. This is why the rapture must take place before the identity of the Antichrist can be unveiled.

Keep in mind, however, that the removal of Spirit-filled Christians does not mean the earth will be devoid of the work of the Spirit from that moment on. For example, the Spirit will seal and protect the 144,000 Jews who serve God during the Tribulation. Likewise, millions who do not reject God by worshipping the Beast and taking his sign of 666 (Revelation 13:15-18) will turn to the Lord and allow themselves to be martyred so as to avoid taking the mark. In the past, prior to Pentecost, the Holy Spirit moved mightily among men without necessarily *indwelling* them. We can see the handiwork of the Spirit working in individuals such as Noah, Moses, Jonah, David, and even John the Baptist. In addition, those prophets who obediently wrote down the Scriptures were of course moved by the Spirit to do so (2 Peter 1:20-21).

The Holy Spirit will continue to do His work during the Tribulation. However those who have the Spirit (the restrainer) living within them—that is, the bride of Christ—will be removed from the earth and reunited with their Groom in heaven.

The Rapture Is Imminent

The rapture of the church has been the hope of believers since it was first revealed in the New Testament. Numerous passages instruct us to watch and be ready for it. It is due to the expectation of Christ's imminent return that we are motivated to live in purity and obedience to Him. And it is the promise of our being reunited with our loved ones "in the air" that brings comfort.

Scripture tells us no one can know the exact time of the rapture. Likewise, there are no prophesied events scheduled to take place between now and the catching away of the church into heaven. So the rapture could come at any moment. Believers should therefore not be looking for the appearance of the Antichrist, the judgments of the Tribulation, or Christ's millennial kingdom. Instead, they should focus on being ready for the rapture.

While we can be certain that Jesus *will* indeed come, we are uncertain as to when. And this has a number of benefits. It motivates us toward holy living because we do not want to be ashamed upon His return. It also encourages us to share the gospel with others. With many signs today suggesting that the Tribulation may be just around the corner, this work of sharing Christ with the lost takes on an even greater urgency. Had the date of the rapture been revealed, this urgency would have been lost to every generation prior.

Placing the rapture at the middle or end of the Tribulation destroys the concept of imminency along with the positive effects it can have on one's life. A posttribulation view of the rapture, for example, means that once the Tribulation begins, believers must suffer through the seven-year Tribulation. This eliminates any comfort, encouragement, motivation, or purifying hope that a pretribulation rapture brings.

Israel versus the Church

The Tribulation will be a time when God once again deals with the nation of Israel. The church will have been removed at the rapture, and God will then turn His attention to the Jewish people who remain on the earth and are about to face the Tribulation. The Old Testament records many promises God made to Israel in times past which have yet to be fulfilled, and many of these prophecies will come to fruition during the Tribulation—for God always keeps His promises:

> When you are in distress, and all these things come
> upon you in the latter days, when you turn to the
> LORD your God and obey His voice (for the LORD
> your God is a merciful God), He will not forsake
> you nor destroy you, nor forget the covenant of
> your fathers which He swore to them (Deuteron-
> omy 4: 30-31).

> The day of the LORD is near in the valley of deci-
> sion. The sun and moon will grow dark, and the
> stars will diminish their brightness. The LORD also
> will roar from Zion, and utter His voice from Jeru-
> salem; the heavens and earth will shake; but the
> LORD will be a shelter for His people, and the
> strength of the children of Israel. So you shall know
> that I am the LORD your God (Joel 3:14-17).

The sealing and protection of 144,000 Jews during the Tribulation is but one promise that the Lord will fulfill during this
time:

> I heard the number of those who were sealed. One
> hundred and forty-four thousand of all the tribes of
> the children of Israel were sealed (Revelation 7:4).

> I will bring the one-third through the fire, will
> refine them as silver is refined, and test them as
> gold is tested. They will call on My name, and I will
> answer them. I will say, "This is My people"; and
> each one will say, "The LORD is my God" (Zecha-
> riah 13:9).

There are some today who believe the church has replaced
Israel in the prophetic scheme of things and is therefore deserv-
ing of the blessings and promises made to the Jews by God in
the Old Testament. This heretical idea, known as replacement
theology, is simply untrue. The Jews and the church remain
two separate groups today, and God has two separate plans for
their futures. The lives of Old Testament patriarchs Enoch and
Noah can be viewed as being in parallel with each of these two

groups. Enoch, for example, was taken up to heaven just before the great flood destroyed the earth (Genesis 5:24). Enoch can therefore be compared to the church, which will be raptured to heaven prior to the Tribulation. Noah, on the other hand, experienced the devastation of the worldwide flood yet was protected throughout the ordeal. Thus Noah can be compared to the many Jews whom God will safely lead through the trials of the Tribulation.

Spared by God's Love

There are at least five key reasons that we as Christians can rest in the fact we will not have to endure the Tribulation:

1. *The Lord promised to deliver us.* In Revelation 3:10, God Himself said He will keep us out of the wrath that is to come upon the world.

2. *Only the pretribulation rapture preserves imminency.* Scripture tells us again and again to watch, be ready, and to look for His coming at any moment. Both the mid- and posttribulation rapture views destroy the concept of imminency and cause Christians to look for the Antichrist and the events of the Tribulation instead of Christ. How could the expectation of these things possibly bring comfort?

3. *The rapture and the glorious appearing are two separate events.* In his letters to the young church in Thessalonica, Paul emphatically explained that Jesus would rescue Christians from the wrath to come. Apparently Paul considered it essential to ground these new believers with information about the imminent rapture, followed by the seven-year Tribulation, and then the glorious appearing (second coming) of Christ. From these and other passages we can conclude that the rapture and the second coming serve as bookends for the Tribulation.

4. *We are not appointed to wrath.* First Thessalonians
   5:9 makes it clear God has not appointed us to
   wrath but will deliver us from it (via the rapture). People left behind to experience the Tribulation will be forced to decide whether or not
   to take the mark of the Beast or repent of their
   self-will and accept Christ. Those who refuse the
   mark will be martyred, and their numbers will be
   astronomical (see Revelation 6:11; 7:14; 20:4).
   It is therefore apparent that people who become
   believers during the Tribulation will *not* be guar-
   anteed safety—only those who are Christians
   before the rapture have that assurance.

5. *The church is absent from Revelation 4–18.* The
   church is mentioned 17 times in the first three
   chapters of Revelation, then does not appear
   again until chapter 19, when she is seen returning to the earth with Jesus at His glorious appearing. Chapters 4–18 describe the events of the
   Tribulation, and it is obvious the church has no
   part in it, for she has been raptured out of it.

The deliverance of Christians from the world's greatest period of devastation can be looked upon as a gift from
God. It is not something the church deserves; rather, the Lord
spares the church out of love—the perfect gift from the perfect
Groom to His bride. A pretribulational view of the rapture is
in keeping with the merciful character of a loving God who
takes His bride to His Father's house in heaven. No wonder
the rapture is often called "the blessed hope" (or confidence)
of the church! (Titus 2:13).

11

HOW TO AVOID
BEING LEFT BEHIND

Ed Hindson

The timing of the last days is in God's hands. From a human standpoint it appears that we are standing on the threshold of the final frontier. The pieces of the puzzle are all in place. As the sands of time slip through the hourglass of eternity, we are all moving closer to an appointment with destiny. The only question is, How much time is left?

The tension between living for today and looking for tomorrow is one of the realities of the Christian life. We often find ourselves caught between the here-and-now and the hereafter. On the one hand, we need to be ready for Jesus to come at any moment. On the other hand, we have God-given responsibilities to fulfill in this world.

We are living in a time of great crisis, but it is also a time of great opportunity. We must be prepared for the challenges that lie ahead of us. New technologies will make our lives more convenient, but they will also make us more dependent on these conveniences. Medical advancements will continue to pose enormous challenges in the area of biomedical ethics. The shifting sands of sociopolitical change will also challenge our national and international policies in the days ahead. We will find ourselves living in a very different world from the one into which we were born. All these changes and challenges will confront us in the days ahead.

Preparing for Christ's return is something each one of us must do on our own. You cannot look to others to get your heart ready to meet God. Each person is responsible for his or her eternal destiny. Jesus urges us to do three things in view of His second coming:

1. Keep watching (Matthew 24:42)
2. Be ready (Matthew 24:44)
3. Keep serving (Matthew 24:46)

Is There Any Hope for Our Generation?

Throughout history, God has often moved to bless His people in a fresh and powerful way. Genuine revival came as God's people were convicted of their sin, repented, and gained a new zeal and devotion for God in their lives. In revival, the self-centered, halfhearted indifference that so often dominates our lives is swept aside by a new and genuine desire to live for God.

Revival renews our values and redirects our lives. It calls us to a more serious walk with Christ and results in substantial and abiding fruit (see John 15:16; Galatians 5:22-23). The changes that occur, both in individual believers and in the church collectively, speak convincingly to the world about what it really means to belong to Christ. Such revival comes when God's people pray, when God's truth is proclaimed, and when God's Spirit moves in our lives.

In the meantime, we can live with our eyes on the skies—watching for Christ to come—and with our feet on the earth, working for Him until He comes. The balance of expectation (that Jesus could come at any moment) and participation (serving Him faithfully until He comes) is what the Christian life is really all about. Living in light of His coming keeps us focused on what is really important. It also keeps our attention on the balance between our present responsibilities and our future expectations.

The hope of the second coming is a powerful incentive for

us to live right until Jesus comes. The ultimate encouragement toward right living is the fact that we will face our Lord when He returns. Each of us needs to be ready when that day comes. If we live out faithfully whatever time is left to us, we will surely hear Him say, "Well done, good and faithful servant."

A Date with Destiny

The world is speeding toward its ultimate date with destiny. Every day that passes moves us closer to the end. The people and the planet have a divine appointment to keep. As the clock of time ticks away, mankind comes closer and closer to earth's final hour.

It is only a matter of time before our planet will experience the most devastating catastrophes imaginable. Global conflagration is clearly predicted in biblical prophecy, and the outcome is certain. How much time is left?

Almost 2000 years ago, the apostle Peter said, "The end of all things is at hand; therefore be serious and watchful in your prayers" (1 Peter 4:7). Peter's reference to the end is expressed by a perfect-tense verb in the original Greek text. This means the action involved is a present reality with future consequences. It could just as appropriately be translated, "The end of all things has already begun." For Peter, the end of the age was already a present reality.

The first coming of Christ initiated the end of the age (see Acts 2:14-21; Hebrews 1:2), and His second coming will terminate the end of the age (Matthew 24:30). Therefore, the entire church age is a "last days," or a "last of the last days."

Scripture also speaks of the end as a future event. The apostle Paul predicted, "In the last days perilous times will come" (2 Timothy 3:1). The opening verse of the Apocalypse refers to "things which must shortly come to pass" (Revelation 1:1 KJV) and goes on to warn us that "the time is near" (Revelation 1:3). Scripture also presents Christ's coming as an imminent reality. "Behold, I am coming quickly!" Christ promised (Revelation 22:7). He will come suddenly, and He could come at any moment.

That leaves us asking this question: What time is it now? Peter referred to the *present*, saying, "[Christ] was manifest in these last times" (1 Peter 1:20). At the same time, Peter referred to the coming of Christ as a future event, "ready to be revealed in the last time" (1 Peter 1:5). It is clear that he viewed the last times as both a present reality and a future event.

The Bible affirms three basic facts about the coming of Christ at the end of the age.

First, *we are living in the last days*. Every generation of Christians has lived with the hope of the imminent return of Christ. We believe that He could return at any moment. There is no prophetic event that remains to be fulfilled before the way can be opened for Him to return. In fact, certain events, such as the return of Israel to her land, indicate that we are close to the end.

Second, *God's timetable is not our timetable*. Peter himself told us that "scoffers will come in the last days," questioning the promise of His second coming (2 Peter 3:3-4). They will reject the idea of God's intervention in human history and suggest that all things are moving forward without any help from God. These skeptics also fail to anticipate God's coming judgment upon the world (2 Peter 3:8-9). God's perspective is not limited to human time. But we dare not mistake the patience of God for a change in His plans. He is waiting, giving people time to repent. The Bible warns: "He who is coming will come and will not tarry" (Hebrews 10:37).

Third, *Christ's coming is always growing closer*. The Bible emphatically promises that Christ is coming again (Luke 12:40; Titus 2:13; Hebrews 9:28). Scripture urges us to be watching, waiting, and ready. Whether Christ returns next week or 100 years from now, we are to be living as though He were coming today.

Looking Ahead

Anticipation is the key to preparation. If you were expecting an important visitor, you would probably keep looking for him as you await his arrival. Chances are that you would also make proper preparations for his visit. Your anticipation would influence your preparation for his visit. The same is true of our anticipation of Christ's coming. If we really believe He is coming, we will want to be ready for Him.

If we take seriously the biblical predictions about the end time, then we must make preparations now. The time for action is now. If you are not sure about your relationship with Christ, make sure before it is too late. That's because all of us will face death at some point. We cannot avoid it.

Death is the great equalizer. It makes no difference how rich or poor, famous or infamous, respected or rejected you are. When you face death, you are facing an impartial judge. The Bible reminds us that "all have sinned" (Romans 3:23) and "the wages of sin is death" (Romans 6:23). When death comes knocking at your door, all that really matters is that you are ready to face it.

The reason Jesus came was to die for our sins. He paid the price for our sins so that we might be forgiven. He is called our Redeemer because He has done what is necessary to redeem us from God's judgment against our sin. Peter wrote: "You were... redeemed...with the precious blood of Christ...He was indeed foreordained before the foundation of the world, but was manifest in these last times for your sake" (1 Peter 1:18-20).

Jesus said: "I am the resurrection and the life. He who believes in Me, though he may die, he shall live" (John 11:25). This is the great promise of Christ. He calls us to faith in Him and promises to reward us with eternal life (John 3:16; 5:24). The Bible pictures eternity as a place of great activity where we serve Christ forever. In the meantime, we are "pilgrims" passing through the temporary domain of earth on our way to our ultimate home. Joseph Stowell writes, "To claim the pilgrim's identity means that we always know we're not home yet. For us, the best is yet to come."[1]

Until the trumpet sounds, or death comes to usher us into eternity, we are to keep our eyes on the Savior (Hebrews 12:2). He is the focus of Bible prophecy. The prophets predicted His first coming with perfect accuracy, and they have done the same for His second coming. Jesus said, "When these things begin to happen, look up and lift up your heads, because your redemption draws near" (Luke 21:28).

Whatever else is coming in the future, we can rest assured that Jesus is coming again. The ultimate question is, Is He coming for you? He came the first time to die on the cross as the sacrifice for our sins. Trusting what Jesus did for us in His first coming prepares us for His second coming.

The promise of the Bible is: "Believe on the Lord Jesus Christ and you will be saved" (Acts 16:31). If you trust Him, you will not be left behind.

12

IS THE RAPTURE FOUND IN 2 THESSALONIANS 2:3?

H. Wayne House

P aul's letters to the Thessalonian church were written early in his ministry (c. AD 51–52). These Christians eagerly accepted the teaching that Paul gave to them in the short time he was with them. But as soon as Paul left, persons came into their midst who perverted the apostle's teaching. Paul had apparently taught that they should be diligent in looking for Christ to come (1 Thessalonians 4–5). Unfortunately, however, someone argued that Jesus had already returned. This puzzled the believers, for they had not been taken in the expected rapture (1 Thessalonians 4:13). Now Paul wrote to provide additional evidence to assure them that Jesus had not yet returned.

How Bible Scholars Have Understood *Apostasia* in 2 Thessalonians 2:3

Bible scholars have understood the Greek word *apostasia* (translated "falling away" in the KJV) in four different ways. How one understands this Greek term will impact how one sees the return of Jesus. Let us examine the different interpretations below.

Apostasia *Refers to the Man of Sin*

This view holds that the word "apostasy" refers to the "man of sin" in verse 3 (what scholars call apposition). This was a common understanding in the first few centuries of the church, but few hold it today. The church father Augustine said, "No one can doubt that he [Paul] wrote this of Antichrist and of the day of judgment, which he here calls the day of the Lord, nor that he declared that this day should not come unless he first came who is called the apostate—apostate, to wit, from the Lord God."[1]

Apostasia *Refers to "Falling Away" from the Faith*

A second view is that adopted by the KJV Bible, namely, "falling away." Under this view, "apostasy" speaks of a falling away or defection from the faith.[2] When this occurs, the Antichrist (man of sin) will arise, showing signs and wonders. This view seems to have originated with the translation of the KJV in 1611, and is popular today. However, there is no consistency regarding who will actually fall away: Does this refer to the church, to Jews during the Tribulation, or to non-Christians? Let us look at examples of those who hold to each view.

PROFESSING CHURCH

Theologian Charles Ryrie believes that the "apostasy" in 2 Thessalonians 2:3 speaks of a future falling away of those within the professing church who never truly believed in Jesus, and believes this view is supported in Revelation 17 and 2 Timothy 3:1.[3]

JEWS DURING THE TRIBULATION

The second view asserts that the "apostasy" refers to Jews who will reject God during the Tribulation. Marvin Rosenthal has argued that even as the word is used in the New Testament when Paul was opposed by Jews (e.g., Acts 21:21), so this is how Jews will act during the Tribulation. He says they will "totally abandon the God of their fathers and their messianic hope in favor of a false religion (humanism) and a false messiah (the Antichrist, 2 Thess. 2:2-12)."[4]

NON-CHRISTIANS

Some view the "falling away" as referring to non-Christians. C.F. Hogg and W.E. Vine, as well as Lewis Sperry Chafer, believed that the term referred to the way in which unsaved humanity failed to embrace the truth of God found in the gospel after the church has been removed from the earth.[5]

Apostasia *Refers to a Revolt or Rebellion Against God*

Understanding *apostasia* as revolt or rebellion stands in strong contrast to the former "falling away." The latter implies a defection from the faith or from God, while the former speaks of a forceful or violent rejection of God.

A.L. Moore explains this view:

> [T]he rebellion comes first: here Paul uses imagery drawn probably from Daniel 11:36 (and cf. Isa. 14:13ff; Ezek. 28:2). Rebellion, *apostasia*, could refer to political apostasy or military revolt in classical Greek, but in the LXX [Greek OT] it denotes religious rebellion against God (cf. Jos. 22:22; Jer. 2:19)...The thought is, we suggest, that when the moment comes for Christ to appear in glory and for all that rebels against God to be unmasked and cast out, the forces of evil will arise as never before in a last desperate effort against God.[6]

The majority of scholars probably hold to this perspective, believing the word "apostasy" expresses deliberate opposition against God and/or His people,[7] and even may be a revolt against public order or government.[8] This disorder would set the stage for the rise of a person who would bring back order, also known as the Antichrist.

Apostasia *as the Rapture*

The final view, held by a minority today, including E. Schuyler English, Stanley Ellisen, Gordon Lewis, and Kenneth Wuest, is that "apostasy" may refer to the departure of the church. Since the view is rarely considered by commentators, it becomes incumbent upon those who hold to it to make a vigorous defense. Whether or not *apostasia* may mean rapture does not rely only upon the meaning of the term in the Greek text, but whether the idea of defection or revolt in the end times is found in Paul's teaching, as well as the likely meaning of the word in the immediate context of the letter to the Thessalonians.

Regarding the idea of defection or revolt in Paul's teaching, Ellisen captures the likely scenario:

> At the risk of being out of step with most commentaries on the subject, may we suggest the greater acceptability of an alternate view: the evidence for a great singular defection from the faith, occurring just prior to the rapture or to the day of the Lord, is really based on questionable ground. In the first reference generally appealed to (1 Tim. 4), Paul does speak of an apostasy from the faith, but not as a unique end-time event. Rather, he described it as a trend or movement that was already present. This he characterized as erroneous doctrine, hypocritical living, and improper legalism. In using the term here, he qualified it with the phrase "from the faith." By itself it meant simply "departure."
>
> In the second reference to defection, 2 Timothy 3:1ff., Paul does not use the term apostasy, but merely speaks of evil men in general in the latter times. His point here is that evil men will become more and more depraved as the age wears on (2 Timothy 3:13). Thus this passage has no real relation to apostasy from the faith and certainly does not warn of some specific final defection that will precede the rapture or introduce the day of the Lord.[9]

In the rest of this chapter, we will focus on the meaning of the technical term "apostasy" and what best meaning fits its usage in 2 Thessalonians 2:3.

How *Apostasia* Has Been Translated

Jerome translated the Greek New Testament into Latin in

the fourth century (the Vulgate). He used the Latin word *discessio*, meaning "departure," for the Greek word *apostasia*. This meaning was continued in the earliest English translations such as the Wycliff Bible (1384), Tyndale Bible (1526), Coverdale Bible (1535), Cranmer Bible (1539), Breeches Bible (1576), Beza Bible (1583), and Geneva Bible (1608). The KJV deviated from this translation, translating *apostasia* as "falling away." No explanation was given for doing this. Moreover, Theodore Beza transliterated *apostasia* as "apostasy," rather than translating it. Since the seventeenth century, the consistent understanding of *apostasia* in modern translations has been rebellion (NIV, NRSV, Goodspeed, RSV, Moffatt, Phillips, Jerusalem Bible, Williams), or falling away (Berkeley, ASV, NKJV).

Arguments that Favor
Apostasia as the Rapture

The Sense of "Departure" in Classical and Biblical Sources

The word *apostasia* is regularly translated "rebellion" or "defection" in Greek literature before the New Testament was written. In a few cases, however, it does have the sense of "departure." The reason for this difference is the context of the passages. At times, the word does not occur in a context in which the matter of rebellion against authority, or defection from a person, ideology, or religious faith is in view. Rather, the noun adheres more closely to the verbal meaning of "depart" or some other spatial sense.[10] The predominant meaning of rebellion and, at times, defection is also found in the Greek Old Testament. One must be careful when deviating from the established meanings in classical and biblical (LXX) writings, yet one must also not be afraid to take the minority meaning with spatial connotation when context warrants. Such may be the case in 2 Thessalonians 2:3.

The Use of the Definite Article with Apostasia

One finds the use of the Greek article with *apostasia* in 2 Thessalonians 2:3. Another example of this is 1 Maccabees

2:15, where defection from the Old Testament faith is gener-ally viewed to be the proper translation of *hee apostasia*. "And those who came from the king were compelling the defection in the city of Modein, in order to sacrifice" (1 Maccabees 2:15). What is the significance of these two instances? Similar to this passage in 1 Maccabees, 2 Thessalonians 2:3 has the article and no qualifiers, such as defection from God, so the context is determinative for the meaning of *apostasia*. In the first two chapters of 1 Maccabees there is a description of the Greek victory over Israel by Alexander the Greek until the time of Antiochus Epiphanes, with the latter king invading Judah and enforcing a desecration of the temple. When one studies the context of 2 Thessalonians 2:13 in the same way, the context speaks of the coming of Christ for the church, after which the man is revealed because the restrainer has been removed.

Idea of Second Coming Throughout 1 and 2 Thessalonians

Paul is deeply concerned that believers understand the coming of Christ. He speaks of Jesus' coming for His people in every chapter in 1 Thessalonians. For example, in 1:9-10a he spoke of how Christ will rescue believers from God's com-ing wrath. The pivotal passage on the rapture is 1 Thessalo-nians 4:13-17, where the apostle revealed that the dead would be "caught up" (from which we get the word rapture) together with living saints to be with Christ. In 5:1-11 he continued the discussion in chapter 4. He said that believers, unlike those in the world, would not be caught unready for Christ's coming.

Paul again discussed Jesus' coming in 2 Thessalonians. In chapter 2 he addressed the false teaching that Christ had already come, and told the Christians they need have no anxi-ety over this teaching.

Contextual Reasons for Apostasia to be the Rapture

What in the context of 2 Thessalonians 2 would lead one to accept that the rapture, rather than defection or rebellion is in view? Let us look at the immediately preceding verses to the reference of an *apostasia*. Second Thessalonians 2:1-2 reads,

> Now we request you, brethren, with regard to the
> coming of our Lord Jesus Christ and our gathering
> together to Him, that you not be quickly shaken
> from your composure or be disturbed either by a
> spirit or a message or a letter as if from us, to the
> effect that the day of the Lord has come (NASB).

The purpose of Paul's teaching on the coming of Christ was
to comfort the church. Each text in 1 and 2 Thessalonians
emphasizes this truth. If *apostasia* carries the sense of departure, following his words in 2:1, this would add to the comfort and assurance. Moreover, in verse 3 he sought to assuage
them of the false notion that the Day of the Lord had already
come. Rather, the Day of the Lord (a time of judgment) would
not come until two events occurred: One is the *apostasia* and
the other the rise of the man of sin. Since neither of these two
had yet taken place, the Thessalonian Christians should not
believe that the time for God's judgment had arrived.

Which makes the most sense in the context: that the Day
of the Lord had not come because a rebellion against government or a defection from the faith had not occurred, or that
the departure to be with Christ had not occurred? Remember,
in 1 Thessalonians 1, the encouragement was that the coming
of Christ would rescue believers from God's coming wrath. In
addition, there are at least three more arguments that favor a
departure rather than a rebellion/defection.

First, in passages where a rebellion or defection is in view,
the context speaks of the rebellion or defection, but such is not
in view in the preceding verses in 2 Thessalonians. Rather, as
we have seen in a brief review of 1 and 2 Thessalonians, the
coming of Christ is in view: "Now we request you, brethren,
with regard to the coming of our Lord Jesus Christ and our
gathering together to Him" (2 Thessalonians 2:1 NASB). Since
the subject of the passage is the coming of Christ, and nothing in this passage, or any other to my knowledge, presents
a rebellion against government or defection from Christianity as being a prerequisite for Christ's coming, the most natural understanding of *apostasia* would be a spatial departure in

concert with 1 Thessalonians 4. Certainly Matthew 24 speaks of many being led to follow the Antichrist (verse 5), but there is nothing about true believers following false Christs as an indication of Christ's coming. Moreover, the events of Matthew 24 refer to Christ's coming in judgment, not salvation, and relate to the time of the Tribulation and afterward. A statement about false teachers in the church is found in Acts 20, but it does not concern the man of sin.

Second, the word *apostasia* has the unusual article occurring with it, signifying that a specific event is in view, one that is known to the readers. The only event that fits with this special sense would seem to be in 2 Thessalonians 2:1 and 1 Thessalonians, particularly chapters 4–5. This would favor also a rapture perspective.

Finally, there is the use of "restrainer" in 2 Thessalonians 2:6-7. What is Paul speaking of when he mentions a "restrainer" that keeps the man of sin from arising (note that the restrainer does not impact the *apostasia*)? The term *apostasia* and the rise of the man of sin are probably not the same event in verse 3, and the contrast of the restrainer and the man of sin lend support to *apostasia* being a departure. Verses 6-7 seem to be parallel of *apostasia* and man of sin. Generally the restrainer in verses 6-7 is understood as a reference to the Holy Spirit or to the church (though some have seen this as a reference to government). What is interesting is that the idea of this restrainer is expressed in both a personal and impersonal sense. The text reads, "You know what restrains him now, so that in his time he will be revealed. For the mystery of lawlessness is already at work; only he who now restrains will do so until he is taken out of the way" (2 Thessalonians 2:6-7 NASB). So there is a *what* that restrains and a *who* that restrains. *What* is it that keeps the man of sin from arising, and *who* keeps him from arising? I believe it is reasonable to conclude that the church's presence on earth restrains him and the presence of the Holy Spirit in the church restrains him. When the Antichrist comes to power, God's redeemed will no longer be present on earth. The Spirit came upon the church in Acts 2, and will leave with the church in 2 Thessalonians 2.[11]

Interaction with Those
Who Reject the Rapture View

The claim is made that *apostasia* never speaks of a departure in Greek literature, specifically the New Testament. I have already dealt with this earlier in the chapter, and in much more depth elsewhere.[12] One key critic against *apostasia* referring to the rapture is Robert Gundry. His arguments have even convinced a stalwart pretribulationist such as John Walvoord.[13]

Gundry recognizes that Schuyler English, an early proponent of the rapture view, discovered *apostasia* as meaning "departure" in the classical period, but considered this discovery to be unimportant for the word in 2 Thessalonians 2:3. Gundry says that the four sources for determining the meaning are found in the New Testament, the Greek Old Testament (LXX), the *koine* (common Greek in time of NT), and classical Greek. He is unconvinced that the word *apostasia* carries this minority meaning in 2 Thessalonians 2:3. Since the predominant meaning of *apostasia* is revolt and religious defection, he believes that this would govern its use in 2 Thessalonians 2:3.

The only other instance of *apostasia* in the New Testament is Acts 21:21, when Paul is challenged as "teaching all the Jews who are among the Gentiles to forsake Moses" (Acts 21:21 NASB). The meaning is clear, religious defection. Gundry believes that the two instances in the New Testament (Acts 21:21 and 2 Thessalonians 2:3) would convey the idea of defection from the faith—*despite* no such reference in 2 Thessalonians 2:3—because even without defection being in the context, the word *apostasia* had inherently come to mean defection. Such is not the case, however. One must always consider context when determining the meaning of words. In the passages where *apostasia* is translated revolt or defection, the context naturally leads one to the translation. This is not the case for 2 Thessalonians. The context does *not* address these negative ideas. Rather, the focus is the coming of Christ and what must precede the Day of the Lord. Consequently, the sense of spatial departure is not outside the possible meaning.

Secure in Hope

To view *apostasia* as speaking of a departure agrees with examples of usage in the Greek world, is consistent with the context of 2 Thessalonians 2, and fits with Paul's objective to provide comfort to believers. This interpretation of 2 Thessalonians 2:3 can also provide hope for Christians today, securing them in the knowledge that they are not destined for wrath, but to meet the Lord in the air and to always be with Him (1 Thessalonians 4:17).

"DEPARTING" RATHER THAN "FALLING AWAY" IN 2 THESSALONIANS 2:3

Tim LaHaye

When it comes to the end times, are you looking for Christ or the Antichrist?

Your answer will likely determine whether you believe the Bible teaches that Christ will rapture His church prior to the beginning of the Tribulation or closer to its end. Personally I believe that many sincere prophecy students and even some scholars have been influenced into accepting a posttribulationalist view as a result of a faulty rendition of 2 Thessalonians 2:3. Consider how the difference in the translation of a *single Greek word* can affect a person's conclusion about the timing of the rapture:

THE PRETRIB RAPTURE	THE MID- OR POSTTRIB RAPTURE
Let no one deceive you by any means; for *that Day will not come* unless the **departing** comes first, and the man of sin is revealed, the son of perdition (2 Thessalonians 2:3).	Let no one deceive you by any means; for *that Day will not come* unless the **falling away** comes first, and the man of sin is revealed, the son of perdition (2 Thessalonians 2:3).

We who believe the rapture will take place before the Trib-ulation readily admit there are at least three Bible passages that predict there will be a global apostasy on the earth when Jesus raptures the church. *But this is not one of them!* Apostasy is not new; it has plagued the church ever since the first cen-tury. In fact, there probably has never been a time in our plan-et's history when some heretic group or cult has not been in the process of turning from the faith "once for all delivered to the saints" (Jude 3). In AD 95, the apostle John, the last living disciple, received the book of Revelation directly from Jesus Christ and predicted that one of the last four church ages would be the church of Laodicea, where the faith would become "lukewarm" (Revelation 3:14-22). But nowhere in Scripture is this "church" used as a sign of our Lord's return.

The Historical Backdrop

In spite of the many verses that urge us to look for Christ to come at any moment, some Christians are instead looking for the Antichrist first. They get this notion principally from the KJV translation of 2 Thessalonians 2:3, which says, "That day will not come unless the falling away comes first, and the man of sin is revealed, the son of perdition." Read that way, you cannot blame Bible students who are watching for the appearance of the Antichrist rather than Jesus to come rap-ture His church. In fact, some Bible and Greek scholars believe the KJV translators were wrong to translate *apostasia* as "fall-ing away" instead of "departing," for there was no real reason to do so. This point was made clear in the last chapter by Dr. Wayne House. No one really knows why subsequent translators have all fallen in line with the KJV rendering of *apostasia*. The KJV is often referred to as the Authorized Version—authorized during the seventeenth century by King James, who was not a Greek scholar. Furthermore, the KJV was not all that well received until it was mandated by the British government over 40 years later as the official Bible of the Church of England.

It has long impressed me that the first seven translators of the Greek Bible into English translated the word *apostasia* to mean "departing" (as in a physical departing) rather than "falling away" or "rebellion," which today's more recent translations hold to. The great fourteenth-century scholar John Wycliffe, in 1384, was the first of the seven English translators to render the text as "departing." Not until three centuries later, with the KJV translators who were hired to do the king's bidding, was the meaning of the word changed.

There seems to be no known reason why most of the modern translators since the time of the KJV have used it as a template. Could it be eschatological bias? At that time in English history most translators held an amillennial or posttribulational view of the return of Christ which did not even include a rapture.

Today many Bible scholars who usually take the Bible in its literal sense can be found on both sides of this issue. What most do not realize is that from the time Jerome translated the New Testament into Latin in the fourth century to the time of the KJV, there was an unbroken record of *apostasia* being translated "departing." To our knowledge, no one in the early church and up to the early seventeenth century saw that word as meaning anything else. We can therefore conclude that is the correct translation, and in all probability, is the original meaning of the word. This cements the idea that the rapture will precede the Tribulation and the revelation of the "man of sin, the son of perdition." It also makes it understandable then that until the KJV translators arrived on the scene, virtually all known ancient translators believed likewise. Until someone can give a convincing reason why the first seven translators of the Greek New Testament into English were wrong to use the word "departing," we are justified in believing they were correct in doing so.

Because no one knows why the KJV translators introduced a totally different translation for *apostasia* in 2 Thessalonians 2:3, the burden is on mid- or posttribulationalists to explain why the change was made. Until they come up with an answer that adequately explains the reason for altering this important word after 17 centuries, it would be good to hear from noted biblical scholar Dr. E. Schuyler English, who pointedly addressed this very subject.

Who Was Dr. E. Schuyler English?

Dr. E. Schuyler English was a highly respected prophecy expert and Greek scholar who served as chairman of the committee that took 12 years to revise and update the influential Scofield Reference Bible. He also served as editor of the popular *Our Hope* prophecy magazine during the late 1940s and the 1950s. As such he succeeded the great Bible and prophecy teacher Dr. A.C. Gaebelein. He was also a prolific author, writing several Bible expositions and the biography of Dr. Harry A. Ironside, a great pastor and Bible-teaching evangelist at Moody Church in Chicago. Later in life, English also wrote the biography of one of the greatest pastoral orators of all time, Dr. Robert G. Lee, and served as editor-in-chief of the Pilgrim Edition of the Bible.

Dr. English probably never dreamed he was throwing a hand grenade into the prophecy debate between pre- and post-tribulationalists when in 1954 he published his 129-page book *Re-thinking the Rapture*. As a young minister in my first full-time pastorate in Minneapolis, Minnesota, I can testify that the debate back then was not always gracious and kind. But Dr. English's book was different. He was more gracious in recognizing that this was a discussion between Christians who loved the same Lord and His appearing. However, he felt their differences with regard to the timing of the rapture had been affected by what he thought was a faulty translation of *apostasia* that had originated with the KJV translators in 1611.

In his overview of the origin of the various rapture views, commentator Richard Reiter states:

> In his series *Re-thinking the Rapture, Our Hope* editor E. Schuyler English concluded that *apostasia* in 2 Thessalonians 2:3 meant "departure" or "withdrawal" rather than the more common translations of "falling away" or "rebellion." English based his case on lexical possibilities and contextual considerations to solve a theological problem. He also published replies by conservative scholars—some agreed but many disagreed. Allan

A. MacRae, President of Faith Theological Seminary in Philadelphia at that time, felt that the interpretation solved a serious problem for pre-tribulational interpretation. Kenneth S. Wuest of Moody Bible Institute approved it, yet most pre-tribulationalists rejected it. Probably none recalled that J.S. Mabie, connected with the earlier Bible conference movement, suggested "a most original answer" to the interpretation of *apostasia* at the Annual Conference on the Lord's Coming, Los Angeles, in November, 1895…it was the Rapture of the Church set forth in 1 Thessalonians 4:14-18.[1]

The late Dr. Stanley Ellisen acknowledged that the term *apostasia* has come to be identified almost universally as referring to a defection usually associated with the retraction from godliness and the gospel as found in passages such as 1 Timothy 4:1; 2 Timothy 3:11; and 1 John 2:18. Due to this, said Ellisen, a doctrine of a major defection from the faith in the last days had been constructed so that dictionaries uniformly define *apostasy* as desertion of one's faith.[2] Ellisen then commented:

At the risk of being out of step with most commentaries on the subject, may we suggest the greater acceptability of an alternate view: the evidence for a great singular defection from the faith, occurring just prior to the Rapture or to the Day of the Lord, is really based on questionable ground. In the first reference generally appealed to (1 Timothy 4), Paul does speak of an apostasy from the faith, but not as a unique endtime event. Rather, he described it as a trend or movement that was already present. This he characterized as erroneous doctrine, hypocritical living, and improper legalism. In using the term here, he qualified it with the phrase "from the faith." By itself it meant simply "departure."[3]

Similarly, the late Dr. David Allen Lewis, a well-respected Bible scholar of the Assembly of God church and former member of the Pre-Trib Research Center, argued that *apostasia* may rightly be translated other than "defection" or "revolt," and referred to a spatial departure like the rapture of the church.

Dr. Wayne House wrote in *When the Trumpet Sounds* (Harvest House, p. 268):

> Among the scholars who have adopted the Rapture understanding of *apostasia* are MacRae, Ellisen, Lewis, English, Pentecost, and Wuest." An internet search revealed that MacRae and Wuest had sent letters (both pro "departure") to Dr. English, which he printed in "Let the Prophets Speak," *Our Hope*, vol. LVI, number 12, June 1950, on pp. 725 and 731 respectively. Presumably, these letters were responses to Dr. English's request for an evaluation of his position on 2 Thessalonians 2:3.

Dr. Larry Crutchfield wrote a personal note to me, saying: "Gordon R. Lewis was my systematic theology professor at Denver Seminary during the mid-70s. He was indeed a 2 Thessalonians 2:3 'departure' proponent. In our class eschatology syllabus under the heading, 'The Time of the Rapture of the Church According to I and II Thessalonians,' he states:

> The Greek usage of "departure" (*apostasia*) is not limited to apostasy from the faith, but includes also departure from a given place. Kittel's *Theological Dictionary of the New Testament* includes an entry for the verb and two related noun forms (*aphistemi*, *apostasia*, and *dichostasia*). The contributor, Heinrich Schlier from Marburg, concludes that the New Testament usage is limited to political and religious alienation from persons. But the root verb, he writes, means "'to remove,' either spatially, or from the context of a state or relationship, or from fellowship with a person." The verb may mean to remove spatially. There is little reason than to deny that the noun can mean such a spatial removal or departure. Since the noun is used only one other

time in the New Testament of apostasy from Moses (Acts 21:21) we can hardly conclude that its biblical meaning is necessarily determined.

The verb is used fifteen times in the New Testament. Of these fifteen, only three have anything to do with a departure from the faith (Luke 8:13; I Timothy 4:1; Hebrews 3:12). The word is used for departing from iniquity (II Timothy 2:19), from ungodly men (I Timothy 6:5), from the temple (Luke 2:37), from the body (II Corinthians 12:8), and from a person (Acts 12:10; Luke 4:13). With Dr. Allan A. MacRae we conclude, "Thus the New Testament instances make it abundantly clear that the verb means depart, or go away, in a very wide sense, and is only in certain instances specialized to the idea of a departure from the faith" (Allan A. MacRae, "New Light on the Second Chapter of Second Thessalonians," *The Bible Today*). Dr. Lewis' position on this issue was published earlier in *BibSac*: Gordon R. Lewis, "Biblical Evidence for Pretribulationism," *Bibliotheca Sacra* 125 (July-Sept. 1968): 216-226.

I believe English saw the apostle Paul's statement of "departure first" in 2 Thessalonians 2:3 to mean that the Rapture would occur first, after which the Antichrist would be revealed. Evidently, some false teachers had sowed seeds of deception in that young Thessalonian church, and Paul sent his letter to correct their thinking by explaining that the persecutions they were experiencing were not part of the coming Tribulation, for the Antichrist had not yet been revealed. Paul wanted to make it clear that they were to be looking first for Christ (in the Rapture), and that the Antichrist would come later. It makes a world of difference. There is good reason to believe Paul meant for this passage to read "Let no one deceive you by any means; for *that Day will not come* unless the departing comes first, and the man of sin is revealed, the son of perdition" (2 Thess. 2:3).[4]

THE SECOND COMING ACCORDING TO 2 THESSALONIANS 2:1-12

Our gathering together unto Him
(verse 1)
John 14:1-3

The Day of the Lord
(verses 2,8)

Rapture

Reign of Peace

Millennium

Christ destroys man of sin (verse 8)

The angel chains Satan and shuts him in the bottomless pit (20:1-3)

Departing
2 Thessalonians 2:3a

Antichrist

7-Year Tribulation

God sends "strong delusion" (verse 11) to those who worship Antichrist and take the mark 666 (13:16-18)

Man of sin desecrates temple (verse 4; Daniel 9:27)

Church Age

Man of sin revealed (verse 3b)

Let Dr. English Speak for Himself

The following is excerpted from *Re-thinking the Rapture*, by Dr. E. Schuyler English, pages 67-71:

> By the very facts made known in the first epistle concerning the coming of our Lord Jesus Christ and our gathering together unto Him, that is, the Rapture as revealed in chapter 4, the Thessalonian Christians are told not to be shaken in mind, or troubled. Evidently a spurious message had come to them, purportedly from Paul, suggesting that the day of the Lord was "already present" (a better rendition than "at hand"). But the tribulation that they were enduring was not a part of God's wrath poured out upon the world. It was persecution from man. God would recompense the offenders with judgment, and those who were being troubled, with rest. Therefore, by the very hope of Christ's coming and the gathering together of the saints unto Him, they could be sure that the day of the Lord was not yet present. Certain things must take place before that day would come, circumstances that had not yet occurred. The nature of these things is revealed in the verses that follow.
>
> "Let no man deceive you by any means," says Paul, "for that day shall not come, except there come a falling away first, and that man of sin be revealed, the son of perdition...Remember ye not, that when I was yet with you, I told you these things?" (vss. 3-5).
>
> Two events must occur, and in a specific order, before the day of the Lord: (1) the (the definite article, *hee*, is in the Greek) falling away; and (2) the revelation of the man of sin. It is the former of these two phenomena that we would discuss as pertaining to the subject of this treatise.
>
> We suggest, for prayerful deliberation, a deviation from the accepted translation and interpretation of this passage. It is never the part of wisdom,

we believe, to discard traditional rendition of the ancient MSS unless we have reasonable proof to support our views. We shall therefore, present, for consideration, such evidence as we are able to produce.

The Greek words, translated "a falling away," are *hee apostasia*. It is directly from the noun that we obtain our English word "*apostasy.*" Apostasy generally carries the meaning of *defection, revolt,* or *rebellion against God.* These are the primary meanings of the word, as found in most lexicons. There is a secondary connotation in Liddell & Scott's *Greek-English Lexicon,*[5] namely: *disappearance,* or *departure.*

In determining the true meaning of a word in the Bible, we must discover its customary usage in the Scriptures. The noun, *apostasy,* occurs in only one other instance in the New Testament, that is, in Acts 21:21, where Paul is accused of teaching the Jews to "forsake Moses," and this assuredly is related to rebellion against God.

Apostasy, or an older form of the noun, *apostasis,* is found frequently in the *Septuagint* (the Greek translation of the Old Testament): Joshua 22:22; 1 Kings 21:13; 2 Chronicles 29:19; 33:19; Isaiah 30:1; and Jeremiah 2:19. Its usage in these passages has to do with departure from God. It is well to bear in mind, however, that in every instance either a descriptive phrase so signifying, or the context in which the word is employed, particularizes its meaning. Having said these things in favor of the traditional translation of *apostasy,* let us look further.

It is from the verb that we obtain the root meaning of a noun. *Apostasy,* or an older form of the noun, *apostasis,* comes from the verb *aphisteemi,* which means *to remove,* or, in the causal sense, *to put away,* or *to cause to be removed.* This root verb, *aphisteemi,* is used fifteen times in the New Testament; Luke 2:27; 4:13; 8:13; 22:29; Acts 5:37,38; 12:10; 15:38;

19:9; 22:29; 2 Corinthians 12:8; 1 Timothy 4:1; 6:5;
2 Timothy 2:19; and Hebrews 3:12. Of these fifteen
occurrences of the verb, only three have any reference to religious departure. In all three of these
cases, by context (Luke 8:13), and by the descriptive
phrases, "from the faith" and "from the living God"
respectively (1 Timothy 4:1; Hebrews 3:12), religious defection is designated. In eleven of the fifteen
N.T. occurrences, the actual word "depart" is used
in translating *aphisteemi,* in relation to such modes
of departure as that of the angel who, having delivered Peter from prison, "*departed* from him" (Acts
12:10), and of Paul's prayer that his thorn in the
flesh "might *depart*" from him (2 Corinthians 12:8).

It is evident, then, that the verb *aphisteemi* does
have the meaning of *to depart* in the New Testament, in a very general sense which is not specialized as being related to rebellion against God
or forsaking the faith. And, since a noun takes its
meaning from the verb, the noun, too, may have
such a broad connotation. "The departure" is assuredly an acceptable translation of *hee apostasia*[6] and
is, in our opinion, the proper one.

The day of the Lord will not come, then, until the
man of sin be revealed. And before he is revealed,
there must be "the departure." Departure from
what or to what? It must have been something concerning which the Thessalonian believers were
informed, else the definite article would hardly
have been employed, and without any qualify-
ing description with the noun.[7] *Why do we assume
that this departure must be from the faith?* It has been
shown that, in its verb form, the word frequently
signifies separation other than religious revolt.
Have we not based our interpretation upon what
may quite possibly be an inappropriate rendition
of the Greek noun? And since the definite article
suggests strongly that the departure was something

with which the Thessalonians were familiar, why do we think of the departure as apostasy? There is nothing in either of the Thessalonian epistles, to this point, about the great apostasy. To submit that, while the apostle did not write to this church about the apostasy he must have talked to them about it, is pure conjecture.

Again, how would the Thessalonians, or Christians in any century since, be qualified to recognize the apostasy when it should come, assuming, simply for the sake of this inquiry, that the Church might be on earth when it does come? There has been apostasy from God, rebellion against Him, since time began. And if it be proposed that the man of sin, sitting in the temple of God and showing Himself to be God, is *the* apostasy, we must ask ourselves a question: Is this act, on the part of the man of sin, apostasy, a falling away, or is it blasphemous denial by one who never at any time acknowledged God?

There is a departure concerning which the Thessalonians had been instructed by letter. This is not conjecture but fact: it is the Rapture of the Church, described in 1 Thessalonians 4:13-17. It was on account of the confusion in the minds of these young Christians, in the matter of events associated with the coming of the Lord, that this epistle was written—for some had sought to deceive them, as by spirit (claiming, perhaps, some new revelation from God), or by word (possibly a misinterpretation of something Paul said), or by letter as from Paul, telling the Thessalonians that the day of the Lord was already present. And how could the apostle set their minds at rest? He could assure them, "by the coming of our Lord Jesus Christ, and by our gathering together unto Him," that the day of the Lord will not come "except there come the departure, the Rapture, first, and that man of sin be revealed, the son of perdition." The day of the Lord was not present; for they themselves, members of Christ's mystical body, were still on earth. The Rapture had not already taken place, they being left behind; for the man of sin was not revealed.

This interpretation corresponds perfectly, in sequence, with that in verses 7 and 8, if the restraining power is, as we believe to be the case, the Holy Spirit. The Church departs, and the man of sin is revealed (vs. 3); the Holy Spirit, the restrainer, is taken out of the way, "and then shall that wicked one be revealed" (vss. 7, 8).

It would be entirely inappropriate for us to be dogmatic in a matter so involved and still open to question as that which we have been discussing. We have expressed our understanding of the passage as fully as we are able. We are persuaded, in our own mind, that this is the correct view of this passage. If we are not mistaken, we have here a final answer to the time of the translation of the Church in relation to the Tribulation.

The Seven Early Greek-to-English Scholars

Let's turn our attention now to the seven early Greek scholars who translated *apostasia* to "departing," or the Old English "departynge," which many scholars admit could mean a spatial departure, as in the rapture, described in 1 Thessalonians 4:16-17. As stated earlier, the first translations of the Bible into English provide strong evidence for *apostasia* referring to a physical departure:

1384	Wycliffe Bible	Departynge first
1526	Tyndale Bible	Departynge first
1535	Coverdale Bible	Departynge first
1539	Cranmer Bible	Departynge first
1576	Breeches Bible	Departing first
1583	Beza Bible	Departing first
1608	Geneva Bible	Departing first

In the centuries that followed, a number of other Bible translators would agree with this rendering, such as John Lineberry, who rendered this, "Except there come the departure [rapture of the church] first." Furthermore, others would concur, including J.R. Major, MA (1831), John James, LLD (1825), John Parkhurst (1851—he wrote a Greek lexicon), and Robert Scott, who wrote, "Properly, a departure."

Greek scholar Dr. Kenneth S. Wuest translated this passage, "Because that day shall not come except the aforementioned departure [of the church to heaven] comes first." Dr. English suggested that *apostasis* has a secondary meaning of "take or go away," which also points to the rapture of the church, which must occur before the "man of sin" (the Antichrist) can be revealed.[8]

Prophecy scholar and teacher Hart Armstrong, in his book *When Is the Rapture?* pointed out there were many others who also held to this position. He concluded:

> So I believe I am honest, logical, and Scriptural to state that what Paul is saying here could be paraphrased to say: "Now we beseech you, brethren, by the coming of our Lord Jesus Christ [or *harpazo*—the Greek word for 'caught up'], and by our gathering together unto him in the rapture of the church. That you be not shaken or troubled that the Day of the Lord (the day of divine judgment) has come. For that day shall not come except first there be the going away of the church, the aforesaid gathering together of the Christians to the Lord in the pretribulation rapture of the church: and that man of sin, Antichrist be revealed."[9]

Many today are finding it difficult to return to the original meaning of *hee apostasia* as "departing"—a position held for thousands of years by many careful Bible scholars throughout the ages. It often requires courage in some Christian circles to take such a position these days. I know two seminary presidents who agree with this position but are reluctant to acknowledge it publicly. One who wrote about it in his graduate school dissertation admitted he believed it, but asked me not to use his name publicly, which I haven't. But it shows how some fear the hostile treatment often exhibited toward those who embrace this position.

Hopefully this book and others in the LaHaye Prophecy Library will clearly explain the logical reasons for believing that the rapture and the glorious appearing are not the same event. In fact, there are at least 15 differences that prove they cannot occur at the same time (see chapter 4 in this book). Those who argue otherwise are not able to reconcile these 15 differences, and yet they continue to promote their "hope stealing" view regarding the rapture.

Why I Favor "Departing" (Rapture) in 2 Thessalonians 2:3

I have come to the conclusion that the weight of evidence favors "departing" as the proper translation of *apostasia* in the original text, not "apostasy" or "falling away" or "rebellion." The following five reasons are based not only on Dr. English's careful analysis in *Re-thinking the Rapture*, but also my own 30-plus years of research and my correspondence with many respected colleagues—some of whom agree and some who do not.

Context, Context, Context!

When there are differences for determining the right meaning of a word, context should be the deciding factor. In this case "our gathering together unto Him" as part of the second coming of Jesus, as it is in 2 Thessalonians 2:1-8, clearly means the rapture or "departing" as in a physical departing, and is unquestionably the context of verse 3, this entire chapter, and both Thessalonian epistles.

"Departing" Translation of Apostasia

Apostasia and other derivatives of departing from the faith is admittedly prophesied for the end times from other passages of Scripture. But deception and the signs of apostasy are not new and have plagued the church ever since the disciples asked, "What will be the sign of your coming and of the end of the age?" (Matthew 24:3). Jesus answered, "Take heed that no one deceives you, for many will come in My name... and will deceive many" (verses 4-5). Such false prophets and christs have come, thousands of them, but none of them introduced the Day of the Lord. That day is yet to come. However, "departing," as in the rapture, would indeed qualify as a prelude to the Day of the Lord. But sliding the original word *apostasia* into the Greek or Latin language as "apostasy" is not a translation; it is a *transliteration*. Up until the seventeenth century the Greek word was translated "departing," and it should still be translated so.

The First Seven English Bible Translations

The fact that all of the first seven scholars who translated this verse into English used "departynge" or "departing" to translate *apostasia* carries great weight in determining the true meaning of the original word. That it was done from the Wycliffe Bible of 1384 to the Geneva Bible of 1608 makes a convincing argument for translating *apostasia* as "departing." Even more significant is the fact in the fourth century Jerome translated *apostasia* into the Latin Vulgate as *discessio* or "departure." All through my research on this subject I've been convinced Jerome and the early Greek-to-English scholars knew something more about the true meaning of *apostasia* than did the translators of the KJV of the seventeenth century.

"Departing in the Rapture" Brings Comfort to the Believer

Both 1 and 2 Thessalonians were written to comfort those who had lost loved ones. It is within this context we find the sad news that those left behind through the death of an unsaved loved one "sorrow as those who have no hope." By contrast, the teaching that raptured believers will one day be reunited with their dead loved ones is "hope" or (a confident expectation). That's why Paul could say, "Comfort one another with these words."

In 2 Thessalonians 2:3 we read of "our gathering together to Him" (an obvious reference to the rapture) and that this day hasn't come (as though the rapture had come and the Thessalonians had missed it), for it will not come unless the departure (rapture) comes first. Then "the man of sin" or Antichrist will be revealed by the signing of the covenant with Israel for seven years, making this event seven years before the end of the Tribulation and the glorious appearing (Matthew 24:29-30). Note the difference the correct translation of that one Greek word makes. This makes the verse uphold the pretribulation view rather than the posttribulation; a position that is also confirmed by noting the 15 differences between various second coming passages. No wonder Paul called the rapture "the blessed hope" in contrast to the "glorious appearing" (Titus 2:13)! Both refer to the second coming, but each is the title for a different phase of the second coming—one in the air for the believers, the other to the earth for the whole world.

"Departing" Gives Us Confidence in Death and Motivation in Life

In both Thessalonian epistles, Paul speaks of the rapture ("departing") to comfort his readers. There is no comfort in looking ahead to the seven-year Tribulation. Nowhere in the Bible are believers taught to look for the Antichrist. Rather, we are challenged many times to look for Jesus' return.

As my friend Dr. Ed Hindson says, "I'm not looking for the Antichrist, I'm looking for Jesus Christ!" To me, the use of the word "departing" in 2 Thessalonians 2:3 to indicate the rapture makes this crystal clear. The apostle John taught us, "Abide in Him, that when He appears, we may have confidence and not be ashamed before Him at His coming" (1 John 2:28).

Looking for the Antichrist and the horrors of the Tribulation only leads to fear, dread, and depression. Looking for Christ's return as promised motivates us to the blessed hope and anticipation of a great future that makes believers want to share Christ with others, giving them a missionary vision and greater desire to serve the Lord.

THE END-TIME APOSTASY IS ALREADY HERE

David R. Reagan

The year was 1980. The man had oversight of more than 400 churches in his denomination. He had called and invited me to come to his office to get acquainted. When I entered, he asked me to sit down, and then said something peculiar: "Excuse me while I find a witness."

He returned a few minutes later with a secretary. He told her to have a seat and to start taking notes. I asked him why he needed a witness.

"Because I'm going to read you the riot act," he responded. He then proceeded to do just that: "I want you to get out of my churches and stay out of them!"

"Why?" I asked.

"Because I don't want any of my people hearing your message."

"But my message is right out of the Bible," I protested. "All I'm doing is preaching the soon return of Jesus."

"I know," he said, "and that's the message I don't want my people to hear."

I was dumbfounded. "Don't you believe in the second coming?"

"Not what you call the second coming," he replied. "I believe the second coming occurs when a person accepts Jesus. He becomes alive in that person's heart. That's all there is to the second coming."

Before I could reply, he added, "And there's another reason I don't want you preaching to my people. You are a salvationist!"

I had been called many names in my life, but never that one. "What do you mean by that?" I asked.

"You are one of those guys who believes a fellow can hear a sermon and come under conviction about sin, and that conviction will ultimately lead him to repent and experience what you call being born again."

"I plead guilty," I replied. "What are you?"

"Well, I'm not a salvationist!" he snapped. "I believe that any person in the world who is growing more mature is in the process of being saved."

"Does that apply to Hindus, Buddhists, and Muslims?" I asked.

"Yes," he said.

"Whether they ever accept Jesus or not?"

"That's right."

One of the most curious things about this whole experience is that on the wall behind this man's desk was a framed quotation that read, "I speak where the Bible speaks, and I am silent where the Bible is silent."

Welcome to the bizarre world of Christian apostasy. And keep in mind that this happened in 1980. In the 30 years since that time, apostasy in the church has increased exponentially.

Apostasy in Prophecy

The Bible clearly prophesies that the church of the end times will be characterized by apostasy, meaning that people will depart from the fundamentals of the Christian faith. Jesus prophesied that "many will fall away" and "most people's love will grow cold" (Matthew 24:10,12 NASB). In like manner, the apostle Paul forecast that in the end times there will be those who "depart from the faith" because they will pay attention to "deceiving spirits and doctrines of demons" (1 Timothy 4:1). Peter joined the chorus in 2 Peter 3:3-4, where he warned that "scoffers will come in the last days" mocking the promise that Jesus will return.

In Revelation, chapters 2–3, John recorded seven letters of Jesus to seven churches in what is now modern-day Turkey. Among other things, these letters present a panoramic prophetic survey of the church in history. The last of the churches mentioned, the one that represents the church of the end times, is the church at Laodicea. It is pictured as a church that is neither hot (healing) nor cold (refreshing), but rather is lukewarm or tepid (3:15-16). In short, it is a church that is apathetic. Jesus also pictures it as a worldly church enamored with its wealth (3:17). The Lord is so dissatisfied with this church that He declares, "Because you are lukewarm, and neither cold nor hot, I will vomit you out of My mouth" (3:16).

Paul supplies us with some strong clues as to why the end-times church will be weak, vacillating, and full of apostasy. One of those clues can be found in 2 Timothy 4:3-4: "The time will come when they [Christians] will not endure sound doctrine; but...because they have itching ears, they will heap up for themselves teachers; and they will turn their ears away from the truth, and be turned aside to fables."

Another clue is found in Paul's famous prophecy about how society will fall apart in the end times. He said people will be "having a form of godliness but denying its power" (2 Timothy 3:5). There will be no lack of religion. Rather, people will deny the true power that is able to transform society for the good, producing peace, righteousness, and justice.

What is that power? First and foremost it is the power of the blood of Jesus—the very power that was blasphemed by the regional minister who confronted me, claiming that salvation can be achieved apart from Jesus. It is also the power that comes from accepting the Bible as the infallible Word of God. It is the power of believing in a Creator God with whom all things are possible. And certainly it includes a belief in the power of the Holy Spirit.

Today, these essential beliefs, which constitute the power

of Christianity, are being subjected to an unparalleled assault from within the church itself.

The Root of Modern Apostasy

How have we reached this crisis point in the church? Much of it is rooted in what is called the German school of higher criticism, which invaded this country in the early 1900s. According to the "scientific approach" of this school of skeptics, the Bible is not the revealed Word of God. Rather, it is man's search for God, and therefore it is filled with myth, legend, and superstition. They therefore approach the study of the Bible as if it were mere literature—not to find God's truth for mankind, but for the purpose of analyzing it critically.

Today this viewpoint dominates in many seminaries. The Bible is studied not as a God-breathed, authoritative text to be believed and obeyed but to be analyzed, dissected, and criticized.

Accordingly, so what difference does it make if Scripture condemns homosexuality? The critics argue that the Bible was written thousands of years ago by men who knew nothing about modern physiology or psychology, and who certainly did not understand that homosexuality is "natural" or genetically determined. They view Paul as a victim of his own prejudices, and they speculate he was probably a homosexual himself who was simply engaged in self-loathing. Absurd? Yes, but not from the viewpoint of those who have rejected the authority of the Scriptures.

Early Apostate Leaders

One of the trailblazers of apostasy in the United States was Harry Emerson Fosdick (1878–1969).[1] He started out as a Baptist minister in 1903 after graduating from Union Theological Seminary. He quickly gravitated to the preaching of liberal theology based on a rejection of the Bible as the inerrant Word of God. He became pastor of the prestigious interdenominational Riverside Church in New York City, a church financed by John D. Rockefeller, Jr.

In the 1920s Fosdick began publicly attacking what he called Fundamentalism. In the process he repudiated the core beliefs of the Christian faith. He declared that belief in the virgin birth of Jesus was unnecessary and argued against the inerrancy of the Scriptures. He also denounced the doctrine of the second coming of Jesus as "absurd."[2]

Fosdick's mantle was inherited by Norman Vincent Peale (1898–1993), who became the father of the positive-thinking, self-esteem gospel, which is a mixture of humanistic psychology, eastern religion, and Bible verses taken out of context. He taught that people—whether Christians or not—could tap into the power of God, which he claimed resided within every person.[3]

In 1984 Peale announced on the Phil Donahue program, "It's not necessary to be born again. You have your way to God; I have mine. I found eternal peace in a Shinto shrine...I've been to Shinto shrines, and God is everywhere."

Phil Donahue was so shocked he actually came to the defense of Christianity. "But you're a Christian minister," he retorted, "and you're supposed to tell me that Christ is the way and the truth and the life, aren't you?"

Peale replied, "Christ is one of the ways. God is everywhere."[4]

Look again at Peale's incredulous statement "It's not necessary to be born again." What did Jesus say? "Most assuredly, I say to you, unless one is born again, he cannot see the kingdom of God" (John 3:3). Who are we to believe?

Rick Miesel of Biblical Discernment Ministries points out that Peale was a modern-day proponent of the fourth-century apostasy called Pelagianism. That is, he was "someone who believed that human nature is essentially good and that human beings are saved by developing their inner potential."[5]

An Apostate Gospel

Peale's leading disciple, Robert Schuller, has outdone his teacher with the development of his "gospel of possibility thinking." In his book *Self Esteem: The New Reformation,*

Schuller stated that the leaders of the Reformation made a mistake in centering their theology on God instead of man.[6]

Schuller teaches that the essence of man's problem is low self-esteem.[7] The Bible teaches it is pride. Schuller says that when Jesus referred in John 7:38 to "rivers of living water" flowing out of believers, He was speaking of self-esteem.[8] But in the Bible, the very next verse says He was speaking of the Holy Spirit. Schuller argues that sin is anything that robs us of our "divine dignity."[9] The Bible says sin is rebellion against God.

Like Peale, Schuller has redefined the meaning of being born again. He says it means being "changed from a negative to a positive self-image—from inferiority to self-esteem, from fear to love, and from doubt to trust."[10] But the Bible doesn't say being born again is the result of changes in attitude. Rather, it says being born again relates to coming alive spiritually through faith in Jesus as Lord and Savior. Being born again is a spiritual phenomenon, not a psychological one. The experience will certainly *result* in changed attitudes, but it is not *produced* by them. Schuller confuses cause and effect.

In a long letter published in the October 5, 1984 issue of *Christianity Today*, Schuller made an astounding comment that has haunted him to this day:

> I don't think anything has been done in the name of Christ and under the banner of Christianity that has proven more destructive to human personality and, hence, counterproductive to the evangelism enterprise than the often crude, uncouth, and unchristian strategy of attempting to make people aware of their lost and sinful condition.[11]

As a writer for *Time* put it in an article in 1985, "For Schuller, an acknowledgment of self-worth, more than a confession of sinfulness, is the path to God.[12]

This stands in strong contrast to the New Testament's explicit calls for people to repent of their sins and seek salvation in Christ alone.

Other Modern-day Apostate Leaders

In recent years, John Spong, a retired bishop of the Episcopal Church, has become the poster boy of Christian apostasy. He has written books in which he denies the virgin birth, denies the miracles of Jesus, denies the resurrection, denies the second coming, and argues that Paul and Timothy were homosexual lovers. Bishop Spong has become so enamored with other religions that he has announced he will no longer witness to those caught up in the spiritual darkness of pagan faiths.[13]

A similar spokesman for apostasy today is R. Kirby Godsey, who served as president of Mercer University in Georgia for 27 years, from 1979 to 2006. During that time the school was affiliated with the Georgia Baptist Convention. Today he continues with the school as chancellor. He denies the inerrancy of the Bible, the unique power and authority of God, the validity of the gospel accounts of the life of Jesus, the efficacy of Jesus' atonement, and the uniqueness of Jesus as the only Savior.[14] In 2005 the Georgia Baptist Convention ended its affiliation with the school, but the school continues to claim to be Baptist in theology.

Another modern-day apostate is the Reverend Bill Phipps, who was elected moderator of the United Church of Canada in 1998. This is the largest Protestant group in that nation. At a press conference following his election, Phipps denied all the fundamentals of the Christian faith, including the deity of Jesus. "I don't believe Jesus was God," he said. "I don't believe Jesus is the only way to God. I don't believe He rose from the dead...I don't know whether these things happened. It's an irrelevant question."[15]

When Phipps denies Jesus is the only way to God, he makes Jesus out to be a liar, for Jesus said, "I am the way, the truth, and the life. No one comes to the Father except through Me" (John 14:6). When Phipps states that the truth regarding the resurrection is irrelevant, he makes a liar of the apostle Paul, who wrote, "If Christ is not risen, then our preaching is empty...if Christ is not risen, your faith is futile" (1 Corinthians 15:14,17).

An Apostate Seminar

The Jesus Seminar was formed in 1985 by Robert Funk, a New Testament scholar at the University of Montana. The avowed purpose of the Seminar was "to renew the quest for the historical Jesus."[16] The Seminar conducted this quest in a very unusual way. Meeting twice a year for six years, the group voted on each of the sayings of Jesus recorded in the Gospels. They voted by dropping colored beads in a box. A black bead meant Jesus definitely did not make the statement in question. A gray bead meant He did not say it, but it might have represented His thinking. A pink bead meant He probably said something like this, but not in the words recorded. A red bead meant He definitely made the statement.[17]

As you can see, the very approach expressed contempt for the veracity of the Gospel accounts. What a spectacle this must have been to the Lord as He watched these so-called scholars vote on passages from His Word. "Professing to be wise, they became fools" (Romans 1:22).

The Seminar began with 30 scholars. Ultimately, more than 200 persons participated in the deliberations. But only 74 hung in to the end. Most of those who dropped out did so because of their disgust with the process and their discomfort with the fact that the radical fringe element of New Testament scholarship in America was disproportionately represented.[18]

The final product of the Seminar, published in 1993, was a blasphemy of God's Word. It was titled *The Five Gospels*.[19] The title comes from the fact that the Seminar decided to grant the apocryphal Gospel of Thomas equal standing with the four traditional Gospels.

Only 15 sayings of Jesus made it into *The Five Gospels* in red. In Matthew's account of the Lord's Prayer, the only words voted as authentic were "Our Father." Only one saying in the entire book of Mark was colored red—Mark 12:17, where Jesus told His disciples to "render to Caesar the things that are Caesar's, and to God the things that are God's." Likewise, only one statement from the Gospel of John qualified for the red coloring: "A prophet has no honor in his own country" (John 4:44).

Equally chilling about all this is that many of the men who produced this spiritual pornography are professors at seminaries across America. They are among those training the current generation of pastors and teachers.

Recent Apostate Developments

- In 1988 the United Church of Canada became the first Christian denomination to authorize the ordination of homosexuals.[20]

- In the 1990s an interfaith conference called Re-Imaging: A Global Theological Conference by Women met with attendees from 16 denominations. The organizers hosted feminist theologians who called upon the participants to repudiate the "male chauvinist God of the Scriptures" in favor of female goddesses like Sophia, Isis, Aphrodite, and the Irish goddess, Brigid.[21]

- In 1999 the Archbishop of Canterbury, George Carey, publicly expressed doubt about the resurrection of Jesus: "I can tell you frankly that while we can be absolutely sure that Jesus lived and that He was certainly crucified on the cross, we cannot with the same certainty say that we know he was raised by God from the dead."[22]

- In 2005 The United Church of Christ became the first American Christian denomination to officially approve same-sex marriage.[23]

- In 2006 the Episcopal Church elected Katharine Jefferts Schori to a nine-year term as presiding bishop of the church. When asked how she could reconcile her support of homosexuality with the Bible's condemnation of it she replied, "The Bible was written in a very different historical context by people asking different questions." In other words, the Bible is irrelevant. To no one's surprise she declared at the 2010 Episcopal Convocation that "there are many roads to God."[24]

- In 2010 The Claremont School of Theology in California, affiliated with the United Methodist Church, announced that it was going to start offering training programs for Muslim Imams and Jewish Rabbis, with the hope of later adding similar clergy programs for Hindus and Buddhists.[25] (After all, if there are many roads to God, what difference does it make which road you take?)

- In 2010 Thomas Nelson Publishers, the world's largest publisher of English-language Bibles, announced the publication of *The Remnant Study Bible*, which was advertised on their website as "The last study Bible you will ever need." What is so distinctive about it? It features the study notes of Ellen G. White, a false prophet whose writings led to the founding of the Seventh Day Adventists.[26]

- In 2011 Adela Yarbro Collins, Buckingham Professor of New Testament Criticism and Interpretation at Yale University, declared that any Jew who has led a good life need not worry about being thrown into the lake of fire at the end of time. She then went even further to state that all people would be judged on the basis of their works and that "those whose names will be erased from the book of life are not those whose beliefs are inadequate. Rather, they are those whose works are not 'full' or 'complete' in the sight of God."[27]

Apostasy Among Evangelicals

These examples of apostasy I have cited thus far are bad enough, but what is more shocking is the apostasy that is currently taking place among those who claim to be evangelicals. Consider, for example, the Emergent Church movement. The leaders of this movement claim to be evangelicals, but they are thoroughly postmodern in their thinking, urging people to question absolute truth and to question what are considered the fundamentals of the Christian faith.

One of their leaders, Brian McLaren, had this to say about the abominable *Da Vinci Code* book: "I don't think *The Da Vinci Code* has more harmful ideas in it than the Left Behind novels."[28] And when asked to define his theology, he stated, "I am a missional, evangelical, post/protestant, liberal/conservative, mystical/poetic, biblical, charismatic/contemplative, fundamentalist/calvinist, anabaptist/ anglican, methodist, catholic, green, incarnational, depressed-yet-hopeful, emergent, unfinished Christian."[29] In other words, he attempts to be all things to all people.

Another spokesman for the Emergent Church is Rob Bell. In his book *Velvet Elvis*, subtitled *Repainting the Christian Faith*, he states, "God is bigger than any religion. God is bigger than any worldview. God is bigger than the Christian faith."[30] That happens to be one of the mantras of those who believe there are many roads to God.

Bell's book demonstrates his low view of Scripture, as illustrated by this statement: "part of the problem [is] continually insisting that one of the absolutes of the Christian faith must be a belief that 'scripture alone' is our guide. It sounds nice, but it is not true...When people say that all we need is the Bible, it is simply not true."[31]

And consider his interpretation of one of Jesus' most famous statements: "When Jesus said, 'No one comes to the Father except through Me,' He was saying that His way, His words, His life is our connection to how things truly are at the deepest level of existence."[32] No, what Jesus was really saying is, "No one comes to the Father except through Me" (John 14:6).

In *Love Wins*, Bell makes statements of a universalist nature. Universalism teaches that ultimately, all people will be saved.[33] Although Bell says he believes some people will go to hell, he pictures hell as a purifying place where people will receive a second chance. He summarizes his position in the preface of his book in this way:

A staggering number of people have been taught
that a select few Christians will spend forever in a
peaceful, joyous place called heaven, while the rest
of humanity spends forever in torment and punishment in hell with no chance of anything better...
This is misguided and toxic and ultimately subverts
the contagious spread of Jesus' message of love,
peace, forgiveness, and joy.[34]

Bell reveals the fundamental reason for his perspectives
when he states, "We have to listen to what our inner voice is
saying."[35] But what if that inner voice contradicts Scripture?

It certainly doesn't help when publications such as *Christianity Today* give voice to individuals like Rob Bell, conveying the
impression he is a part of the evangelical community. More and
more the magazine has adopted an ecumenical tone rather than
one that is distinctly and biblically evangelical. When Billy Gra-
ham established *Christianity Today* in 1956, he said the purpose
of it was "to plant the evangelical flag in the middle-of-the-road,
taking a conservative theological position."[36]

But over the years the magazine has strayed from its more
conservative theological roots. It has consistently featured
content that takes a liberal approach to social issues, it has
incorporated Catholic writers as contributing editors, and it
has given voice to postmodern thinking, open theism, and
Replacement Theology with regard to Israel and the Jewish
people.

Both quoting and responding to the February 2004 issue of
Christianity Today (CT), which inaugurated a series of articles
titled "Evangelicals: The Next 50 Years," Phil Johnson made
this observation:

Whereas "the evangelicalism of 50 years ago focused
narrowly on issues that emerged from the confronta-
tion with modernism," CT's editors tell us the new
evangelicalism "has become 'an ecumenically significant reality'" (p. 76). The truths today's evangelicals are concerned with are no longer "a series of
facts, but truth understood in a dynamic, relational,

and personal fashion" (p. 75)—i.e., subjective ideas rather than objective facts.[37]

So as *Christianity Today* professes to speak for evangelicals yet assumes what has become a more ecumenical mantle, the result is a broadened redefinition of what evangelicalism really stands for or represents. Ultimately this causes a kind of confusion that blurs the distinctives of biblical Christianity—which stands contrary to open theism, postmodern thinking, and certain Catholic teachings, among other things.

Apostasy in Reference to Bible Prophecy

Particularly disturbing to me as a Bible prophecy teacher is the rapidly developing apostasy regarding God's prophetic Word. I see this development as a fulfillment of Bible prophecy. Consider, for example, the warning in 2 Peter 3:3-4 (NASB):

> Know this first of all, that in the last days mockers will come with their mocking, following after their own lusts, and saying, "Where is the promise of His coming? For ever since the fathers fell asleep, all continues just as it was from the beginning of creation."

In other words, in the end times, many will mock God's prophetic Word. I used to think such scoffing would come solely from nonbelievers. But tragically, some of the open scoffing today is coming from Christian circles.

For example, in December of 2008 the National Council of Churches issued a denunciation of all those who "consider the state of Israel to be divinely ordained and scripturally determined, with a central role in ushering in the end of history…"[38]

Rob Bell added his voice to the chorus of condemnation with the following statement:

> I would argue that in the last couple hundred years, disconnection has been the dominant way people have understood reality. And the Church has contributed to that disconnection by preaching

horrible messages about being left behind and that thisplace is going to burn—absolutely toxic messages that are against the teachings of Scripture, which state that we are connected to God, we are connected to the earth, we are connected to each other.[39]

Yet another example is Brian McLaren, who claims to have been raised on Dispensational teaching, but now attacks it with a vengeance, arguing that it is "morally and ethically harmful."[40]

Writing in *Sojourners* magazine in April 2009, he stated that any theology that stresses a special end-time role for Israel is "terrible," "deadly," "distorted," and "biblically unfaithful." He further stated that those who take end-time prophecies about Israel seriously use a " bogus end-of-the-world scenario to create a kind of death wish for World War III, which—unless it is confronted more robustly by the rest of us—could too easily create a self-fulfilling prophecy."[41]

Or consider this statement from his book *Everything Must Change*:

> The phrase "the Second Coming of Christ" never actually appears in the Bible...If we believe that Jesus came in peace the first time, but that wasn't his "real" and decisive coming—it was just a kind of warm-up for the real thing—then we leave the door open to envisioning a Second Coming that will be characterized by violence, killing, domination, and eternal torture.
>
> This vision reflects a deconversion, a return to trust in the power of Pilate, not the unarmed truth that stood before Pilate, refusing to fight. This eschatological understanding of a violent Second Coming leads us to believe that in the end, even God finds it impossible to fix the world apart from violence and coercion...
>
> If we remain charmed by this kind of eschatology, we will be forced to see the nonviolence of the Jesus

of the Gospels as a kind of strategic fake out, like a feigned retreat in war, to be followed up by a crushing blow of so-called redemptive violence in the end.

The gentle Jesus of the First Coming becomes a kind of trick Jesus, a fake-me-out Messiah, to be replaced by the true jihadist Jesus of a violent Second Coming. This is why I believe that many of our current eschatologies, intoxicated by dubious interpretations of John's Apocalypse, are not only ignorant and wrong, but dangerous and immoral.[42]

McLaren's reference to "the gentle Jesus of the First Coming" immediately reminded me of Jesus' words in Revelation 2, where He gives a strong warning to the church at Thyatira for tolerating a false prophetess in their midst:

Indeed, I will cast her into a sickbed, and those who commit adultery with her into great tribulation, unless they repent of her deeds. I will kill her children with death, and all the churches shall know that I am He who searches the minds and hearts. And I will give to each one of you according to your works (Revelation 2:22-23).

That statement alone should be sufficient to dispel the myth of the supposedly "gentle Jesus of the First Coming."

A Revival of Postmillennialism

What appears to be happening today is that evangelicalism is being hijacked by people who are advocating the old liberal social gospel combined with Dominion theology. Increasingly, they talk about the responsibility of the church to "restore God's creation." The mission of the church, according to them, is to take the world for Christ, solve all the world's political, economic, social, and ecological problems, and then present a restored earth to Jesus.

In April 2010, when Rick Warren unveiled his PEACE plan before 30,000 people at Angel Stadium in what he called his "Sermon on the Mound," he said, "I'm looking at a stadium full of people who are telling God they will do whatever it takes to establish God's kingdom on earth as it is in heaven."[43]

Standing Firm for the Truth

The truth is that the church was never given the task of conquering the world for Christ or solving all the world's political and social problems. We were commanded to preach the gospel and make disciples (Matthew 28:18-20). And yes, we were instructed to stand for righteousness (Matthew 5:13-16). But the restoration of God's creation is a task that will be accomplished by Jesus when He returns to reign in glory and majesty from Mount Zion in Jerusalem (Matthew 19:28-29; Acts 3:18-21).

What's sad about the apostasy concerning Bible prophecy is that we are living right on the threshold of the Tribulation, when God will pour out His wrath on those who have rejected His grace, mercy, and love. Satan must be very pleased; because that is a truth he does not want anyone to know.

One of the greatest events prophesied in Scripture—the rapture of the church—is imminent, and yet apostate teachers are directing people's attention away from that blessed hope and focusing their eyes instead on a false hope of establishing the kingdom of God on earth without the presence of the King.

The formidable task we face as believers in God's prophetic Word is to stand firm and continue to proclaim the truth of the Lord's soon return to as many people as we can, as quickly as we can.

Test Everything by God's Word

There is only one basic defense against the apostasy that is epidemic in the church today, and that is a knowledge of God's Word. Unfortunately, public opinion polls show that the average professing Christian today is biblically illiterate, and that conclusion applies also to those who consider themselves to be "born again evangelicals."[44]

Too many of our churches have surrendered the preaching of the Bible to the proclamation of pop psychology in an effort to keep from offending anyone, when the reality is that people need to be lovingly confronted with their sins and then pointed to faith in Jesus as their only hope. And they also need to be taught how to test everything by the standard of God's Word, as the Bereans did with the teachings of the apostle Paul (Acts 17:10-11). Then, and only then, will the tidal wave of apostasy be contained.[45]

15

THE LITERAL INTERPRETATION OF SCRIPTURE AND THE RAPTURE

Thomas Ice

When the literal interpretation of the Bible is held in high esteem and practiced consistently, it usually follows that one is attracted to pretribulationism. The opposite is also usually true as well. Tim LaHaye has long championed Dr. Cooper's golden rule of biblical interpretation, which is as follows:

> When the plain sense of Scripture makes common sense, seek no other sense; therefore, take every word at its primary, ordinary, usual, literal meaning unless the facts of the immediate context, studied in the light of related passages and axiomatic and fundamental truths, indicate clearly otherwise.[1]

"If you follow this rule, it is relatively easy to understand Scripture; if you ignore it, you will always be in error," declares LaHaye. "That is particularly true of the prophetic sections of Scripture."[2]

However, critics of our theology have often distorted what

we mean by the literal interpretation of prophecy. This matter is a vitally important one and determines for individuals whether pretribulationism is true.

Interpretation of Scripture

Literal Interpretation Defined

The dictionary defines *literal* as "belonging to letters." It also says literal interpretation involves an approach "based on the actual words in their ordinary meaning...not going beyond the facts."[3] The mother of all dictionaries, *The Oxford English Dictionary*, says, "Pertaining to the 'letter' (of Scripture); the distinctive epithet of that sense or interpretation (of the text) which is obtained by taking its words in their natural or customary meaning and applying the ordinary rules of grammar; opposed to *mystical, allegorical,* etc."[4]

"Literal interpretation of the Bible simply means to explain the original sense of the Bible according to the normal and customary usages of its language."[5] How is this done? It can only be accomplished through the grammatical (according to the rules of grammar), historical (consistent with the historical setting of the passage), contextual (in accord with its context) method of interpretation.

Literalism looks to the text, the actual words and phrases of a passage. Allegorical or nonliteral interpretation imports an idea not found specifically in the text of a passage. Thus, the opposite of *literal* interpretation is *allegorical* interpretation. As Bernard Ramm said in his classic and authoritative book on biblical interpretation, "the 'literal' directly opposes the 'allegorical.'"[6]

Literal Interpretation Illustrated

Isaiah 2:1-5 is a passage that many have interpreted allegorically instead of literally. As you read the passage, make a mental note as to whom Isaiah was addressing. What does the text actually say?

> The word which Isaiah the son of Amoz saw concerning Judah and Jerusalem.

Now it will come about that in the last days, the
mountain of the house of the LORD will be established as the chief of the mountains, and will be raised
above the hills; and all the nations will stream to it.
And many peoples will come and say, "Come, let us
go up to the mountain of the LORD, to the house of
the God of Jacob; that He may teach us concerning
His ways, and that we may walk in His paths." For
the law will go forth from Zion, and the word of the
LORD from Jerusalem. And He will judge between
the nations, and will render decisions for many peoples; and they will hammer their swords into plow-
shares, and their spears into pruning hooks. Nation
will not lift up sword against nation, and never again
will they learn war. Come, house of Jacob, and let us
walk in the light of the LORD (NASB).

The text of this passage addresses "Judah and Jerusalem"
(verse 1), "Zion," "Jerusalem" (verse 3), and "house of Jacob"
(verse 5). Yet many allegorical interpreters read this passage
and simply substitute "the church" for the aforementioned syn-
onyms for Israel. Nowhere does the text say anything about the
church, yet too often the idea of the church is simply imported
in. Those who read this passage and note that it is referring
to historical Judah and Jerusalem are interpreting it literally—
that is, according to what the letters of the text actually says.
Those who say that it refers to the church, or something similar, are interpreting it allegorically—that is, importing an idea
about the text when there is no basis for such a thought in the
actual letters or words of the text.

Allegorical interpreters take phrases like "the mountain
of the house of the LORD," "all the nations will stream to
it," "many peoples," and "the house of the God of Jacob" and
say this passage is teaching the conversion of the Gentiles to
the Christian faith and their ingathering into the Christian
church.[7] Such an understanding is not found at all in this passage. Such ideas have to be imported from outside the text.
When this is done it results in a nonliteral interpretation.

A literal interpretation of this passage is one that is given in the *Tim LaHaye Prophecy Study Bible* as follows:

> Isaiah envisions the Kingdom Age, when the nations of the world will come to the Holy City (Jerusalem) to learn the ways of God. Christ Himself is the Judge who will direct the affairs of nations, and peace shall prevail. Then the instruments of war and bloodshed will be refashioned into instruments of peace and prosperity.[8]

This interpretation is literal because it understands Jerusalem to refer to Jerusalem, and so on. This is what is meant by the system of literal interpretation, or hermeneutics.

Grammatical-Historical Interpretation

Dr. Charles Ryrie, an advocate of literal interpretation, notes that literal interpretation is the same as the grammatical-historical method of interpretation:

> It is sometimes called the principle of *grammatical-historical* interpretation since the meaning of each word is determined by grammatical and historical considerations. The principle might also be called *normal* interpretation since the literal meaning of words is the normal approach to their understanding in all languages. It might also be designated *plain* interpretation so that no one receives the mistaken notion that the literal principle rules out figures of speech.[9]

The literal system of interpretation takes into consideration the following elements of a text: grammatical, historical, contextual, and semantics. Let's examine each of these categories more closely.

GRAMMATICAL

The grammatical aspect of literal interpretation considers the impact that grammar plays on a passage. This means that a student of the text should correctly analyze the grammatical relationships of words, phrases, and sentences to one another. Literal interpreter Roy Zuck wrote,

> When we speak of interpreting the Bible grammatically, we are referring to the process of seeking to determine its meaning by ascertaining four things: (a) the meaning of words (lexicology), (b) the form of words (morphology), (c) the function of words (parts of speech), and (d) the relationships of words (syntax).[10]

Dr. Zuck taught biblical interpretation for many years at Dallas Theological Seminary and his book *Basic Bible Interpretation* is a great place to start for anyone interested in learning how to interpret the Bible. He provides further amplification on the four areas he noted above:

> In the meaning of words (lexicology), we are concerned with (a) etymology—how words are derived and developed, (b) usage—how words are used by the same and other authors, (c) synonyms and antonyms—how similar and opposite words are used, and (d) context—how words are used in various contexts.
>
> In discussing the form of words (morphology) we are looking at how words are structured and how that affects their meaning. For example the word *eat* means something different from *ate*, though the same letters are used. The word *part* changes meaning when the letter *s* is added to it to make the word *parts*. The function of words (parts of speech) considers what the various forms do. These include attention to subjects, verbs, objects, nouns, and others...The relationships of words (syntax) are the way words are related or put together to form phrases, clauses, and sentences.[11]

Even though the grammatical aspect of literal interpretation is just one aspect of hermeneutics, it lets us know that any interpretation that conflicts with grammar is invalid. Grammar is an important and foundational aspect of literal interpretation.

Historical

Proper interpretation of the Bible takes into account the text's historical context. This means one must consider the historical setting and circumstances in which the books of the Bible were written. Dr. Paul Lee Tan explains:

> The proper concept of the historical in Bible interpretation is to view the Scriptures as written during given ages and cultures. Applications may then be drawn which are relevant to our times. For instance, the subject of meat offered to idols can only be interpreted from the historical and cultural setting of New Testament times. Principles to be drawn are relevant to us today.[12]

Contextual

"A passage taken out of context is a pretext." This slogan is certainly true! One of the most common mistakes made by those who are found to have misinterpreted a Bible passage is that of taking a verse out of its divinely ordered context. A sentence excerpted from Scripture is not the Word of God if it is placed into a context which changes the meaning from that which God intended in its original context.

Dr. Zuck says, "The context in which a given Scripture passage is written influences how that passage is to be understood. Context includes several things:

- the verse(s) immediately before and after a passage
- the paragraph and book in which the verses occur
- the dispensation in which it was written
- the message of the entire Bible
- the historical-cultural environment of that time when it was written."[13]

An example of a passage often taken out of context is Proverbs 11:30, which says, "The fruit of the righteous is a tree of life, and he who is wise wins souls" (NASB). This is sometimes used as a verse to advocate Christian evangelism. We are all for anyone who preaches the gospel to the lost. But when studied in context, the wise one who wins souls is one who is able to draw others to oneself and teach them wisdom. Wisdom, as used in Proverbs, refers to skill in everyday living. New Testament Christian evangelism is nowhere to be found in the context. If this passages is taken out of its context in Proverbs and the phrase "he who is wise wins souls" is placed by itself in a contemporary context, then it would be understandable that it could be thought to be a statement advocating evangelism. However, such a meaning is impossible in the original context.

SEMANTICS

The principles of literal interpretation recognize that a biblical word or phrase can be used either plainly (denotative) or figuratively (connotative), just as in our conversations today. For example, we might use plain speech to say, "He died yesterday" (denotative use of language). Or we could say this in a more colorful way—"He kicked the bucket yesterday" (connotative use of language). Every word or phrase in every language is used in at least one of these two ways.

LITERAL INTERPRETATION

One Meaning

Either | Or

Plain—Literal | **Figurative—Literal**

The literal interpretation is the explicit *assertion* of the words—DENOTATIVE | The literal interpretation is the specific *intention* of the figure—CONNOTATIVE

Created by Earl Radmacher and used with permission.

It is important to realize that even though we may use a

figure of speech to refer to someone's death, we are using that figure to refer to a literal event. Some interpreters are mistaken to think that just because a figure of speech or a symbol is used to describe an event (e.g., Jonah's experience in the belly of the great fish in Jonah 2), that the event was not literal. Such is not the case.

Literal interpreters, for instance, understand that Isaiah used a figure of speech in Isaiah 55:12. He was teaching that the Adamic curse upon nature would be reversed in the Millennium: "All the trees of the field shall clap their hands." This figure is discerned by specific factors in the context in which it was written. Trees don't have hands and thus do not clap. Humans do have hands and can clap them. Isaiah, wishing to communicate the joy that nature will experience, does so by attributing an expression of human joy to trees. This figure of speech is called *personification* and relates to the removal of the curse upon nature at a future time. Such an understanding is supported by the preceding and subsequent contexts surrounding verse 12. That this is a figure of speech is decided by factors within the text itself. If the decision about whether a tree can clap its hands were made on the basis of an idea imported from outside the text, then it would be an allegorical interpretation. Even though figurative language is employed, this event of the curse being reversed will have a literal fulfillment.

Therefore, we see that within the interpretative process the word *literal* is used in a second way, different from the first way in which we used it when referring to the system of *literal interpretation*. This second use relates to *semantics* and whether a word or phrase is used literally or figuratively. This is an important point to keep in mind because later I will demonstrate that this relates to how opponents of pretribulationism distort and misrepresent biblical prophecy.

Dr. Ryrie drives this point home:

> Symbols, figures of speech and types are all interpreted plainly in this method and they are in no way contrary to literal interpretation. After all, the very existence of any meaning for a figure of speech

depends on the reality of the literal meaning of the terms involved. Figures often make the meaning plainer, but it is the literal, normal, or plain meaning that they convey to the reader.[14]

Notice that figures of speech or symbols are *not* a synonym for allegorical interpretation. Therefore, the presence of a figure of speech in a passage does not justify allegorical interpretation. Remember, allegorical interpretation involves the importing of an idea not actually stated by the words found in a text. A figure of speech is simply a connotative expression made by the words or phrases within the text itself.

Literal versus Literal

Dallas Seminary professor Elliott Johnson, in his book on biblical interpretation, notes that much of the confusion over literalism is removed when we understand the two ways it is used: "(1) the clear, plain sense of a word or phrase as over against a figurative use, and (2) a system that views the text as providing the basis of the true interpretation."[15] Pretribulationists by and large use *literal* to refer to their *system* of interpretation (the consistent use of the grammatical-historical system), and once inside that system, in the area of semantics, *literal* refers to whether a specific word or phrase is used in its context figuratively or literally. Thus, literal interpreters considering semantics will discuss whether a word or phrase is meant by the biblical authors to convey a literal or figurative meaning.

The Allegorical Shell Game

Some who use the allegorical approach to Bible prophecy are known to attack pretribulationists by using a hermeneutical shell game to misrepresent and distort literal interpretation. Hank Hanegraaff provides an example of this shell game in his book *The Apocalypse Code*.[16] On the one hand, he attempts to make his point by arguing that since literal interpreters take some words and phrases as figures of speech, they are not consistent with literal interpretation. On the other hand, he says these same interpreters do not know how to properly understand figures of speech and symbols. Thus, Hanegraaff moves back and forth between the two connotations of literal in order to show that pretribulationists like Tim LaHaye are irrational and mixed up when it comes to understanding Bible prophecy. Hanegraaff plays a shell game with pretribulationists as he moves back and forth between the two nuances of *literal*. He often labels pretribulationists as practicing "literalism" or that they see figures of speech as "wooden literalists." Professor Bernard Ramm, in his widely acclaimed book on biblical interpretation, says,

> The program of literal interpretation of Scripture does not overlook the figures of speech, the symbols, the types, the allegories that as a matter of fact are to be found in Holy Scripture. It is not a blind letterism nor a wooden literalism as is so often the accusation.[17]

Literal versus Allegorical

Why do antipretribulationists like Hanegraaff misrepresent literal interpretation? If the literal interpretation of prophecy were left standing, he would have no basis for disagreeing with our view of the end times. Apparently Hanegraaff does not believe that he would have a strong case against our view of Bible prophecy apart from misrepresenting or distorting the view.

In some of their more candid moments, opponents of literal interpretation admit that if our approach is followed then it does rightly lead to the dispensational view. For example, Floyd Hamilton declared,

> Now we must frankly admit that a literal interpretation of the Old Testament prophecies gives us just such a picture of an earthly reign of the Messiah as the premillennialist pictures. That was the kind of Messianic kingdom that the Jews of the time of Christ were looking for, on the basis of a literal interpretation of the Old Testament promises.[18]

In the same vein, Old Testament scholar Oswald Allis

admits "the Old Testament prophecies if literally interpreted cannot be regarded as having been yet fulfilled or as being capable of fulfillment in this present age."[19]

Vindicating Literal Interpretation Through Prophetic Fulfillment

One way that the literal interpretation of prophecy can be vindicated is by examining how past prophecies were fulfilled. Pretribulationist Paul Tan says that at "the first coming of Christ, over 300 prophecies were completely fulfilled." Tan concludes that "every prophecy that has been fulfilled has been fulfilled literally. On the basis of New Testament attestations and the record of history, the fulfillment of Bible prophecy has always been literal."[20]

Ryrie also argues that the literal fulfillment of past prophecy affirms that future prophecy should be interpreted literally. He holds that "the prophecies in the Old Testament concerning the first coming of Christ—His birth, His rearing, His ministry, His death, His resurrection—were all fulfilled literally. That argues strongly for the literal method."[21]

As early as the book of Genesis, God demonstrates that prophecy is fulfilled literally even when figures of speech and symbols are employed. A number of dreams and visions are depicted throughout Genesis in which God shows the future to some of His people. A classic example is found in Joseph's dreams about his ascendancy over his family (Genesis 37:5-11). In both dreams, God used symbols to communicate what the future held. In one dream sheaves of grain represented Joseph and his brothers; in the other dream, the sun represents Jacob, the moon stood for Rachel, and the stars are his brothers. Even though symbols were used, these dreams were fulfilled literally in the life of Joseph and his family as he later ruled over them when he rose to second-in-command over Egypt.

In Revelation 12, some of the prophetic symbols that appeared in Joseph's prophetic dreams are mentioned again. The sun refers to Jacob, the moon stands for Rachel, and the stars are the 12 tribes of Israel. Even though symbols are used here, biblical precedent dictates that the prophecy should be interpreted literally and will be fulfilled literally as well.

History of Hermeneutics

The well-known truism that ideas have consequences certainly applies to the issue of how to properly interpret Scripture, especially Bible prophecy. The book of Proverbs speaks of the end of a matter[22]—in other words, where does one's viewpoint lead? A good way to examine this issue is to see where interpretive methods have led in the past. We believe that if allegorical or nonliteral interpretive approaches were to become widely accepted, the church would go back to the Dark Ages hermeneutically.

Ancient History

During the first 200 years of church history, two competing schools of interpretation arose. The Syrian School of Antioch championed a literal and historical interpretation, whereas a school in Alexandria, Egypt, advocated an allegorical or spiritual hermeneutic. Bernard Ramm says, "The Syrian school fought Origen in particular as the inventor of the allegorical method, and maintained the primacy of the literal and historical interpretation."[23] Clement of Alexandria (150–215) and Origen (185–254) developed the allegorical approach to biblical interpretation in the early third century.

"The fundamental criticism of Origen, beginning during his own lifetime," notes Joseph Trigg, "was that he used allegorical interpretation to provide a specious justification for reinterpreting Christian doctrine in terms of Platonic philosophy."[24] Origen believed that "Proverbs 22:20 authorizes interpreters to seek a three-fold meaning in each passage of Scripture: fleshly, psychic and spiritual." Since Origen believed that "the spiritual meaning belongs to a higher order of ideas than the literal,"[25] he was attracted to the spiritual or allegorical meaning of the text. Ronald Diprose explains the implications of an allegorical interpretation as follows:

He motivated this view by appealing to the principle of divine inspiration and by affirming that often statements made by the biblical writers are not literally true and that many events, presented as historical, are inherently impossible. Thus only simple believers will limit themselves to the literal meaning of the text.[26]

The adherents of allegorical interpretation sound just like a twenty-first century Origen when they exhibit just such a rationale in their rejection of a literal interpretation of Bible prophecy. For example, Hank Hanegraaff labels Tim LaHaye's view of Revelation 14:20 as a "literal-at-all-costs method of interpretation." There, the text says the blood from the slaughter at Armageddon will run "up to the horses' bridle" for a distance of 200 miles. Hanegraaff declares: "Interpreting apocalyptic imagery in a woodenly literal sense inevitably leads to absurdity." Why does he think this is the case? He explains: "Since it is difficult to imagine that the blood of Christ's enemies could create a literal river reaching as high as 'the horses' bridles for a distance of 1,600 stadia,' LaHaye exercises extraordinary literary license."[27] A page later Hanegraaff says, "Figurative language requires readers to use their imagination...Such imaginative leaps are the rule rather than the exception."[28]

Hanegraaff imagines that the blood in this passage, rather than just emanating from the subjects of God's judgment, as the text says, is also a symbol "of blood that flowed from Immanuel's veins."[29] As his imagination continues to speculate, we find out that "the number sixteen hundred is pregnant with meaning." He quotes preterist commentator David Chilton, who explains "that the number sixteen hundred is a number that uniquely emphasizes Palestine. Four squared symbolizes the land and ten squared is emblematic of the largeness of the land."[30] How does he know that is what four squared, or sixteen hundred, refers to? This is a clear importation of meaning into the text. Where is the evidence that his explanation of 1600 is the meaning? Why could it not be a multiple of eight, instead of four and ten? And how does Hanegraaff know this will not happen literally? Literalists believe it will because that is what the text says.

The bottom line for the interpreters at the Syrian School at Antioch is their assertion that "the literal was plain-literal and figurative literal." By this they meant that "a plain-literal sentence is a straightforward prose sentence with no figures of speech in it. 'The eye of the Lord is upon thee,' would be a figurative literal sentence."[31] Such an approach had a tremendous impact on Bible prophecy, and liberal commentator R.H. Charles notes "the Alexandrians, who, under the influence of Hellenism and the traditional allegorical school of interpretation which came to a head in Philo, rejected the literal sense of the Apocalypse, and attached to it a spiritual significance only."[32]

Hanegraaff's downgrade of the modern state of Israel as prophetically significant also has roots in Origen and an allegorical hermeneutic. Diprose notes as follows:

> An attitude of contempt towards Israel had become the rule by Origen's time. The new element in his own view of Israel is his perception of them as "manifesting no elevation [of thought]." It follows that the interpreter must always posit a deeper or higher meaning for prophecies relating to Judea, Jerusalem, Israel, Judah and Jacob which, he affirms, are "not being understood by us in a 'carnal' sense."
>
> In Origen's understanding, the only positive function of *physical* Israel was that of being a type of *spiritual* Israel. The promises were not made to physical Israel because she was unworthy of them and incapable of understanding them. Thus Origen effectively disinherits physical Israel.[33]

Hanegraaff's treatment of Israel follows the same course as Origen's. Hanegraaff, in his model of eschatology, clearly disinherits physical Israel and replaces her with what he regularly calls "spiritual Israel,"[34] or the church. "Origen likens Israel to a divorced wife in whom an unseemly thing had been found," notes Diprose. Origen said, "A sign that she has received the bill of divorce is this, that Jerusalem was destroyed along with what they called the sanctuary."[35] Hanegraaff holds a similar view, as he depicts Israel "as an insatiable prostitute,"[36] while the church is "the purified bride."[37] In spite of all the evidence in his book, from a historical perspective, Hanegraaff says he has "never argued for Replacement Theology."[38] Norman Geisler provides a more reasonable assessment when he says, "Ideas do have consequences, and the typological-allegorical idea has had severe consequences in the history of the church. Denying a literal fulfillment of God's promises to Israel has led to anti-Semitism." Geisler concludes that those "who replace literal Israel with a spiritual church nullify the literal land and throne promises, thus opening the door to Liberalism and cultism."[39]

Although the Syrian school had great influence during the first few centuries, the Alexandrian school eventually won out with the help of Jerome and Augustine, who were advocates of the allegorical approach to Bible prophecy. Liberal historian Henry Preserved Smith concluded concerning Augustine that "with his endorsement allegory may fairly be said to have triumphed."[40] This influence paved the way for the dominance of allegorical interpretation during much of the Middle Ages, especially in the area of Bible prophecy. Augustine, by the way, developed a dual hermeneutic. He tended to interpret the Bible literally, but when it came to eschatology, he interpreted it spiritually or allegorically.

The Middle Ages

The allegorical method of interpretation dominated through the Middle Ages. Since Origen taught that the spiritual is the deeper or real meaning of a text, why deal with the inferior literal meaning of a passage when one can see so much more in the spiritual realm? One dominant late-medieval belief was that every sentence in the pages of Scripture had to be understood as referring to Christ. This erroneous interpretive dictum was based upon a misinterpretation and misapplication of Luke 24:44, where Jesus said, "These are the words which I spoke to you while I was still with you, that all things must be fulfilled which were written in the Law of Moses and the Prophets and the Psalms concerning Me."

This passage does not say that every word or sentence in the Old Testament has to refer to Jesus, the Messiah; but rather, that Jesus is the one being referenced in the Old Testament when it speaks of the Messiah. This would mean that a clearly historical passage like 1 Chronicles 26:18, which says, "As for the Parbar on the west, there were four on the highway and two at the Parbar," would have to be interpreted as referring to Christ. This sentence is *not* speaking about Christ, but through allegorical alchemy it was explained in some kind of Christological way. "During these nine centuries we find very little except the 'glimmerings and decays' of patristic exposition," notes Farrar. "Much of the learning which still continued to exist was devoted to something which was meant for exegesis, yet not one writer in hundreds showed any true conception of what exegesis really implies."[41]

The Reformation

It was not until the dawning of the Reformation that biblical interpreters began to return to the sanity of literal interpretation. The Reformation could not have occurred if the reformers did not have the confidence that they knew what God's Word was saying. "The tradition of the Syrian school... became the essential hermeneutical theory of the Reformers."[42]

Ramm points out that in Europe "there was a hermeneutical Reformation which preceded the ecclesiastical Reformation."[43] Thus, we see demonstrated once again in history that one's interpretive method precedes and produces one's exegesis, and finally, a theological belief. Luther and Calvin generally returned the church to literal interpretation. Had they not done this, then Protestantism would have never been born and reformation would have never taken place. Luther said, "The literal sense of Scripture alone is the whole essence of faith and of Christian theology."[44] Calvin said, "It is the first business of an interpreter to let his author say what he does, instead of attributing to him what we think he ought to say."[45] However, like most of us, Luther and Calvin did not always follow their own theory, but they and like-minded reformers turned the hermeneutical tide in the right direction. Unfortunately they did not include taking the text literally when the plain sense of the original obviously stated what was meant.

The Post-Reformation

During the post-Reformation period many Protestants slowly cast off 1000 years of allegorical interpretation of the Bible. First they applied literal interpretation to issues relating to the doctrine of salvation, and then they began to apply it increasingly across the entire Bible. In the early 1600s there was a return to premillennialism because some started applying the literal hermeneutic to Revelation 20.[46] At the same time, many Protestants began to see that there was a literal future for national Israel,[47] which was spearheaded by reading the premillennialism of the early church fathers,[48] and for the English-speaking world, the notes in the Geneva Bible.[49]

Even though literal interpretation was being restored during the Reformation and post-Reformation periods, it still took a while for biblical interpreters to more consistently rid themselves of medieval allegorical influences. For the influential Puritan theologian William Perkins, "the medieval four-fold sense was reduced to a two-fold or double-literal sense."[50] This would be similar to Augustine's dual hermeneutic. However, most Protestant Bible interpreters were increasingly moving toward the literal hermeneutic and functioning within that framework so that the historical, grammatical, contextual method is labeled the Protestant hermeneutic.[51]

By the 1600s most Bible scholars preferred a literal method of interpretation; nevertheless, a couple hundred years passed before that understanding influenced all areas of Bible interpretation, especially Bible prophecy. Even though premillennialism had been restored, it was still dominated, to a large extent, by the blend of literal and allegorical interpretation that is known as historicism, which calculated time within a contrived day/year theory. To historicists, when the Bible cites 1260 days from Daniel and Revelation, it really means 1260 years. This is not literal interpretation!

It was not until the late 1700s and early 1800s that biblical interpreters grew more consistent in applying a literal hermeneutic. Wilber B. Wallis tells us that "a consistent futurism, which completely removes the necessity for calculating the times, did not emerge until the early nineteenth century."[52] In general, the evangelical church, especially in the English-speaking world, returned to the premillennial futurism of the early church. Now they would apply the literal method and develop it beyond that found in the early church. As Wallis notes, the views of Irenaeus (c. 185) contained the basics of the literal and futurist understanding of Bible prophecy as seen in modern dispensationalism.[53] The important point to note here is that as interpreters became more consistent in applying a literal hermeneutic to the entire Bible, especially to biblical prophecy, it undoubtedly yielded a futurist view of prophecy. "We have returned to Irenaeus' conception of the futurity of Daniel's seventieth week,"[54] says Wallis.

Implications for Today

If the evangelical church continues to follow its current trend of moving away from literal interpretation, the only direction it can move is back toward the mysticism of the Alexandrian school and the hermeneutical trends of the Middle Ages. This is not progress; if it were to happen, it would be retrogression and a downgrade.

A shift toward the interpretive trends of the Middle Ages would have serious consequences. Beryl Smalley, a scholar specializing in medieval views of biblical interpretation, tells us that "they subordinated scholarship meanwhile to mysticism and to propaganda."[55] "Again the crisis was reflected in biblical studies. The speculation of Joachim signified a new wave of mysticism."[56] "Revolution and uncertainty have discouraged biblical scholarship in the past and stimulated more subjective modes of interpretation," she contends. "Conditions today are giving rise to a certain sympathy with the allegorists. We have a spate of studies on medieval 'spirituality'."[57] Too many within evangelicalism are following the overall trends of secular society and are moving away from literal interpretation into the shadowy darkness of nonliteral hermeneutics.

It has been observed that culture cycles back and forth between rationalism and mysticism over the years. Since the 1960s, American culture has definitely moved in the direction of and is now firmly dominated by a mystical worldview, especially in the area of personal beliefs. However, biblical Christianity is not based on reason or mysticism as its starting point for truth; instead it is built upon revelation or God's Word. When mysticism dominates a culture's mind-set, it predisposes one hermeneutically toward mysticism and nonliteral interpretation.

Some years ago Dr. John Walvoord was asked, "What do you predict will be the most significant theological issues over the next ten years?" He answered, among other things, "the hermeneutical problem of not interpreting the Bible literally, especially the prophetic areas. The church today is engulfed in the idea that one cannot interpret prophecy literally."[58]

Veteran evangelical scholar Walt Kaiser suggested almost 30 years ago that the church is "now going through a hermeneutical crisis, perhaps as significant in its importance and outcome as that of the Reformation."[59] In this crisis, "the meaning of the text lies in its subject matter, rather than in what an author meant by that text."[60] Kaiser explains further:

> The process of exegesis of a text is no longer linear but circular—one in which the interpreter affects his text as much as the text (in its subject matter) somehow affects the interpreter as well. Clearly, there is a confusion of ontology with epistemology, the subject with the object, the "thereness" of the propositions of the text with the total cultural and interpretive "baggage" of the interpreter.[61]

Norman Geisler has also expressed concern with the direction of evangelical hermeneutics and said that it "is based on an allegorical method of interpreting prophetic Scripture that if applied to other teachings of Scripture, would undermine the salvation essentials of the Christian Faith."[62] It is clear from

2000 years of church history that if we do indeed continue to adopt current evangelical trends for interpreting Bible prophecy, then we will return to the subjectivism and mysticism of the Dark Ages. Could our current downgrade lead us toward the false mysticism that will be widespread during the Tribulation?

16

WHY CHRIST WILL COME BEFORE THE TRIBULATION

Tim LaHaye

At this point it should be apparent that the seven-year Tribulation will be the most horrific period in all of human history. Our Lord Himself spoke about it in His great Olivet Discourse: "For then there will be Great Tribulation, such as has not been since the beginning of the world until this time, no, nor ever shall be" (Matthew 24:21).

This is, in fact, the most important description ever given about this devastating period, making it obvious that it has yet to occur. Keep in mind that the Tribulation receives more space in the Bible than any other historical period described, whether it be past or future.

Compare, for example, the period known as the millennial kingdom. We would be hard-pressed to find a dozen chapters in the Bible that describe this incredible 1000-year period. And yet the short seven-year Tribulation is mentioned 49 times in the Old Testament, given two chapters each in both Matthew and Luke, one chapter in Mark, and 13 chapters in the book of Revelation, among others. In fact, the only subject in the New Testament that is given more space than the Tribulation is the subject of Jesus Himself. He is, after all, the principle reason for the existence of the Bible, yet the subject of the Tribulation runs second to the Lord in regard to the allocation of space. That in itself demonstrates just how important this soon-to-come period of time is.

While on the subject, I would like to explain the reason for this outpouring of calamity. It is a time of judgment—a time when man's false gods of materialism, unbelief, and libertine living are dashed to pieces. And though God's wrath takes center stage during the Tribulation, after having studied prophecy for over 60 years, I have come to the conclusion that the supreme purpose of the Tribulation is for God to exhibit His great mercy to mankind. For the judgments He will place on unsaved people are intended to warn them of their need to turn to the Lord while they still can. With Christ's millennial kingdom rapidly approaching, time is of the essence. People must make a decision whether to believe in Jesus as the Messiah or to reject Him. The seven-year Tribulation will present people with one last chance to salvation before the arrival of the millennial kingdom.

There are a number of acts God will perform during the Tribulation that will clearly demonstrate His great mercy, including the sealing of the 144,000 servants of God in Revelation 7:4-8; the saving of "a great multitude [of Tribulation saints] that no one could number" in Revelation 7:9-17; and the release of the "angel flying in the midst of heaven, having the everlasting gospel to preach to those who dwell on the earth" in Revelation 14:6-7.

These and other acts of God will occur during this most traumatic period in our planet's history, and they will prove just how merciful our God is in desiring that all men be saved. The events of the Tribulation will cause multiplied millions to call on the name of the Lord and prepare them for the wonderful eternity He has in store for them.

Reasons the Rapture
Will Precede the Tribulation

There must be a reason the majority of evangelical Christians who take the Bible literally believe that the Bible's prophetic passages indicate the rapture will occur prior to the beginning of the Tribulation. And there is. In fact, I have found at least 14 such reasons. Consider them carefully and see if you agree.

1. Commonsense Meaning of Scripture

When all the end-time prophetic passages are taken literally for their commonsense meaning, they clearly teach the pretribulational coming of Christ to rapture His church to the "Father's house" before the Tribulation begins. Centuries ago, a belief in the pretribulation rapture naturally grew out of the distribution and study of the Bible following its translation into the language of the common people. During the first 300 years after the birth of Christianity, few people had access to the written Word. This was due to a number of factors, including a lack of education resulting in an inability to read, an inability to afford the texts, the durability of papyrus, and so on. Consequently, when persecution hit the early church, what little the people had heard about the Tribulation caused them to think they might actually be in it, except for those who knew about what the apostle Paul had told the Christians in Thessalonica regarding the rapture taking place before the Tribulation. Otherwise, many people became victims of the deception promoted by false teachers.

By the third century, those teachers who preferred to allegorize or spiritualize the Word rather than take it at face value had gained a foothold in the expanding church, to the detriment of the people. And by the fifth century, the teachings of Augustine, coupled with the influence of Greek philosophy (which insisted that all beliefs possessed more than one interpretation), continued to keep the truth shrouded in mystery and confusion. By the sixth century, the Roman government, acting as the head of Christendom, had seen fit to confine all biblical manuscripts to museums and libraries, prohibiting access by the common people and thus ushering in the Dark Ages—dark because people were cut off from the light and truth of God's Word.

All of that changed by the sixteenth century. The first book to come off the newly invented Gutenberg press was the Bible. Individuals such as Wycliffe, Tyndale, Beza, and Coverdale took upon themselves the task of translating the Bible into the language of the people and distributing it around the world. Tragically, some of these men of God were labeled heretics and were rewarded for their efforts by being burned at the stake! Nevertheless, their valiant acts forever changed the world. For the first time in history, the common man could now read the Word of God for himself. During the seventeenth century, the Bible became the most popular book in the world, and it remains so to this day.

The Bible's ready availability during the last few centuries has resulted in a rapid spread of biblical truth, and this includes truths about the rapture and the second coming. For many, the personal knowledge of Bible teaching has had a threefold effect: It has given believers a renewed evangelical zeal for soul winning; it has given them a greater vision for reaching the world for Christ through missions work; and it has cultivated a desire to live a godly life in the midst of an increasingly unholy society. The teaching of the pretribulation rapture—the most popular view among Bible students—has played a vital role in influencing the church for good.

2. The Golden Rule of Interpretation

When all the facts about the return of Christ are taken at face value, the pretrib position is the most logical conclusion to take regarding this critically important future event. The golden rule of biblical interpretation is "When the plain sense of Scripture makes common sense, seek no other sense. Take every word at its primary literal meaning unless the facts of the immediate context clearly indicate otherwise." Detractors to this position often claim this does not allow for figures of speech, and accuse adherents of "wooden literalism."

But those who interpret Scripture literally recognize there are figures of speech used in every language. What's more, even when the Bible speaks in symbolic terms, the context usually explains itself. The Bible is its own best resource when it comes to understanding what it means.

3. Harmonizing the Two Phases of the Second Coming

The pretribulation rapture view is the only perspective that clearly and logically untangles the seemingly contradictory events of the second coming.

We have already seen how the rapture passages are distinct from the glorious appearing passages. Because they both come from the Word of God, we can be certain that both will take place, but they speak of two different sets of events. For example, Christ cannot come for His church suddenly without warning and be seen only by believers (the rapture), and simultaneously come in full view of the whole world (the glorious appearing). Nor can He come "in the air" (the rapture) and "to the earth" (the glorious appearing) at the same time. Anyone seeking the truth on this matter must face the fact that many times Jesus promised to return at any moment, and yet He cannot come in His glorious appearing for at least seven years following the beginning of the Tribulation. The rapture, however, could take place at any time. So although the rapture and the glorious appearing are both classified as occurring in the last days as part of Christ's second coming, they are clearly two separate events.

4. The Expectation that Christ Could Return Any Moment

The pretrib perspective is the only view that holds to an imminent expectation that Christ could come at any moment. It's significant that the early church of the first three centuries was driven by a belief that Christ could come at any moment. And He could, but only *if* His coming is pretribulational. The church that is looking for Jesus to return at any moment is a more evangelistic, soul-winning church than the church that is looking for the Tribulation to occur next on the prophetic calendar.

A good illustration of that is the church I pastored for 25 years in San Diego. God blessed it greatly, and we were able to start two satellite churches—one of them being Shadow Mountain Community Church, where Dr. David Jeremiah has pastored now for over 30 years. In other words, that church has had only two pastors in its 55-plus years. Both of us have made a point to preach the prophetic Word of God and in particular, the pretribulational return of Jesus Christ. Today, under Pastor Jeremiah's teaching, that church has experienced staggering growth. The people there are serious about soul winning, world missions, and holy living. All that is the result of consistent rapture-expectation teaching. To all pastors I would admonish to "go and do likewise."

5. Honoring the Biblical Distinction Between Israel and the Church

The pretribulation rapture view is the only one that distinguishes clearly between Israel and the church. One of the strange views of the amillenialists and postmillennialists is the merging of Israel and the church together, in spite of the many scriptures that clearly differentiate between these two groups. Numerous prophetic passages call for the regathering of Israel in the end times. In fact, the recognition of Israel as a sovereign state by the United Nations in 1948 is surely a fulfillment of biblical prophecy in our time (see Ezekiel 36–37, particularly 37:11, where the prophet identifies the re-gathering of the dry bones of the nation Israel as "the whole house of Israel"). As often has been said of various other end-time theories: They want to transfer the *promises* of God which are meant for Israel to the church, but are not willing to accept the *curses*. That seems illogical. The church is in fact the bride of Christ and has a future that is clearly shown to be unique from that of Israel.

6. Allowing Time for Believers in Heaven

The pretrib view allows enough time for church-age Christians to be taken to the Father's house as Jesus promised (John 14:1-3). All true believers have been promised a dwelling place there. A rapture that occurs at the end of the Tribulation only allows time for a momentary visit. That would be akin to an elevator trip that quickly goes up and then comes right back down. In such an event there would be no opportunity for the Judgment Seat of Christ, the marriage of the bride, or the marriage supper of the Lamb—all promised to take place before

Jesus Himself returns to the earth in power and great glory. The pretrib view allows at least seven years for these events to take place in heaven while the Tribulation is unfolding on earth.

7. A Blessed Future, Not Cursed

The pretrib view is the only view of "the blessed hope" that allows it to indeed be a blessing and not a curse. In Titus 2:11-12, the rapture, or "the blessed hope," is distinguished from the "glorious appearing." Both events, as we have already seen, are distinct and are separated by the seven-year Tribulation (see Revelation 4–19). Realistically speaking, how can anyone get excited about and look forward to seven horrific years of tribulation and define it as a "blessed hope"? Rapture, ecstasy, and being in the presence of the Lord, yes! Tribulation, suffering, and death, no!

8. The Silence Regarding Preparation

Not one word of instruction is given to believers on how to prepare for life during the Tribulation, when the Antichrist will severely persecute Christians. Why? Because we won't be around. God did not intend for those who believe on Him to suffer the judgments of the Tribulation.

9. The Silence About the Church

The church is mentioned 17 times in Revelation 1–3. But after John, a member of the church, is invited up to heaven in Revelation 4:3 prior to the start of the Tribulation, the church is not mentioned even once—all the way through chapter 19. Yet Israel and the Israelites are mentioned numerous times. Why? Because the Tribulation is "the time of Jacob's trouble" and has nothing to do with the church. According to Daniel 9, the Tribulation involves Israel.

10. Taking God's Promise Literally

The pretrib view is the only one that takes literally God's promise to "keep [us] from the hour of trial which shall come upon the whole world" (Revelation 3:10). This planet has never experienced such worldwide testing. It is called a time of wrath several times in the Old Testament, and again in Romans 5:9 and I Thessalonians 1:10. Our Lord describes that period in Matthew 24 and it is covered in great detail in Revelation 6–19. This hour of trial is not for believers but for the unconverted.

11. The Magnitude of the Event

The pretrib stance views the rapture of the church as a major event. Keep in mind we are talking about many millions of people suddenly being removed from the face of the earth. Then there are the countless multitudes of dead believers of past ages (AD 33 to the present) who will meet the Lord in the air as well. From there, Christ will take the raptured church and formerly dead believers to the Father's house. The entire world will watch the resulting chaos on the news. Imagine the confusion and devastation as drivers are snatched from their vehicles, police officers and firemen and medical personnel disappear instantaneously, and so much more.

And what about air travel? With an estimated 40,000 takeoffs and landings occurring each day around the world, what will happen when Christian pilots are suddenly snatched up to heaven? Some flights will be fortunate enough to have an unsaved copilot ready to take over the controls to get the plane back safely on the ground.

The rapture will change *everything* in countries where the gospel has been taught. And that's just the tip of the iceberg!

The rapture will be the most astounding event in all of history. And soon after, the Antichrist will bring together his global government, global economy, and global religion as described in the book of Revelation.

12. Watching in Expectation for Jesus

The pretrib view is the only one that has the church watching out for the coming of Christ, which is what Scripture urges us to do. Those who have bought into the posttrib view aren't looking for Jesus, but for the Antichrist, the False Prophet, and other false christs.

13. No Signs Left to Fulfill Before the Rapture

Only the pretrib view assures us that Jesus could come today—not to set up His millennial kingdom, but to take His church (the "bride of Christ") to His Father's house. The second phase of His coming, the glorious appearing, cannot occur today, according to Daniel 9:24-27, for it must take place at least seven years after the signing of the covenant between the Antichrist and the nation of Israel. This will signal the beginning of the final seven-year period of 70 *heptads* (70 "sevens"), or 490 years. Daniel prophesied that 483 years (or 69 "sevens") were determined until the Messiah came and was rejected by the nation of Israel. However, the last *heptad* or seven-year period (the Tribulation) has yet to occur.

14. Repopulation of the Earth During the Millennium

Not too long ago I was "sandbagged" by a Christian TV personality who invited me on his show to discuss Bible prophecy along with two others I did not know. I had been led to believe we would talk about the chaos in the Middle East and Islamic terrorism against the tiny nation of Israel. Instead, one of the men launched into a well-rehearsed speech about the rapture taking place at the end of the Tribulation. I didn't want to be rude and interrupt his rapid-fire presentation, but I finally managed to stop him in his tracks with a question he could not answer: If Jesus raptures His church at the end of the Tribulation and takes them to His Father's house as promised in John 14:1-3, and if all unbelievers are cast into hell as promised in Matthew 25:31-46, then who at the end of the Tribulation will be left in their natural bodies to populate the 1000-year kingdom?

Of course, this posttribulationist had no answer. No one does. The pretrib position provides a simple answer. Those Gentiles and Jews who come to faith during the Tribulation and escape the Antichrist's attempts to kill them will go directly into the millennial kingdom and help repopulate the earth. In fact, many scholars believe they will retain their natural bodies and launch an unprecedented population explosion.

The majority of those who find themselves in Jesus' millennial kingdom—which will be free of war, crime, and satanic deception—will readily accept Jesus as their Savior. But not all. At the end of that 1000-year period, according to Revelation 20:7-10, Satan will be released from his prison and go out into the world to tempt the people of the earth one last time. Many will respond to his deceptions and ultimately be cast with him, the Antichrist, and the False Prophet into hell. So why would God briefly release Satan? To level the playing field between all generations of humanity, from Adam to the end of time as we know it. Even those who choose to remain unsaved at the end of the millennial kingdom will have had the same opportunity all people have had to call on the name of the Lord and be saved.

Making the Right Choice Today

The choice is yours to make! God leaves the choice of receiving the Savior up to the individual. And so will it be for those living during the Tribulation and the millennium.

> The Lord is not slack concerning His promise, as some count slackness, but is longsuffering toward us, not willing that any should perish but that all should come to repentance (2 Peter 3:9).

ISRAEL AND THE CHURCH AND WHY THEY MATTER TO THE RAPTURE

Michael J. Vlach

God is a God of truth and order. Not only can we be assured that all He reveals is true, we can also know that the many facets of His revelation fit in perfect harmony with each other. No revealed truth in one area ever contradicts a revealed truth in another. Nor will His purposes in one area contradict His purposes in another. We find this to be true when we come to the matter of how Israel and the church relate to the rapture. These categories, while distinct, fit together.

The issue of Israel and the church relates to a broader theological category called "the people of God." When we look at biblical history, we can see different categories of believers. There are pre-Israel saints, saved Israelites, Gentiles who became saved before the church age, and Gentiles who became saved after the church age. And of course, there is the church itself. These peoples of God are all saved the same way—by grace alone, through faith alone, in Christ alone, based on the atonement of Christ alone. It is in these areas that there is unity. Yet these peoples of God still retain distinctions. Israel, for example, is distinct from other nations and the church.

This unity/diversity motif is found elsewhere in Scripture. It is true of the Trinity, in which there is unity (one God) and diversity (three Persons). The family unit is one, yet there are individual members within that family with differing responsibilities (i.e., father, mother, and children). With regard to salvation, men and women are equal (see Galatians 3:28), yet there are still functional distinctions between the genders (see 1 Timothy 2:11-15). As these examples show, both unity and diversity can co-exist in a wonderful harmony. This is true for the concept of the people or peoples of God as well, including the relationship between Israel and the church. Both Israel and the church can participate equally in salvation yet remain distinct in identity and function.

The rapture, on the other hand, is an *event*. Or to be more specific, it is an eschatological event in which Jesus will "snatch" His church to meet Him in the air, then bring her to heaven.[1]

Passages that many believe refer to the rapture include John 14:1-3; 1 Corinthians 15:51-52; and 1 Thessalonians 4:13-18. This event includes the resurrection of both living and deceased members of the church.

Now the rapture is not an isolated event. It occurs in the context of another event—the Tribulation. Also known as Daniel's seventieth week or the Day of the Lord, the Tribulation is a unique period during which God will unleash His divine wrath on an unbelieving world and resume His plan to save and restore Israel. This era is discussed in detail in Matthew 24; 2 Thessalonians 2; and Revelation 6–19.

This leads us to our main topic in this chapter—the relationship of Israel and the church to the rapture. To address the question, Why and how do Israel and the church matter to the rapture? we need to look at three key issues: (1) the distinction between Israel and the church; (2) Israel's relationship to the rapture and the Tribulation; and (3) the church's relationship to the rapture and the Tribulation. Our study of these issues will help us better understand the rapture and its purpose.

The Distinction Between Israel and the Church

Israel

A proper understanding of the rapture is related to a correct understanding of the distinction between Israel and the church. Israel, as a nation, has deep roots in the Old Testament. Abraham was promised that a "great nation" would come from him (Genesis 12:2), and it would be this great nation that provided the means for bringing blessings to "all the families of the earth" (Genesis 12:3). As the book of Genesis unfolds we see that Israel would comprise the physical descendants of Abraham through Isaac and Jacob. Jacob's sons would then become the basis for the 12 tribes of Israel. Later, as a result of the exodus from Egypt, the Israelites would become a nation of their own under the leadership of Moses. Deuteronomy 28–29 details the promised blessings and curses that would come upon Israel in relation to her obedience (or lack thereof) to the Mosaic Covenant. And in Deuteronomy 30 God declared that Israel would be punished and scattered throughout the earth, but then would be saved and restored to her land with both spiritual and physical blessings (verses 1-6).

Israel officially became a kingdom under Saul, David, and Solomon, and the nation later became divided, then was taken captive by nations such as Assyria, Babylon, Medo-Persia, Greece, and Rome. All of this fulfilled what was predicted for the nation back in Deuteronomy 28–30, where captivity and dispersion were predicted. With no king on the throne, the prophets of Israel came to the fore with messages of judgment and then hope for a future restoration. They foretold of a coming Servant and Messiah who would restore Israel and bring blessings to the nations (see Isaiah 42:6; 49:6).

As the passages above show, the bulk of the Old Testament witness focuses on Israel. This is true for Genesis 12 through Malachi. There are periods of obedience and triumph for Israel, but the downward spiral into disobedience and judgment is more dominant. Yet even during the bleakest of times, the prophets foretold of blessings coming to Israel (see Isaiah 60–66). At the end of the Old Testament, Malachi prophesied that a future restoration of Israel would take place (4:5-6).

The Gospels, too, focus much attention on Israel. The angel Gabriel told Mary that her Son would sit on the throne of His father David and that He would reign over the house of

Jacob forever (Luke 1:32-33). Jesus Himself told the disciples they would someday sit on 12 thrones judging the 12 tribes of Israel (Matthew 19:28). Jesus' earthly ministry was primarily directed to Israel, so much so that He told His disciples at one point to preach only to the cities of Israel (Matthew 10:6). Jesus mourned over Israel for missing the time of her divine visitation (see Luke 19:41-44), but He also predicted that a day was coming when Israel would cry out to Him in repentance (Matthew 23:37-39). Jesus' Olivet Discourse, found in Matthew 24-25, Mark 13, and Luke 21, describes events that will take place in Israel during the last days leading up to His return.

Throughout the Gospels, the emphasis is on Jesus' dealings with Israel. Yet late in His earthly ministry Jesus foretold of the church's coming when He declared, "I will build my church" (Matthew 16:18). This verse, along with Matthew 18:17, is the only reference to "church" in the four Gospels and highlights Jesus' relations with Israel. Even on Jesus' day of ascension the apostles were thinking of Israel when they asked, "Lord, will You at this time restore the kingdom to Israel?" (Acts 1:6). In Acts 3:12 Peter told the "men of Israel" that if they would "repent and return" Jesus would return again and the "times of refreshing" and the "restoration of all things" would occur (verses 19-21 NASB). These refer to kingdom blessings associated with the return of the Messiah and His kingdom reign upon the earth. So even in the early chapters of Acts, much of the attention is on Israel.

The Church

The New Testament's shift in emphasis from Israel to the church begins later in Acts. The church begins to take center stage from Acts 8 onward, and remains there until Revelation chapters 1–3. While there are only two references to the church in the Gospels, there are 107 references in the Acts, the epistles, and Revelation. This emphasis, however, is not at the expense of national Israel's importance. Paul affirmed the significance of Israel in God's plans in Romans 9–11 and John detailed the significance of the 144,000 saved Jews from the 12 tribes of Israel (Revelation 7:4-8). So while the church is the primary focus of the New Testament after Acts 8, the nation Israel is not forgotten or viewed as being superseded by the church. Both the church and Israel have ongoing roles to play in God's purposes.

Unlike Israel, the church is a New Testament entity. The church began in Acts 2 on the Day of Pentecost when the Holy Spirit was poured out on believers. In Ephesians 2:20 Paul said the church was "built on the foundation of the apostles and prophets." Both "apostles" and "prophets" here are New Testament persons upon which the church is built, showing that the church had its origins in the New Testament era.[2] Also, the spiritual gifts that are linked with the church are tied to Jesus' ascension in Ephesians 4:7-8. It was when Jesus "ascended on high" that He "gave gifts to men" (verse 8). When we remember that Jesus said, "I will build My church" (Matthew 16:18), we see that the church did not begin in the Old Testament, but is rather a New Testament entity.

Key Observations About the Distinction

To properly understand the rapture, we must understand the scriptural distinction between Israel and the church. Not recognizing this distinction brings confusion. In fact, a key reason many Christians do not properly understand the rapture is because of a supersessionist theology that views the church as a replacement of Israel. But over the last two centuries, the supersessionist view has been rightly challenged and soundly refuted.[3] Several points highlight this distinction between Israel and the church:

First, the title *Israel* in the Bible refers only to ethnic Jews and never to believing Gentiles. Never are Gentiles or Gentile Christians ever referred to as "Israel" or "Jews." It has been claimed by some that passages like Romans 9:6 and Galatians 6:16 refer to believing Gentiles as "Israel," but this is not true. Both passages refer to Jews who are believers. Within the broader pool of ethnic Jews there is a narrower subset of Jews who have placed their faith in Christ. These are the "Israel of

God" that Paul refers to in Galatians 6:16 and the Israel within Israel mentioned in Romans 9:6. So the designations "Israel" and "Jew" can be used of both the nation Israel and Jews as an ethnic group or as believing Jews in particular (see Romans 2:28-29), but they do not refer to Gentiles.

Second, the New Testament writers strategically use the term "church" in such a way as to avoid the idea that the church is now the new Israel. I have already pointed out that the Gospels mention the church in only two verses (Matthew 16:18 and 18:17). But Acts, the epistles, and Revelation 1–3 mention the church over 100 times. The Gospel writer Luke is also relevant in this regard. It is no coincidence that Luke included zero references to the church in his Gospel, yet mentioned the church 23 times in Acts. It does not appear that Luke viewed the church as existing during Jesus' earthly ministry; rather, the church was an entity that began in the Acts. At no point does Luke indicate that the church is the new Israel.

Third, on the day of Jesus' ascension, both Jesus and the apostles still believed in a future restoration of the nation Israel. Acts 1:3 states that Jesus gave the disciples a 40-day lesson on the kingdom of God. Then in Acts 1:6 the apostles asked Jesus, "Lord, will You at this time restore the kingdom to Israel?" After 40 days of kingdom instruction from the risen Lord, the apostles still expected a restoration of the nation Israel. To them, there was no doubt that the kingdom would be restored to Israel, but the time this would happen was still unknown. Jesus did not rebuke their understanding; instead, He said, "It is not for you to know times or seasons" (verse 7). Thus their understanding of Israel's restoration was correct, but they were not to know when it would happen. One thing we can know for sure: After Jesus' resurrection and on His day of ascension, the apostles were convinced the kingdom would be restored to Israel. Jesus did not correct this understanding and appeared to reaffirm their expectation. This is evidence that the nation Israel still has a role to play in God's plans, and that the church does not supersede Israel.

Fourth, even after the church was well underway, the

apostle Paul indicated in Romans that the Old Testament promises and covenants still belonged to Israel:

> I could wish that I myself were accursed from Christ for my brethren, my countrymen according to the flesh, who are Israelites, to whom pertain the adoption, the glory, the covenants, the giving of the law, the service of God and the promises; of whom are the fathers, and from whom, according to the flesh, Christ came, who is over all, the eternally blessed God (9:3-5).

Even in a current state of unbelief, the nation Israel is still related to the "covenants," "service of God," and "promises." Notice that Paul used the present tense—"to whom pertain." Israel still belongs to these matters. This shows a continuing relevance of these things to the nation Israel. If the church had replaced Israel, Paul would not have made such a statement.

Notice that Israel's relationship to these matters is because of "the fathers." Paul links the perpetuity of Israel in the plan of God with the promises God made to Israel's patriarchs, a sure reference to Abraham, Isaac, and Jacob. Paul again made this point in Romans 11:28-29: "Concerning the gospel they [Israel] are enemies for your sake, but concerning the election they are beloved for the sake of the fathers. For the gifts and the calling of God are irrevocable." God cannot revoke His promises to Israel, for if He did so, He would be going back on His Word and the promises He made to Israel's fathers. Is there doubt as to why Paul could exclaim in Romans 11:1, "Has God cast away His people? Certainly not!"

Fifth, Paul, after a period he refers to as "the fullness of the Gentiles" (Romans 11:25), predicted the salvation of the nation Israel: "all Israel will be saved" (verse 26). This is an explicit prediction that Israel will experience salvation. Romans 11:27 ties Israel's salvation with the new covenant promises of the Old Testament that predicted Israel's restoration to her land—"This is My covenant with them, when I take away their sins." Walter Kaiser points out, "This [Romans 11:27] is nothing less than a reference to the New Covenant of

Jer. 31:31-34, which is itself an expansion of the very promises God had made with Abraham and David. Thus, we are back to the promise-doctrine again, which also includes the promise of the land."[4]

Sixth, John indicated that 144,000 Jews will be saved during the Tribulation (Revelation 7:4-8). This consists of 12,000 from each of the 12 tribes of Israel. These Jews are distinct from the "great multitude" from the nations (Revelation 7:4-9). There is no good reason for not interpreting this section as referring to the salvation of 144,000 Jews and is further evidence that God has future plans for Israel.

The points above highlight two important truths: (1) the nation Israel still has a future in God's plan; and (2) Israel and the church are distinct. The Bible does not promote any replacement theology in which the church replaces Israel. Instead, the Bible indicates that both the church and Israel have different roles in the purposes of God.

Understanding this distinction between Israel and the church is crucial for understanding the purpose of the rapture. As we will see, the rapture relates differently to the church and Israel. If one confuses Israel and the church by viewing the church as the new Israel, one will miss the significance of the rapture.

Israel's Relationship to the Rapture and Tribulation

During the tribulation, God will pour out His wrath on an unbelieving world. Isaiah 13:9 states, "Behold, the day of the LORD comes," and then God states, "I will punish the world for its evil and the wicked for their iniquity" (13:11). This judgment of an unbelieving world is the first purpose of the Tribulation. But second, the Tribulation is also related to Israel. The Bible indicates the Tribulation is a time for God to resume His plan for Israel, saving and restoring her through a time of intense turmoil and persecution. The 70-weeks prophecy in Daniel 9—which describes the Tribulation period—is for "your people," or Daniel's people, Israel. Jeremiah refers to this period as "the time of Jacob's distress" (30:7). Israel will have to go through this time of distress but Daniel also says that Israel "will be saved from it" (Jeremiah 30:7). Zechariah 12–14 indicates Jerusalem will come under siege from her enemies, but God will save and defend Israel. The 144,000 Jews preserved during the Tribulation gives further evidence of Israel's presence in the Tribulation.

Israel's relationship to the Tribulation is clearly seen in Jesus' Olivet Discourse in Matthew 24–25. Jesus spoke of the coming "abomination of desolation, spoken of by Daniel the prophet, standing in the holy place" (verse 15). Drawing upon the words of Daniel 9:24-27, Jesus referred to a coming abomination that would occur in the Jewish temple in Jerusalem. This horrible event will be a reason for "those who are in Judea" to "flee to the mountains" (Matthew 24:16). Thus, while the events described in the Olivet Discourse will have global consequences, this period is also closely related to Jerusalem and Israel. In 2 Thessalonians 2 Paul reminded his readers that in the coming Day of the Lord, a "man of lawlessness" will take "his seat in the temple of God, displaying himself as being God" (verses 3-4 NASB). Both Jesus and Paul affirmed Daniel's prophecy that Israel, Jerusalem, and the temple have future significance in God's plan. This shows that the Old Testament expectations have not been transcended or reinterpreted by the New Testament.

Israel's place in the coming Tribulation is based partly on the nation's refusal of her Messiah, Jesus Christ. Jesus indicated that Israel missed its "time of...visitation" (Luke 19:41-44). Peace could have come to Israel, but instead judgment would soon happen. Jesus stated that He wanted to gather Israel "as a hen gathers her chicks under her wings," but Israel was "not willing." This led Him to declare, "See! Your house is left to you desolate; for I say to you, you shall see Me no more till you say, 'Blessed He who comes in the name of the LORD!'" (verses 38-39). This indicates that a day is coming when Israel will be saved. Israel missed her Messiah and in doing so brought a temporary judgment on herself. But during the Tribulation, God will draw Israel to himself.

So what is Israel's relationship to the rapture? The answer is that the nation Israel is not related—at least not as a participant. The purpose of the rapture is to deliver the church from the Tribulation, and Israel is destined to go through this period. We can say that the remnant of Israel—the "Israel of God" (Galatians 6:16) who comprise the church with believing Gentiles—will participate in the rapture, but the nation Israel as a whole will not. Israel will face the turmoil of the Tribulation until she looks on the One whom she pierced and mourns for Him with tears of repentance (Zechariah 12:10).

The Church's Relationship to the Rapture and Tribulation

Unlike Israel, the church has a direct relationship to the rapture—it will participate in the event. The reason is because God promised the church it will not have to undergo this time of divine wrath. Three passages explicitly teach this truth:

> ...to wait for His Son from heaven, whom He raised from the dead, even Jesus who delivers us from the wrath to come (1 Thessalonians 1:10).

> God did not appoint us to wrath, but to obtain salvation through our Lord Jesus Christ (1 Thessalonians 5:9).

> Because you have kept My command to persevere, I also will keep you from the hour of trial which shall come upon the whole world, to test those who dwell on the earth (Revelation 3:10).

These passages teach a great truth: God has promised the church deliverance from the divine wrath of the Tribulation. Yes, Jesus indicated that in this present age His followers will experience tribulation (John 16:33), but part of the church's reward for faithfulness in this age is deliverance from the Day of the Lord.

The first two passages mentioned above (1 Thessalonians 1:10; 5:9) discuss rescue from wrath and not being destined for wrath. The "wrath" in this context is specifically Day of the Lord wrath. As 1 Thessalonians 5:2-3 states:

> You yourselves know perfectly that the day of the Lord so comes as a thief in the night. For when they say, "Peace and safety!" then sudden destruction comes upon them, as labor pains upon a pregnant woman. And they shall not escape.

When we look at this passage carefully we see Paul is not talking about God's general wrath upon unbelievers.[5] This is the wrath of the Day of the Lord, and it is this wrath from which the church will be rescued. The fact this is a "wrath to come" shows it is an eschatological wrath.

Revelation 3:10 refers to the coming tribulation as an "hour of trial" that "shall come upon the whole world." But Jesus promised, "I...will keep you from the hour of trial." There has been much debate over what "keep you from" (Greek, *tereo ek*) actually means. Is this a promise of removal from the earth so that the church is not around when this period breaks forth? Or, is it a promise that the church will remain on the earth but be protected from the events of the Tribulation? The former interpretation is preferred, and is bolstered by the fact that the church is never mentioned in Revelation 4–19, which gives explicit detail concerning the Tribulation. Israel is mentioned, as are unsaved Gentiles, but the church is not. It seems odd that if God intended for the church to endure the Tribulation, it was not mentioned in Revelation 4–19. As Richard Mayhue has stated: "It is remarkable and totally unexpected that John would shift from detailed instructions for the church to absolute silence about the church for the subsequent 15 chapters if, in fact, the church continued into the tribulation."[6]

The church simply does not seem to fit God's purposes for the Tribulation. If that purpose is to judge an unbelieving world and resume His plans for Israel, then where does the church fit? The answer is that it doesn't—at least not on the earth. The expectation of the church is the "blessed hope" which is the "glorious appearing of our great God and Savior Christ Jesus" (Titus 2:13). The New Testament does not indicate that the church should be preparing for the Tribulation. Instead, it is to look for the any-moment return of Jesus, which takes place with the rapture.

God's Two Different Purposes

To properly understand the rapture and the Tribulation, one must understand how Israel and the church relate to these events. Israel and the church are distinct entities. Israel will not take part in the rapture, but will undergo the Tribulation as part of the process by which God saves and restores her. The church, on the other hand, is not destined for the Tribulation and will be rescued from this "wrath to come" by Jesus Himself, who will rapture His church to heaven. In sum, Israel fits God's purposes for the Tribulation, and is not a participant in the rapture. The church fits God's purposes for the rapture, but not the Tribulation.

THE RAPTURE, CHURCH, AND ISRAEL IN END-TIMES PROPHECY

Paul Wilkinson

Israel is called *The Everlasting Nation*—a bold thing to say of any people. Throughout their long history they have been threatened many a time with extinction. They have been crushed and humbled, massacred by the million, banished from their home, scattered in all countries, yet have never lost their identity. They cannot be rooted out. Some of the most powerful nations have conquered and enslaved them: the conquerors have ceased to exist, the conquered live and thrive. Even now we watch them renewing their youth and seeking to regain their home-land which they had lost two thousand years ago—a nation whose very existence is a miracle.[1]

These stirring words were penned by the Reverend Samuel Schor in his book *The Everlasting Nation and their Coming King* (1933). Born in Jerusalem to Jewish believers in 1859, Schor was the first native of Palestine to be ordained in Saint Paul's Cathedral in London (1889). Interestingly, he was the only Jewish believer present at the first Zionist Congress held in Basel, Switzerland, in 1897. His book, which was reprinted in 1971, is inspirational in that it lays great emphasis on two of the fundamental doctrines of the faith that have been under considerable attack: belief in the continuing importance of Israel in God's prophetic purposes, and belief in the any-moment catching away of the church, when all true believers will, in the twinkling of an eye, find themselves "gazing in rapture upon the face of the Bridegroom."[2]

Samuel Schor died in 1933 and never witnessed the rebirth of the Jewish nation for which he had longed and prayed, but he was certain it would come to pass because he read the Scriptures in their plain, literal sense, and thus "saw" the promised restoration from afar.

God's Peculiar Affection for Israel

One of the earliest pioneers of belief in a restored Jewish State was Sir Henry Finch (c.1558–1625), who caused an enormous stir with his influential treatise *The World's Great Restauration, or the Calling of the Jewes, and with them of all the Nations and Kingdomes of the Earth, to the Faith of Christ* (1621), arguably the most important Puritan-era work on the restoration of the Jews.

Finch was legal officer to King James I and was made a knight in 1616. However, the publication of his book so incensed the king that Finch and his publisher, William Gouge, were arrested. Finch had argued from Scripture that all nations would one day be subservient to a restored Jewish kingdom. His book was one of a number of Puritan writings banned by the then-Archbishop of Canterbury, William Laud, who, in a sermon preached before James I in June 1621, con-demned belief in a restored Jewish homeland as "monstrous opinions." Laud labelled Finch as the man who could "out-dream the Jews."[3]

In *The World's Great Restauration*, Finch encouraged the Jews of the Diaspora (at a time when no Jew was permitted residence in Britain) to hold fast to the belief that "out of all the places of thy dispersion, East, West, North, and South, his

[God's] purpose is to bring thee home again, and to marry thee to himself by faith for evermore." A man of prayer, Sir Henry Finch assured the Jews that he would "never fail to pray" for their prosperity:

> Bowing my knees to the Father of our Lord Jesus Christ, the God of glory, that he would hasten that which he hath spoken concerning thee by the Prophets of old, and by the Apostles sent by his son. Whose counsels are without repentance, his love never changes.[4]

Two centuries later, following his mission of inquiry to Palestine in 1839, Church of Scotland minister Robert Murray M'Cheyne (1813–1843) preached a sermon in which he posed a question that is as relevant for today's Christian as it was for his own congregation:

> Now the simple question for each of you is, and for our beloved church, Should we not share with God in His peculiar affection for Israel? If we are filled with the Spirit of God, should we not love as He loves?[5]

Lewis Sperry Chafer (1871–1952), founder and first president of Dallas Theological Seminary, was as convinced as M'Cheyne that only one answer to that question was acceptable to God. In his book *He That Is Spiritual* (1918), he wrote:

> The love of God is toward Israel: "Yea, I have loved thee with an everlasting love" (Jeremiah 31:3). So the Spirit-filled believer will learn to rejoice in the great prophecies and purposes of God for that people with whom He is in everlasting covenants, and for whom He has an everlasting love.[6]

God's Everlasting Name

Samuel Schor, in his book on Bible prophecy, highlighted the remarkable fact that next to the name of God, Israel is mentioned more frequently than any other name in the Old Testament—over 200 times:

> This in itself is significant. The people of Israel are the everlasting nation with whom God made an "everlasting covenant" (1 Chron. xvi. 17) and though they—the people of Israel—"have broken the everlasting covenant" (Isa. xxiv. 5), yet— "Israel shall be saved with an everlasting salvation" (Isa. xlv. 17). How deliberately God's Word declares the continuity of the people of Israel.[7]

Scripture teaches that God set Israel apart that it might be "a special treasure above all the peoples on the face of the earth" (Deuteronomy 7:6; cf. Amos 3:2). He chose the Jews not because they were more numerous than the peoples of other nations, but because He loved them and remembered the oath He had sworn to their fathers Abraham, Isaac, and Jacob (Deuteronomy 7:7-8). King David, a man after God's own heart (1 Samuel 13:14), rejoiced in the special relationship Israel enjoyed with the Lord and declared,

> Who is like Your people, like Israel, the one nation on the earth whom God went to redeem for Himself as a people, to make for Himself a name…For You have made Your people Israel Your very own people forever; and You, LORD, have become their God…So let your name be magnified forever, saying, "The LORD of hosts is the God over Israel" (2 Samuel 7:23-24,26).

God reinforces His unique relationship with the Jewish nation by repeatedly joining their name to His, as the following examples illustrate. He is…

- the Stone of Israel (Genesis 49:24)
- the Shepherd of Israel (Psalm 80:1)
- the Lord God of Israel (Psalm 106:48)
- the Holy One of Israel (Isaiah 43:3)

- the Creator of Israel (Isaiah 43:15)
- the Hope of Israel (Jeremiah 14:8)
- a Father to Israel (Jeremiah 31:9)
- the King of Israel (Isaiah 44:6)

The title "King of Israel" was ascribed to Jesus by Nathanael in his first encounter with the Lord (John 1:49), and proclaimed by the Passover crowds who welcomed Jesus into Jerusalem (Luke 19:38-40). On the day of Jesus' death, a sign nailed above His head announced to the whole world that He was "Jesus of Nazareth, the King of the Jews" (John 19:19). This was no accident of history, nor the whim of a Roman procurator, but the express will of the Father.

An Everlasting Covenant

When God commanded Moses to deliver His people from Egypt, He revealed to him the name by which He was to be known: "You shall say to the children of Israel, 'I AM has sent me to you.'" But the Lord did not stop there:

> God said to Moses…"Thus you shall say to the children of Israel, 'The LORD God of your fathers, the God of Abraham, the God of Isaac, and the God of Jacob, has sent me to you. This is My name forever, and this is my memorial to all generations'" (Exodus 3:14-15).

When Jesus discussed the resurrection with the Sadducees, He said, "Have you not read what was spoken to you by God, saying, 'I am the God of Abraham, the God of Isaac, and the God of Jacob'? God is not the God of the dead, but of the living" (Matthew 22:31-32). In the course of affirming the reality and hope of the resurrection, Jesus underlined the everlasting relationship that exists between God and Israel, emphasizing the fact the Lord does not identify Himself with a people who have no future. In Exodus 3, the Hebrew word translated "forever" is *'ôlām*, which can mean "eternal," "ancient," "perpetual," "indefinite," "unlimited," "distant" or "remote," depending on the context. In the majority of cases, 'ôlām is used to depict an indefinite period of time that continues into the distant future, and it is frequently applied to God's covenant with Israel. For example, we read in Genesis that the Lord gave Abraham and his descendants the land of Canaan "forever" (13:15)—it was to be theirs as an "everlasting possession" by virtue of an "everlasting covenant" (17:7-8). As the psalmist said:

> He remembers His covenant forever ['ôlām], the word which He commanded, for a thousand generations, the covenant which He made with Abraham, and His oath to Isaac, and confirmed it to Jacob for a statute, to Israel as an everlasting ['ôlām] covenant, saying, "To you I will give the land of Canaan as the allotment of your inheritance" (105:8-11).

Commenting on this psalm, David Baron (1857–1926), cofounder of the London-based Hebrew Christian Testimony to Israel, laid particular emphasis on the fact God declared the Abrahamic covenant to be *His* covenant that *He* will remember forever. This was the ground upon which He would still act "in grace and blessing at every juncture of failure and faithlessness on the part of His people."[8] In a similar vein Paul rhetorically asked if God had "cast away His people," responding to his own question with an emphatic: "Certainly not!" (Romans 11:1). Such an idea was "a monstrous thought to the apostle,"[9] according to Methodist preacher, author, and student of biblical prophecy Arthur Skevington Wood (1917–1993). John Nelson Darby (1800–1882), the principal founder of Plymouth Brethrenism, was equally convinced that

> Israel is always the people of God...Israel cannot cease to be the people of God. "The gifts and calling of God are without repentance," and it is of Israel that this is said. God never ceases to consider Israel as His people...In all times, Israel is His people, according to His counsels, and the thoughts of His love.[10]

Blessings and Curses

In the blessings and curses chapters of Leviticus 26 and Deuteronomy 28–30, God set before the people of Israel "life and good, death and evil" (Deuteronomy 30:15). In these chapters the entire history of the Jewish nation is prophetically laid out in stark and unambiguous detail: promised blessings for obedience, incremental judgments for disobedience. These chapters are foundational to our understanding of God's dealings with Israel—past, present, *and* future. Those who are shackled to a system of teaching that rejects, replaces, reinterprets, or redefines Israel in favor of the church need to understand God's heart for His people, even in judgment:

> Yet for all that, when they are in the land of their enemies, I will not cast them away, nor shall I abhor them, to utterly destroy them and break My covenant with them; for I am the LORD their God" (Leviticus 26:44; cf. Jeremiah 31:37; 33:19-26).

This point is reinforced by Skevington Wood, who, in his comments on the vision of the valley of dry bones, highlights "the repeated address of the Almighty to Israel: 'Oh my people,'" in response to their despairing cry, "Our bones are dry, our hope is lost, and we ourselves are cut off!" (Ezekiel 37:11). He points out,

> The reiteration is deliberately forceful. It underlines the fact…that God has not cast off His chosen people, the Jews. They will always be His people. His eternal covenant He will never break. They may have broken it, but He abideth faithful. Even when they lie in humiliation as dry bones scattered among the nations, the Lord tenderly calls them His people and graciously claims them as such.[11]

The righteous and equitable Judge of the whole earth has established an irrevocable covenant with Israel that will stand firm as long as night and day endure. Calling on the sun, moon, and stars as witnesses, He solemnly declared:

"If those ordinances depart from before Me, says the
LORD, then the seed of Israel shall also cease from
being a nation before Me forever." Thus says the
LORD: "If heaven above can be measured, and the
foundations of the earth searched out beneath, I
will also cast off all the seed of Israel for all that they
have done, says the LORD" (Jeremiah 31:36-37).

God's Indignation

One of the most important themes the Old Testament
prophets addressed was the way Israel's neighbors responded
to her plight when she fell into the hands of her enemies. God
burned with righteous indignation when He saw how the
nations acted, and passed judgment on them accordingly:

Because you [Ammon] clapped your hands, stamped
your feet, and rejoiced in heart with all your dis-
dain for the land of Israel, indeed, therefore, I will
stretch out my hand against you (Ezekiel 25:6-7).

Because Moab and Seir say, "Look! The house of
Judah is like all the nations," therefore, behold, I
will clear the territory of Moab of cities (verses 8-9).

Because of what Edom did against the house
of Judah by taking vengeance, and has greatly
offended by avenging itself on them, therefore thus
says the Lord GOD: "I will also stretch out My hand
against Edom" (verses 12-13);

Because the Philistines dealt vengefully and took
vengeance with a spiteful heart, to destroy because
of the old hatred, therefore thus says the Lord GOD:
"I will stretch out my hand against the Philistines"
(verses 15-16);

Son of man, because Tyre has said against Jerusalem,
"Aha! She is broken who was the gateway of the peoples; now she is turned over to me; I shall be filled;
she is laid waste." Therefore thus says the Lord GOD:
"Behold, I am against you, O Tyre" (26:2-3).

As John Nelson Darby put it, "When God chastises His people, the world thinks to possess everything; whereas chastisement is but the precursor of the world's judgment."[12]

The day will dawn when Israel will no longer "hear the taunts of the nations anymore, nor bear the reproach of the peoples anymore" (Ezekiel 36:15), but until then we can expect God to continue to raise up nations against His beloved people. According to the Mosaic law, this is one of the disciplinary measures which God has used, and will again use, to cause His people to return to Him (Deuteronomy 30:1-3). But those nations that go further than God intends must face the consequences of their sin. As the Lord declared through the prophet Zechariah, "I am exceedingly angry with the nations at ease; for I was a little angry [with Israel], and they helped—but with evil intent" (1:14-15).

Contemporary English minister James Ayre expresses God's heart in this way:

> He is greatly displeased with those who have the nerve to sit back and enjoy themselves, and have peace and comfort and fulness; those that are at rest and are quiet while Israel is tormented...And is it not true that the nations have continued to exploit God's anger against the Jew, going far beyond the limits of God's wrath? The record is appalling.[13]

The record is indeed appalling. Massacred by the Romans under Titus; whole communities destroyed by Crusaders acting under papal authority; expelled from England in 1290 by royal edict; exiled, killed, and forced to "convert" during the Spanish Inquisition; butchered in the Russian pogroms of the late nineteenth and early twentieth centuries; two-thirds of European Jewry exterminated during the Nazi era...and yet against all odds, the Jewish people have survived. As Anglican Bishop Thomas Newton (1704–1782) wrote in the eighteenth century, "The Jewish nation, like the bush of Moses, hath been always burning, but is never consumed."[14] The first Anglican Bishop of Liverpool, J.C. Ryle (1816–1900), expressed similar sentiments when he said,

Why is it that...this singular race still floats alone, though broken to pieces like a wreck, on the waters of the globe...and after the lapse of 1800 years is neither destroyed, nor crushed, nor evaporated, nor amalgamated, nor lost sight of; but lives to this day as separate and distinct as it was when the arch of Titus was built at Rome? I have not the least idea how questions like these are answered by those who profess to deny the divine authority of Scripture...God has many witnesses to the truth of the Bible, if men would only examine them and listen to their evidence. But you may depend on it there is no witness so unanswerable as one who always keeps standing up, and living, and moving before the eyes of mankind. That witness is the Jew.[15]

The Inspired Volume

For those who continue to stumble over the nation of Israel by subscribing to Replacement or Fulfillment Theology, Bishop Ryle has left a simple but effective remedy: Allow the Bible, written by the Holy Spirit with a pen that was "held by Jewish fingers,"[16] to speak to your heart:

The inspired volume which you have in your hands supplies a full and complete explanation. Search it with an honest determination to put a literal meaning on its prophetical portions, and to reject traditional interpretation, and the difficulty will vanish away...Cultivate the habit of reading prophecy with a single eye to the literal meaning of its proper names. Cast aside the traditional idea that Jacob, and Israel, and Judah, and Jerusalem, and Zion must always mean the Gentile church, and that predictions about the second Advent are to be taken spiritually, and first Advent predictions literally. Be just, and honest, and fair...The Protestant Reformers were not perfect. On no point, I venture to say, were they so much in the wrong as in the interpretation of Old Testament prophecy. Even our venerable Authorized Version of the Bible has many "tables of contents" which are sadly calculated to mislead, in the prophetical books.[17]

The Chicago businessman turned Methodist minister William Eugene Blackstone (1841–1935) advocated the same remedy in his best-selling book *Jesus Is Coming* (1878):

Divest yourself of prejudice and preconceived notions, and let the Holy Spirit show you, from His word, the glorious future of God's chosen people, "who are beloved" (Rom. 11:28), and dear unto Him as "the apple of His eye" Zech. 2:8.[18]

One lady who did divest herself of such prejudice was the former English suffragette leader and "Queen of the Mob," Christabel Pankhurst (1880–1958). Convicted of sin through reading a book on Bible prophecy at the end of World War I, she went on to write several books on the signs of the times, and in 1924 made the following declaration: "The Jew in Palestine! It is the most joyful thing that has happened since the resurrection and ascension of the Lord, because it is the decisive sign of His return."[19]

A Perpetual Memorial

The story of Israel is, first and foremost, the story of a merciful and faithful God whose love endures forever, even in judgment. To ignore Israel is to ignore God; to reject Israel is to reject God; and to condemn Israel is to condemn God. Cyrus Scofield (1843–1921) once confessed "with shame" that there had been a time in his life *as a believer* when he considered prophecy irrelevant and cared little for the Jewish people. Everything changed once he realized that by doing so he was "refusing the most intimate fellowship with the Lord."[20] From that point onward he began to see the Jew as "the miracle of history," who can "no more be understood apart from God than the universe can."[21]

In 1840, a century before the rebirth of Israel, Mrs. J.B. Webb wrote the best-selling novel *Naomi: or The Last Days of*

Jerusalem, which she set in the days of the destruction of the Second Temple. It was written to attract "the attention of the young and thoughtless to the wonderful fulfilment of the prophetic word of God." Like many of her contemporaries, Webb understood God's heart for Israel and expressed complete confidence in His covenant-binding Word:

> The threatened judgments have been awfully and literally accomplished, and shall not the promises of God be found to be equally sure?...The children of Israel are now a despised and humble race, but they are a perpetual memorial to the whole world of God's unsparing justice, and a standing miraculous proof of the truth of His word. Soon may we look for their restoration, and then they will be a splendid monument of His mercy and His faithfulness to Abraham and to his seed forever. Let us then be zealous in our humble efforts to awaken this interesting people, and call on them unceasingly to "arise from the dead, that Christ may give them light."[22]

The witnesses I have called upon in this chapter are drawn from a variety of church traditions, some of which are at odds with premillennial and pretribulational truth. However, they all shared an unshakeable belief that the Jews matter to God, and should therefore matter to the church. Another such witness was Francis Atterbury (1663–1732), the Anglican Bishop of Rochester and Dean of Westminster, who, in 1722, was held in the Tower of London on a charge of conspiracy to set the "Jacobite Pretender" James Stuart (son of James II) on the English throne. In a sermon preached on Good Friday, 1715, in St. James' Chapel, Atterbury described the history of the Jewish nation as "the History of Divine Providence."[23] He went on to proclaim how God

> has kept them [the Jewish people] in a Separate State, not suffering them to incorporate with any other Nation, in order by this means to render the

Triumphs of his Justice more conspicuous, and in order also to preserve them ready for that gracious Call, which, we piously believe, shall one Day summon them from all Parts of the Earth, *and gather together the Outcasts of Israel*—that so *We* and *They* may become one Fold, under One Shepherd, Christ the Righteous![24]

The God Who Cares

Scripture teaches that God is deeply concerned for His people Israel. After pronouncing judgment upon the southern kingdom of Judah, God promised He would one day heal His people and restore them, in part because of the attitude of those who cared little about their plight: "I will restore health to you and heal you of your wounds, says the LORD, because they called you an outcast saying: 'This is Zion; no one seeks her'" (Jeremiah 30:17).

The Hebrew word for "seeks" in this verse is *dârash*, which also occurs in Psalm 142:4, where David exclaimed, "Look on my right hand and see, for there is no one who acknowledges me; refuge has failed me; no one cares [*dârash*] for my soul." The nations, or "lovers" (Jeremiah 30:14) Israel had turned to for help, were nowhere to be seen when the Babylonian armies invaded Jerusalem, but God still cared for them. The Lord declared that despite His judgment, the day would dawn when Zion would be known by the special Hebrew word *dârash*: "They shall call them The Holy People, The Redeemed of the LORD; and you shall be called Sought Out [*dârash*], A City Not Forsaken" (Isaiah 62:12).

One man whose heart was deeply moved by God's everlasting love for Israel—and who sought out the Jewish people—was the Reverend William Henry Hechler (1845–1931). In 1881, Hechler published a broadsheet entitled *The Restoration of the Jews to Palestine*, in which he outlined his belief that the return of the Jewish people to their promised land was inextricably linked to the second coming of Jesus. Although we may disagree with certain aspects of his eschatology, Hechler rightly insisted that it was the duty of every Christian "to *pray earnestly* and to long for the restoration of *God's chosen race*, and to *love the Jews*." He issued the following warning to those who did not: "Blessed shall that nation be, which *loves the Jews*... And let us not forget the *terrible punishments* which await those who *'hate'* and *'persecute'* the Jews."[25]

In March 1914, Hechler visited the renowned Jewish philosopher Martin Buber in Berlin to deliver a solemn warning: "Dr. Buber, your fatherland will soon be given back to you. For a severe crisis will break out, the deep meaning of which is the liberation of your messianic Jerusalem from the yoke of the pagan nations."[26] Sadly, in the years prior to his death, Hechler grew increasingly despondent as his repeated warnings of impending calamity went unheeded. He died in 1931, and his contribution to the cause of the Jewish people has only recently been recognized. At a ceremony held on January 31, 2011 in New Southgate Cemetery, London, Hechler was honored by representatives of both the Jewish and Christian communities. I was privileged to attend the service, and witnessed the raising of a memorial stone at his unmarked grave on which the words "Has God Rejected His People?" are boldly inscribed. Like all true friends of Israel, Hechler longed for the day when Abraham's descendants would finally look upon the One they have pierced and mourn for Him, as for an only son (Zechariah 12:10).

~

Is Ephraim my dear son? Is he a pleasant child? For though I spoke against him, I earnestly remember him still; therefore My heart yearns for him; I will surely have mercy on him, says the LORD...How can I give you up, Ephraim? How can I hand you over, Israel?...My heart churns within Me; My sympathy is stirred...I will not again destroy Ephraim. For I am God and not man, the Holy One in your midst" (Jeremiah 31:20; Hosea 11:8-9).

19

THE BASIS OF THE SECOND COMING OF THE MESSIAH

Arnold G. Fruchtenbaum

I n this volume, some contributors have presented the many distinctives that make it evident the rapture and the second coming are two phases of Christ's return. For example, one distinctive is that we can never predict the date of the rapture, although some have tried to do so. The rapture can come anytime between now and the signing of the seven-year covenant that will trigger the Tribulation. On the other hand, once that covenant is signed and the Tribulation starts, we know when the second coming will occur—exactly seven years later. It will come exactly 1260 days after the abomination of desolation.

The distinctive this chapter will focus on is the precondition of the second coming as it relates to Israel. And because there are no preconditions attached to it, the rapture can come at any time. The second coming of the Messiah, however, does have a major precondition attached to it. A certain condition must be met before the Messiah will return to establish the kingdom.

The purpose of this study is to determine the basis for the second coming of the Messiah. This will be discussed in two main divisions: the rejection of His messiahship, and the prerequisite to the second coming.

Closely connected with God's kingdom program is the first coming of the Messiah. Both John the Baptist (Matthew 3:1-2) and Jesus (Matthew 4:17) came proclaiming that the kingdom of heaven was at hand. Neither John nor Jesus, nor the Gospel writers who recorded these statements, tried to define the nature of this kingdom. Obviously they expected the audience to understand what was meant by that term; and well they might because Jewish audiences had common knowledge of the Old Testament and understood the nature of the messianic kingdom. Even Covenant Theologians of all stripes admit that the common Jewish understanding of the kingdom in first-century Israel was that of a literal, earthly kingdom centered in Jerusalem and ruled by the Messiah. The obvious origin of such a view was the literal understanding of the Old Testament prophets. If either John or Jesus meant something totally different, which all Covenant Theologians insist on, including Covenant Premillennialists, then why did neither one explain such a distinction from the beginning? The very fact they did not shows that the common Jewish understanding of the coming kingdom was a correct one.

> Suddenly in Matthew 3 John the baptizer, the Lord's forerunner, appears on the scene. His message was, "Repent, for the kingdom of heaven is at hand." What does the word *kingdom* mean here? It certainly cannot be some *spiritual* kingdom in the hearts of people. That kingdom was always present (cf. Psalm 37:31). Furthermore, the fact that John never explained what the term meant when the Jews clearly expected an earthly kingdom would imply that he was expecting the same type of kingdom.[1]

However, the common Jewish understanding that all Israel has a share in the age to come was an incorrect one and so both John and Jesus proclaimed that the need to repent for righteousness was the means of entering the kingdom. Furthermore, to see the messianic kingdom established in their day required Israel's acceptance of Jesus as the messianic King.

"The gospel of the kingdom" proclaimed by Christ in Matthew 9:35 must be the same as that preached by Him in 4:23. It was the good news of the nearness of the kingdom and freedom of access by repentance. The kingdom was proximate in two senses. First, the Messiah was here on earth, and second the kingdom's coming was contingent on Israel's response to her Messiah.[2]

When Jesus was rejected, a key change took place in the kingdom program. Toussaint has stated the dispensational viewpoint quite well:

Very often the dispensationalist school of interpretation will refer to "the offer of the kingdom" to Israel. By this is meant the contingency of the coming of the kingdom to Israel in the first century based on Israel's acceptance of Jesus as its Messiah. This concept is clearly found in the New Testament. For instance, Peter openly states the coming of the Messiah rests on Israel's repentance (Acts 3:19-21). The Lord Himself said that John the Baptist could have been the fulfillment of the Elijah prophecy of Malachi 4:5-6 if Israel had repented (Matthew 11:14)...

However, dispensationalists may want to clarify their terminology. The New Testament does teach the contingency of the coming of the kingdom premised on the response to the Jews. But every Israelite wanted the kingdom to come. To say Christ offered the kingdom to Israel is true, but it leaves the impression the Jews did not want the kingdom to come. It would be far better to say Jesus offered Himself as Israel's Messiah and the coming of the kingdom was contingent on their acceptance or rejection of Him.[3]

The King was rejected and, along with Him, the messianic kingdom. This point, so important to Israelology, needs to be expanded.

The Rejection of His Messiahship

To fully understand the basis of Christ's coming, one must first understand what occurred when the messiahship of *Yeshua* (Jesus) was rejected.[4] In Matthew, He began His ministry in chapter 4. From chapters 4 through 12, He was seen going around Israel proclaiming the kingdom and preaching the gospel of the kingdom and performing many miracles. The purpose of His miracles was to authenticate His Person and His message. They were signs intended to force the nation of Israel to come to a decision about two things: first, His Person, that He is the Messiah; and second, His message, the gospel of the kingdom. He was offering to Israel the kingdom that the Jewish prophets had prophesied about. Then in Matthew 12, the purpose of His miracles and ministry underwent a radical change. The rejection of His messiahship occurred in Matthew 12:22-37.

Among the many miracles Jesus performed was the casting out of demons. According to verse 27, Judaism also had exorcists. In Jewish exorcism, one first had to establish communication with the demon in order to find out his name. Then using that demon's name, the exorcist could cast him out. On other occasions Jesus used the Jewish method, as in Luke 8:30. When demons speak, they use the vocal cords of the person under their control. However, in the case of the dumb demon, Jewish exorcism was to no avail, for communication with that kind of demon was impossible. The Jewish observation that dumb demons were different was validated by the Messiah in Mark 9.

The Messiah was able to exorcise that kind of demon: "Then one was brought to him who was demon-possessed, blind, and mute; and He healed him, so that the blind and mute man both spoke and saw" (Matthew 9:22). Jesus performed a miracle that had never been done before.

"All the multitudes were amazed and said, Could this be the Son of David?" (verse 23). That is, they asked, "Can Jesus really be the Messiah?" This was one of the key purposes of this miracle—to get them to see that He was indeed "the Son of David." The people, however, were not willing to judge His Person by themselves. They were looking to their religious leaders, the Pharisees, to come up with some kind of judgment concerning Him. They were waiting for the Pharisees to conclude either that He was the Messiah or that He was not. If He was not, then the Pharisees must offer some kind of alternative explanation as to how He was able to perform these miracles.

Verse 24 tells us, "When the Pharisees heard it, they said, 'This fellow does not cast out demons except by Beelzebub, the ruler of the demons.'" They refused to accept Jesus as the Messiah because He did not fit the pharisaic mold or idea of what the Messiah was supposed to say and do. Their alternative explanation for His miracles was that He was possessed by Beelzebub. This, then, became the official basis of the rejection of Jesus' messiahship. This is "the leaven of the Pharisees" (Luke 12:1), the false teaching about which the Messiah would warn His disciples.

The Messiah's response is recorded in verses 25-29:

> Jesus knew their thoughts, and said to them, "Every kingdom divided against itself is brought to desolation; and every city or house divided against itself will not stand. If Satan casts out Satan, he is divided against himself. How then will his kingdom stand? And if I cast out demons by Beelzebub, by whom do your sons cast them out? therefore they will be your judges. But if I cast out demons by the Spirit of God, surely the kingdom of God has come upon you. Or how can one enter a strong man's house and plunder his goods, unless he first binds the strong man? And then he will plunder his house.

The Messiah responded to the Pharisees' accusation by telling them it couldn't be true because it would mean that Satan's kingdom was divided against itself.

Judgment was then pronounced on the generation of that day in verses 30-37:

> He that is not with me is against me, and he that gathers not with me scatters...Every sin and blasphemy will be forgiven men, but the blasphemy

254 ~ THE POPULAR HANDBOOK ON THE RAPTURE

against the Spirit will not be forgiven men. Anyone who speaks a word against the Son of Man, it
will be forgiven him; but whosoever speaks against
the Holy Spirit, it will not be forgiven him, either
in this age, or in the age to come...Brood of vipers!
How can you, being evil, speak good things? For out
of the abundance of the heart the mouth speaks.
A good man out of the good treasure of his heart
brings forth good things, and an evil man out of
the evil treasure brings forth evil things. But I say
to you that every idle word that men may speak,
they will give account of it in the day of judgment.
For by your words you will be justified, and by your
words you will be condemned.

In verse 31, Jesus said the unpardonable sin was blasphemy
of the Holy Spirit. It should be clearly understood exactly what
the blasphemy of the Holy Spirit is given this sole context in
which it is found, and it must be interpreted accordingly. The
unpardonable sin is not an individual sin, but a national sin. It
was committed by that generation of Israel in Jesus' day and
cannot be applied to subsequent Jewish generations. The content of the unpardonable sin was the national rejection of the
messiahship of Jesus while He was present on earth, and this
rejection was on the grounds that He was demon possessed.
This sin was unpardonable, and judgment was set. The judgment came 40 years later in AD 70 with the destruction of
Jerusalem and the worldwide dispersion of the Jewish people.
This does not mean that individual members of that generation could not be saved, for many were. It did mean, however,
that nothing they could do would avert the coming destruction of Jerusalem.

There were four ramifications of the unpardonable sin. First,
this was a national sin and not an individual one. Even for
individual members of that generation it was possible to escape
the judgment for the unpardonable sin by repenting (chang-
ing their mind about Jesus). No individual could commit this
sin today for two reasons: First, it was not an individual sin to

begin with; and second, all sins are forgivable to those who come to God through Jesus the Messiah. But for the nation as a nation, this sin was unpardonable.

The second ramification was that the sin was limited to "this generation," the Jewish generation of Jesus' day. The third ramification was that no nation can commit this sin today because the Messiah is not physically present with any nation, offering Himself as that nation's Messiah. This was unique to His relationship to Israel and to no other. The fourth ramification was twofold: The commitment of the unpardonable sin by that generation meant, first, the offer of the kingdom was rescinded and it would be reoffered to a later Jewish generation that will accept it (the Jewish generation of the Great Tribulation detailed in Matthew 24–25). And second, it meant that specific generation was under a special divine judgment, the physical judgment of the destruction of Jerusalem, fulfilled in AD 70.

The Sign of the Resurrection: Matthew 12:38-40

> Some of the scribes and Pharisees answered, saying, "Teacher, we want to see a sign from You." But He answered and said to them, "An evil and adulterous generation seeks after a sign, and no sign will be given to it except the sign of the prophet Jonah. For as Jonah was three days and three nights in the belly of the great fish, so shall the Son of Man be three days and three nights in the heart of the earth."

The Pharisees were stunned by Jesus' pronouncement of judgment. They tried to retake the offensive by demanding a sign, as though the Messiah had done nothing so far to substantiate His messiahship! But Jesus said there would be no more signs for the nation, except one. While the Messiah would continue to perform miracles, the purpose for them had changed. No longer were they for authenticating His Person and His message in order to get the nation to come to a decision. That decision had already been made. Rather, His miracles would be for the purpose of training the 12 disciples for the new kind of ministry they would need to conduct as a result of the Jewish leaders' rejection. It is the ministry the disciples performed in the book of Acts.

For that generation, there would be no sign but one: the sign of Jonah, the sign of resurrection. This sign would come for Israel on three occasions: at the resurrection of Lazarus (John 11:1-46); at Jesus' resurrection (Matthew 16:1-4); and at the resurrection of the two witnesses (Revelation 11:3-13). The first two signs were rejected. The third will be accepted, for the resurrection of the two witnesses will lead to the salvation of the Jews of Jerusalem.

Swept, Garnished, and Empty: Matthew 12:41-45

> The men of Nineveh will rise up in the judgment with this generation and condemn it, because they repented at the preaching of Jonah; and indeed a greater than Jonah is here. The queen of the south will rise up in the judgment with this generation and condemn it, for she came from the ends of the earth to hear the wisdom of Solomon; and indeed a greater than Solomon is here. When an unclean spirit goes out of a man, he goes through dry places, seeking rest, and finds none. Then he says, "I will return to my house from which I came. And when he is come, he finds it empty, swept, and put in order. Then he goes and takes with him seven other spirits more wicked than himself, and they enter and dwell there; and the last state of that man is worse than the first. So shall it also be with this evil generation."

This passage concludes with more words of judgment for that generation. In verse 41 Jesus compared this generation with Nineveh and showed why Nineveh will stand in judgment of it. The same is true in verse 42 with the Queen of Sheba. The people in both these cases were Gentiles. With much less revelation to go on, they responded even without miracles. But the generation Jesus spoke to did not.

Then in verses 43-45 the words of judgment conclude with Jesus' account of a demon who, of his own volition, left a man that he had possessed. But when he was unable to find a new body to indwell and control, he returned to his original abode. Although he found it "swept," he also found it still "empty." The individual never took the opportunity to fill his life with the Holy Spirit. Nor had another demon entered him. So the demon re-entered the man and invited seven other demons to join him. So the last state of the man was worse than the first. He was originally possessed by only one demon. Because he failed to fill his life with the Spirit of God, he was possessed by eight demons.

The point of this story is often missed. Jesus was saying that whatever was true of the man was also true of that particular evil generation. When that generation began, it did so with the preaching of John the Baptist. John's ministry was to prepare the people for the reception of the Messiah. But the Messiah came, and they rejected Him. The nation that was swept and put in good order remained empty on account of its rejection of Jesus the Messiah. And because it remained empty, the last state of that generation was worse than the first.

When that generation began, it was under Roman domination. Nevertheless, it had a national entity. It had a semiautonomous form of government in the Jewish Sanhedrin. Jerusalem stood in all its Herodian glory, and the religious worship system in the temple remained intact. But later, as a result of the rejection and judgment in AD 70, the national entity of Israel ceased to exist. In the place of bondage, the people were dispersed by the Roman armies. The temple, the center of Judaism, was completely destroyed so that not one stone stood upon another. Eventually, the Jews were dispersed all over the world. So, indeed, the last state of that generation became worse than the first. They went from bondage to worldwide dispersion.

After the rejection in Matthew 12, because of the nature of the unpardonable sin, the ministry of Jesus changed radically in four areas. The first change was the purpose of His miracles. They were no longer to serve as signs of His messiahship. Rather, they were to train the disciples for their ministry described in the book of Acts (Matthew 16:1-4).

The second change concerned the people for whom Jesus performed these miracles. Until Matthew 12, He performed miracles for the benefit of the masses without requiring them to have faith first. After Matthew 12, He performed miracles only in response to needs of individuals and began requiring them to have faith. Furthermore, before Matthew 12, those He healed were free to proclaim what had been done for them. But after Matthew 12, Jesus forbade those He healed to tell anyone about it (Mark 7:36; Luke 8:56, et al.)

The third change concerned the message that Jesus and the disciples would now proclaim. Until Matthew 12, both He and they went throughout the land of Israel proclaiming Jesus to be the Messiah. In Matthew 10 the disciples were sent out two by two to do just that. After Matthew 12, they were forbidden to tell anyone that Jesus was the Messiah. In Matthew 16, after Peter made his famous confession, "You are the Christ [Messiah], the Son of the living God," Jesus ordered Peter to tell that to no one (verse 20). The disciples were to stay silent (Matthew 17:9) until this was rescinded with the Great Commission (Matthew 28:18-20).

The fourth change concerned Jesus' teaching method. Until Matthew 12, whenever He taught the masses, He did so in terms they could understand. One example is the Sermon on the Mount in Matthew 5-7. Not only did the people understand what Jesus was saying, they also knew how He differed from the scribes and the Pharisees. But in Matthew 13, Jesus began teaching in parables to hide the truth from the masses. This very act of teaching in parables was a sign of judgment against them.

The first series of parables Jesus taught was on the mystery kingdom, the facet of God's kingdom program that was inaugurated as a result of the people's rejection and the rescinded offer of the messianic kingdom. To clearly comprehend what is happening in Matthew 13, one must understand the relationship between Matthew 12 and 13. Matthew 12 records the national rejection of Jesus, in which the people were guilty of the unpardonable sin. From that point on they were under the judgment of AD 70, the year in which Jerusalem was destroyed. In Matthew 13, Jesus taught a series of parables. These parables were spoken on the very same day Jesus was rejected (Matthew 13:1-3).

Matthew 13:10-18 states the purpose of these parables. Verse 10 begins, "The disciples came, and said to Him, 'Why do you speak unto them in parables?'" That the disciples asked this indicates this was the beginning of Jesus' teaching in parables. This, of course, surprised the disciples because up until that point, Jesus had taught them clearly. So why had He begun speaking to them in parables? Jesus gave the answer in verses 11-14:

> He answered and said to them, "Because it has been given to you to know the mysteries of the kingdom of heaven, but to them it has not been given. For whoever has, to him more will be given, and he will have abundance; but whoever does not have, even what he has will be taken away from him. Therefore speak I to them in parables; because seeing they do not see, and hearing they do not hear, nor do they understand. And in them the prophecy of Isaiah is filled."

There were three main reasons Jesus began to teach in parables. First, for His disciples, the parabolic method of teaching would illustrate the truth. Second, however, the parables would hide the truth from the masses. Since the nation had rejected the light they had, no more light would be given. Instead of teaching the people clearly in terms they could understand, He would now teach in parables so they could not and would not understand. Third, this change would fulfill prophecy. Jesus quoted Isaiah 6:9-10, which prophesied that the Messiah would speak in such a way that the Jewish people would not understand Him.

Later, Matthew 13:34-35 states:

> All these things Jesus spoke to the multitudes in parables; and without a parable He did not speak

> to them, that it might be fulfilled which was spo-
> ken by the prophet, saying, "I will open my mouth
> in parables; I will utter things kept secret from the
> foundation of the world."

These verses re-emphasize that Jesus spoke to the multitudes only in parables. This was not true *before* the rejection of
Matthew 12, but it is very true *after* the rejection. This affirms
the second purpose for His parabolic method of teaching—to
hide the truth from the masses. In verse 35 Jesus pointed out
this change was a fulfillment of prophecy, and this time He
quoted Psalm 78:2. This affirmed the third purpose of teaching
in parables, which was to fulfill Old Testament prophecy that
declared His messiahship would be rejected.

In the parallel account found in Mark 4:33-34, the same
point is made:

> With many such parables He spoke the word to
> them as they were able to hear it. But without a
> parable He did not speak to them. And when they
> were alone, He explained all things to His disciples.

Mark 4:34 affirms the first purpose of the parables—that
they would illustrate the truth for the disciples. From Matthew
13 onward, this was how Jesus taught. And when He spoke parables to the masses, it hid the truth from them.

The Sign of Jonah: John 11:1-57

Even after the events in Matthew 12, the Pharisees
approached the Messiah and demanded a sign to authenticate
His Person and His message (Matthew 16:1-4). He refused to
give them any more signs but promised them only "the sign of
the prophet Jonah" (verse 4), which is the sign of resurrection.

The resurrection of Lazarus, recorded in John 11:1-44, is
the presentation of the first sign of Jonah. The Messiah had
raised others from the dead, yet all the other resurrections are
described in just a few verses. But the apostle John used 44
verses to give great detail about the resurrection of Lazarus.
Why? This was the sign of Jonah that Jesus had promised.

In verse 42 Jesus, while speaking to the Father, made it very clear for whom Lazarus was raised—namely, the Jewish multitudes: "I know that you always hear Me, but because of the people who are standing by I said this, that they may believe that You sent Me."

And how did the people respond? "Many of the Jews who had come to Mary, and had seen the things Jesus did, believed in him. But some of them went away to the Pharisees, and told them the things Jesus did" (verses 45-46). Some Jews responded correctly to this first sign of Jonah and believed that Jesus was who He claimed to be. But others still wanted some kind of word or judgment from their leaders, and so they reported to the Pharisees what Jesus had done. Because this was the sign the Messiah had promised them, they had to respond in some way or another.

The Sanhedrin's Verdict: John 11:47-50,53

> The chief priests and the Pharisees gathered a council and said, "What shall we do? For this man works many signs. If we let Him alone like this, everyone will believe in Him, and the Romans will come and take away both our place and nation." And one of them, Caiaphas, being high priest that year, said to them, "You know nothing at all, nor do you consider that it is expedient for us that one man should die for the people, and not that the whole nation perish"…Then from that day on, they plotted to put Him to death.

The Pharisees responded in keeping with their original verdict of Matthew 12. The Sanhedrin gathered together to decide to respond to the sign of Jonah given in the resurrection of Lazarus. They issued a decree of rejection and sought an opportunity to put Jesus to death. Their rejection of His messiahship was now complete—they now condemned Him to death.

Verses 54-57 give the results of the Sanhedrin's verdict. First, the Messiah went into hiding for a short time, because the hour of His death had not yet come. Second, the people still raised questions concerning His Person, a logical thing for them to do in light of the resurrection of Lazarus. And third, the Sanhedrin's verdict filtered down to the masses: "Now both the chief priests and the Pharisees had given a command, that if anyone knew where He was, he should report it, that they might seize Him" (verse 57).

The Triumphal Entry: Luke 19:41-44

> As He drew near, He saw the city and wept over it, saying, "If you had known, even you, especially in this your day, the things that make for your peace! But now they are hidden from your eyes. For the days will come upon you when your enemies will build an embankment around you, surround you and close you in on every side, and level you, and your children within you, to the ground; and they will not leave in you one stone upon another, because you did not know the time of your visitation."

Further light is shed here on the nature of the unpardonable sin in the rejection of Jesus' messiahship. This passage is in the context of the triumphal entry of Jesus into Jerusalem. As Jesus arrived, thousands of Jews cried out, "Blessed is the King who comes in the name of the LORD!" (verse 38). Given the Jewish frame of reference, this is an official messianic greeting based on the messianic context of Psalm 118:26. The Jewish masses proclaimed Jesus' messiahship as He approached Jerusalem. But the Jewish leaders had already committed the unpardonable sin. Judgment had already been set on that generation. Since the sin was unforgivable, there was no way of alleviating that judgment. So in spite of the masses proclaiming Jesus to be the Messiah, Jesus pronounced words of judgment upon Jerusalem.

The Pharisees Denounced: Matthew 23:1-36

Matthew 23 is devoted to a denunciation and condemnation of the scribes and the Pharisees, the leadership of Israel, for various sins. In verses 1-12 they are condemned for their hypocrisy. In verses 13-14 they are condemned for leading the nation in the rejection of Jesus' messiahship. In verse 15 they are condemned for corrupting the proselytes. In verses 16-22 they are condemned for making the Mosaic law ineffectual through pharisaic traditions. In verses 23-24 they are condemned for majoring in the minors. In verses 25-28 they are condemned for being concerned with externals only. And in verses 29-36 they are condemned for rejecting the prophets.

There are two key passages in Matthew 23 that are of special relevance to our study.

MATTHEW 23:13

> Woe unto you, scribes and Pharisees, hypocrites! For you shut up the kingdom of heaven against men: for you neither go in yourselves, nor do you allow those who are entering to go in.

Jesus not only held the Pharisees accountable for rejecting His messiahship, but also for leading the entire nation to reject Him. This is an important factor to note in understanding the basis for the second coming of the Messiah.

MATTHEW 23:29-36

> Woe to you, scribes and Pharisees, hypocrites! Because you build the tombs of the prophets and adorn the monuments of the righteous, and say, "If we had lived in the days of our fathers, we would not have been partakers with them in the blood of the prophets." Therefore you are witnesses against yourselves that you are sons of those who murdered the prophets. Fill up, then, the measure of your fathers' guilt. Serpents, brood of vipers! How can you escape the condemnation of hell? Therefore, indeed, I send you prophets, wise men, and scribes: some of them you will kill and crucify, and some of them you will scourge in your synagogues and persecute

> from city to city, that on you may come all the righ-
> teous blood shed on the earth, from the blood of
> the righteous Abel to the blood of Zachariah, son of
> Berechiah, whom you murdered between the tem-
> ple and the altar. Assuredly, I say to you, all these
> things will come upon this generation.

These verses emphasize the severity of the judgment on that generation. It is primarily upon the leaders, but it is also upon the nation whom the leaders led to reject the Messiah. And the leaders would also be held accountable for the blood of the Old Testament prophets from Abel to Zechariah. In that day, the books of the Old Testament began with Genesis, which mentions Abel, and ended with 2 Chronicles, which mentions Zechariah. So that generation was guilty of the blood of all the prophets. That's because everything God intended to say about the Messiah had already been said by the Jewish prophets. That generation possessed in their hands the entire Old Testament canon. Furthermore, they had the preaching of John the Baptist, which announced the soon coming of the Lord. Finally, they had the physical manifestation and presence of Jesus the Messiah, who performed signs and miracles that authenticated His messiahship.

Nevertheless, the Jewish leaders rejected Jesus. Thus they would be held accountable for the blood of all the prophets who spoke about the Messiah. This is something unique for that generation, for Jesus said in verse 36, "Assuredly, I say to you, all these things will come upon this generation." This judgment came because they had committed the unpardonable sin. The leaders had rejected Jesus' messiahship, and had led the nation to reject it as well on the basis of demon possession.

A few days after these words were spoken, the second sign of Jonah was given in the resurrection of the Messiah, and this second sign was rejected in Acts 1–7. The stoning of Stephen by the Sanhedrin in Acts 7 marked the official rejection of the second sign of Jonah. That is why, in Acts 8, the gospel is spread to the non-Jewish world for the first time.

The book of Hebrews was written to a group of Jewish

believers who, because of persecution, were contemplating a return to Judaism. The writer warned them that they must separate themselves completely from the Judaism that rejected the Messiah. If they failed to do so, they would be caught up in the judgment of AD 70 and suffer physical death. Only if they separated themselves would they escape the judgment upon that generation. Of course, from the book of Hebrews it is not known what the results were, but it is known from Josephus and Eusebius, quoting Hegisippius, a believing Jewish historian of the second century. These men recorded how the Jewish believers, in obedience to the writer of the book of Hebrews, separated themselves from Judaism. When the revolt against Rome began in AD 66, the entire messianic Jewish community left the country and waited out the war in the town of Pella, on the east bank of the Jordan. Although 1.1 million Jews died in the Jewish revolt against Rome, not one Jewish believer was killed. Had they not obeyed the writer of the book of Hebrews, they would have died. But because they did obey, they escaped with their lives and were freed from the judgment upon that generation.

When Jesus was rejected, the offer of the messianic kingdom was rescinded and the mystery kingdom replaced it. This concept is ridiculed by Covenant Theologians and is the basis of their claim that Dispensationalism minimizes the cross and makes it an afterthought in the plan of God. This is far from the truth. Dispensationalism strongly believes that the Messiah's death was inevitable, for it was absolutely necessary for the atonement. *Yeshua* would have died even if Israel had accepted Him. The nation would have proclaimed *Yeshua* as their King, which would have been viewed by Rome as a rebellion against Caesar. *Yeshua* would then have been arrested, tried, and crucified for treason against Rome, as was the case anyway. Three days later, following His resurrection, He would have dispensed with Rome and set up the messianic kingdom. His death would have occurred regardless of what Israel did.

However, it was already known, on the basis of Old Testament prophecy, that Israel would reject His messiahship. The simple fact is that Israel could not reject that which was not offered. And that which was offered had to be more than just a spiritual kingdom of God's rule in their hearts, for many Jews *did* accept Jesus as the Messiah and *did* have God's rule in their hearts. The spiritual kingdom is offered to individuals, not nations, and received by individuals by means of faith. What was offered to the nation had to be much more tangible than the intangible spiritual kingdom. What was offered was the messianic kingdom. In God's plan, it was by means of the rejection of Jesus' messiahship that the death of the Messiah was accomplished. As every good Calvinist should know (and all Covenant Theologians are Calvinists), God ordains both the ends and the means.

Understanding the various facets of God's kingdom program can help to understanding which facet was offered to Israel and rejected, and which facet temporarily took its place. All of these things will have ramifications as to the precondition to the second coming and the establishment of the messianic kingdom.

The Prerequisite to the Second Coming
Leviticus 26:40-42

> If they confess their iniquity and the iniquity of their fathers, with their unfaithfulness in which they were unfaithful to Me, and that they also have walked contrary to Me, and that I also have walked contrary to them and have brought them into the land of their enemies; if their uncircumcised hearts are humbled, and they accept their guilt—then I will remember My covenant with Jacob, and My covenant with Isaac and My covenant with Abraham I will remember; I will remember the land.

In Leviticus 26, Moses predicted the Jews would be scattered all over the world because of their disobedience to God's revealed will. According to the New Testament, this came as a direct result of their rejection of *Yeshua*. By verse 39 the worldwide dispersion is a fact. Up to this point, Leviticus 26 has been fulfilled.

In verse 42, Moses stated that God had every intention of giving Israel all the blessings and promises of the Abrahamic Covenant, especially as the covenant pertains to the Promised Land. But before the people can begin to enjoy these blessings during the messianic age, it is first necessary for them to fulfill the condition of verse 40: "If they confess their iniquity and the iniquity of their fathers." Notice that the word "iniquity" is singular and specific. There is one specific iniquity Israel must confess before she can enjoy the benefits of the Abrahamic Covenant. This iniquity was committed by their fathers or ancestors, and must now be confessed by a subsequent generation.

Jeremiah 3:11-18

> The LORD said to me, "Backsliding Israel has shown herself more righteous than treacherous Judah. Go and proclaim these words toward the north, and say, 'Return, backsliding Israel,' says the LORD; 'I will not cause My anger to fall on you. For I am merciful,' says the LORD; 'I will not remain angry forever. Only acknowledge your iniquity, that you have transgressed against the LORD your God, and have scattered your charms to alien deities under every green tree, and you have not obeyed my voice,' says the LORD. 'Return, O backsliding children,' says the LORD; 'for I am married to you. I will take you, one from a city and two from a family, and I will bring you to Zion. And I will give you shepherds according to My heart, who will feed you with knowledge and understanding. Then it shall come to pass, when you are multiplied and increased in the land in those days,' says the LORD, 'that they will say no more, "The ark of the covenant of the LORD." It shall not come to mind, nor shall they remember it, nor shall they visit, nor shall it be made any more. At that time Jerusalem shall be called The Throne of the LORD; and all the nations shall be gathered to it, to the name of the LORD, to Jerusalem. No more

> shall they follow the dictates of their evil hearts. In those days the house of Judah shall walk with the house of Israel, and they shall come together out of the land of the north to the land that I have given as an inheritance to your fathers.'"

In the verses above, Jeremiah described the blessings that await Israel in the messianic kingdom. This will be a time of tremendous blessing and restoration for the Jewish people. But all these blessings are conditioned by verse 13, where the people must acknowledge or confess one specific iniquity that they committed against the Lord their God.

Zechariah 12:10

Zechariah 12, 13, and 14 are one prophetic revelation, a unit of thought that develops one theme. Chapter 13 speaks of the national cleansing of Israel from their sin. Chapter 14 describes the second coming of the Messiah and the establishment of His kingdom. But the cleansing of Israel followed by the second coming and the messianic kingdom are all conditioned on Zechariah 12:10:

> I will pour on the house of David and on the inhabitants of Jerusalem the Spirit of grace and supplication; then they will look on Me whom they pierced. Yes, they will mourn for Him as one mourns for his only son, and grieve for Him as one grieves for a firstborn.

Before Israel will receive cleansing and before the Messiah will return to establish His kingdom, Israel must first look to the One whom they pierced and plead for His return. Once they do this, then, and only then, will they receive their cleansing and begin to enjoy the blessings of the messianic age.

Hosea 5:15

> I will return again to my place till they acknowledge their offense. Then they will seek My face; in their affliction they will earnestly seek Me.

In Hosea 5, God is speaking. And there are certain presuppositions behind the understanding of this verse. Before anyone can return to a place, he must first leave it. In this passage, God states He is returning to His place. God's place is heaven. Before He can return to heaven, He must first leave it. The question is, When did God ever leave heaven? At the incarnation, in the Person of Jesus of Nazareth. Then, because of one specific offense committed against Him, He returned to heaven at the ascension from the Mount of Olives.

Hosea 5:15 further states God will not return until the offense that caused Him to return to heaven is acknowledged or confessed. What is this national offense committed against Jesus? It is not, as many believe, the act of killing Him. That was done by Gentile hands, not Jewish. He was condemned and sentenced by a Gentile judge. He was crucified by Gentile soldiers. But all that is ultimately irrelevant for, regardless of Jewish acceptance or rejection, Jesus would have to die anyway to become the sacrifice for sin. The national offense of Israel was in the rejection of Jesus' messiahship. According to Hosea 5:15, only when this offense is confessed will the Messiah return.

Matthew 23:37-39

> O Jerusalem, Jerusalem, the one who kills the prophets and stones those who are sent unto her! How often I wanted to gather your children together, as a hen gathers her chicks under her wings, but you were not willing! See! Your house is left unto you desolate; for I say unto you, you shall see Me no more till you say, "Blessed is He who comes in the name of the LORD!"

As was shown earlier, Matthew 23 documents the Messiah's denunciation of the scribes and Pharisees for leading the nation to reject His messiahship. Still speaking to the Jewish leadership, Jesus reiterated in verse 37 His desire to gather them if only they would accept Him. Because of their rejection, they would be scattered instead of gathered. According to verse 38, their "house"—the Jewish temple—will be left desolate and be destroyed, with nothing remaining. Then Jesus declared they would not see Him again until they said, "Blessed is He who comes in the name of the LORD!" This is a messianic greeting, and it will signify their acceptance of His messiahship.

So Jesus will not return to the earth until the Jewish leaders and people ask Him to come back. For just as the leaders led the nation to reject His messiahship, they must someday lead the nation to accept it.

This, then, is the twofold basis of the second coming of the Messiah: First, Israel must confess her national sin. Second, Israel must then plead for Messiah to return, to "mourn for Him as one mourns for his only son."

What This Means for the Church and Israel Today

All this explains why the rapture is distinct from the second coming. The rapture is part of God's program for the church. And the second coming is part of God's program for Israel.

Not only is all this relevant to the topic of the rapture, but it's also pertinent to the principles of Jewish evangelism. Here's why:

First, it helps to understand the biblical foundations of anti-Semitism, and why Satan has had this long unending war against the Jews so as to destroy them at every opportunity. Satan knows that once the second coming occurs his career is over. But he also knows there will be no second coming apart from the Jewish request for it to happen. So if he can succeed in destroying the Jews once and for all, before they have a chance to plead for the Messiah to return, then there will be no second coming, and Satan's career will be forever safe. That's the reason Satan has sought to destroy the Jews all through history. That's why the Crusades occurred; it's why the Russian pogroms occurred; it's why the Nazi Holocaust occurred; and it's why today, both Arab Muslims and non-Arab Muslims seek to destroy Israel. Anti-Semitism in any form—whether it is active or passive; whether it is racial, ethnic, political, social, economic, religious, or theological—is ultimately part of the satanic war to avoid the second coming.

Second, it explains why Satan used one name more than any other name to persecute Jews. Since about the fourth century, over 90 percent of the persecution against the Jews has been done in the name of Christ, the cross, and the church. Satan knows the one name they need to call upon for national salvation and the second coming, so he mapped out a strategy to make that name odious in the Jewish community—and he's been very successful so far. By and large, the vast majority of the Jewish people's reactions to Jesus today is not based upon any knowledge of the *Yeshua* of the New Testament, but upon the Jesus of anti-Jewish "Christian" persecutors through history, who is not the biblical Jesus at all. That is why Jewish reaction to a Jew who believes in Jesus is very different than to a Jew who accepts Buddhism or some other religion. For these reasons, even some evangelical Christians have followed the policy of simply being nice to Jewish people but never sharing the gospel with them because they have fallen for the faulty premise that they have lost the right to do so.

This brings us to the third point: the need for Jewish evangelism today. There is obviously nothing wrong with seeking to do nice things for Jewish people, helping them move to Israel, or providing for their specific needs. But there is everything wrong if these are done at the sacrifice of presenting the gospel. The basic fact is that the call of the church is not merely to help Jews, but to present the gospel to the Jew first and also the Greek. Jewish evangelism is necessary because it helps to provide Jewish people with a correct and biblical understanding of Jesus.

In Acts 4:12, when Peter declared there was no other name given under heaven whereby one could be saved, he was speaking to a Jewish audience, not a Gentile one. Furthermore, he was speaking to religious Jews and not secular. What that means is that even the most Orthodox Jew will not find salvation apart from conscious faith in the messiahship of *Yeshua*, who died for his sins, and rose again. Scripture promises there always was and still is a remnant of Israel coming to faith in

Jesus, but that remnant comes to faith only when they hear and believe the gospel.

So at the present time, Jewish evangelism is essential for the sake of building up the remnant of Israel. Such evangelism can also lay down the seeds of Israel's future national salvation—the seeds we plant now may begin to produce fruit as we enter the latter days as God works to draw Jewish people as a nation to Himself, and that, in turn, will bring about both the second coming and messianic kingdom. If the basis of the second coming of the Messiah teaches anything, it teaches the importance of Jewish evangelism both for the present and the future.

THE DATE OF THE
BOOK OF REVELATION

Andy Woods

Most would consider the arguments surrounding the dating of a New Testament book to have little relevance to their lives today—they would not view it as much more than a scholarly exercise. However, with regard to *when* the end-times scenario revealed in Scripture will take place, the position one holds can rise or fall depending upon the date he ascribes to the composition of the book of Revelation. The reason for this contingency relates to the rise of modern-day preterism. This view teaches that the events in the book of Revelation are not still future. Rather, preterists contend that most, if not all, the contents of the Apocalypse were fulfilled in the events surrounding the fall of Jerusalem in AD 70.[1] In other words, the vision John saw on the Isle of Patmos is not still future, but was largely fulfilled back in the first century. What does the preterist approach to prophecy have to do with the date Revelation was written? Everything!

There are two dates commonly proposed for the writing of Revelation. Advocates of the early date contend Revelation was written in the mid-AD 60s during the reign of Nero. Proponents of a late date for the writing of the book argue it was written in the mid-AD 90s during the reign of Domitian, who regularly sent prisoners to the Isle of Patmos.

Who is right, and why should we care? Well, if you are a preterist, the issue is monumental. Revelation obviously cannot be describing the fall of Jerusalem in AD 70 if it was written in the mid-90s, or after Jerusalem fell. In other words, preterism *needs* the early date of Revelation in order to remain credible. If the early date is not at all possible, the preterist view collapses.

By contrast, it matters very little to other end-times perspectives when one dates Revelation. For example, I am a futurist. This means I believe the events of Revelation 4–22 have not occurred yet. The futuristic view remains unaffected regardless if one holds to a Neronian (AD 65) or Domitianic (AD 95) date. However, the preterist enjoys no similar flexibility. He must date the book early or his view is destroyed. Preterists themselves admit this dilemma. R.C. Sproul concedes, "If the book was written after AD 70, then its contents manifestly do not refer to events surrounding the fall of Jerusalem— unless the book is a wholesale fraud, having been composed after the predicted events had already occurred."[2]

Given the significance of Revelation's date to the preterist scenario, the goal of this chapter is to demonstrate Revelation was written during the reign of Domitian, or 25 years after Jerusalem fell. This would discredit preterism's contention that Revelation predicts Jerusalem's first-century fall. Rather, the book's prophetic content awaits a future fulfillment.

There are two primary approaches scholars use to date a book. First, they consider external evidence, or evidence from outside the biblical book itself. Second, they examine internal evidence, or dating clues found within the book under consideration. This chapter will show that neither the external nor internal evidence favors a Neronian date for Revelation, but rather leans heavily in favor of the Domitianic date.[3]

Arguments for an Early Date

External Evidence

Preterists rely on various pieces of external evidence, or evidence from outside the book of Revelation to build their case for an early date of composition. These sources include the Muratorian Canon, Tertullian, Epiphanius of Salamis, Syriac versions of Revelation, Arethas, and Theophylact. For example, the Muratorian Canon contains a manuscript written between AD 127–200, which says, "the blessed Apostle Paul, following the rule of his predecessor John, writes to no more than seven churches by name."[4] Early-date advocates believe this statement indicates John preceded Paul chronologically in writing Revelation. Because Paul died in the late 60s,[5] early-date proponents claim Revelation must have been written before the late 60s.[6]

Furthermore, Tertullian, while speaking of the church in Rome wrote this: "where Peter had like passion with the Lord; where Paul hath for his crown the same death with John; where the apostle John was plunged into boiling oil, and suffered nothing, and was afterwards banished to an island."[7] Early-date proponents believe this statement indicates John's banishment took place at the same time as Peter and Paul's martyrdom. They claim Revelation must have been written before the late 60s because Paul died in AD 67–68.[8]

In addition, Epiphanius of Salamis (AD 315–403) said John's banishment took place during the emperorship of Claudius.[9] Because Nero and Claudius used one another's names, some scholars have concluded Epiphanius was referring to Nero when he spoke of Claudius.[10] Thus, early date proponents believe that Epiphanius's statement indicates John was banished—and wrote Revelation—during the Neronic reign.[11] Moreover, a subscription in two Syriac versions of Revelation (AD 508, 616) clearly states that Nero exiled John.[12] Also, Arethas (AD 914), the bishop of Caesarea, wrote a commentary on Revelation that favors a pre-AD 70 date.[13] Finally, eleventh-century bishop Theophylact places John's exile at the time of Nero's reign in *Preface to Commentary on the Gospel of John.*[14] Early-date advocates believe all these external sources point to John's exile under Nero and thus a pre-AD 70 date.[15]

However, most of the external evidence preterists rely on to argue for an early date can either be given an alternative interpretation, demonstrate gross inaccuracies, or are dated far too late to effectively further the early-date cause. For example, the Muratorian Canon, which says "the blessed Apostle Paul, following the rule of his predecessor John, writes to no more than seven churches by name," need not be understood as indicating that John preceded Paul in writing seven letters to seven churches. Rather, it's possible John was called Paul's predecessor simply because John became an apostle before Paul. Thus, the statement need not be understood as saying John wrote before Paul.[16]

Moreover, Tertullian's statement "where Peter had like passion with the Lord; where Paul hath for his crown the same death with John; where the apostle John was plunged into boiling oil, and suffered nothing, and was afterwards banished to an island" need not be understood, as preterists assume, as saying John's banishment took place at the same time as Paul and Peter's martyrdom. It is possible the statement simply means the martyrdom of Peter, Paul, and John occurred in the same *place* rather than at the same time.[17] Also, Epiphanius of Salamis' statement that John's banishment took place during the reign of Claudius—which preterists believe is a reference to Nero—is so "notoriously inaccurate" and "widely at variance with all tradition" that scarcely any scholar has accepted it as authoritative.[18]

As for the Syriac versions of Revelation (AD 508, 616), which indicate Nero exiled John; Arethas' (AD 914) commentary on Revelation favoring a pre-AD 70 date; and Theophylact's *Preface to Commentary on the Gospel of John* (AD 1107), which places John's exile at the time of Nero's reign, we should note all these "witnesses" wrote centuries later. The Syriac versions are from the sixth century, and the other two are from the tenth and eleventh centuries. Their date of origin is far too late to be persuasive or compelling on the issue of Revelation's date. As Ritchie Smith observes, "When witnesses are summoned from the tenth and eleventh centuries, the case is plainly hopeless."[19]

Internal Evidence

The internal evidence preterists use includes Revelation's references to "time texts," the temple, the beast, the sixth reigning king, and Jewish Christianity. Preterists also note Revelation's failure to mention the events of AD 70. For example, because Revelation makes use of the words "shortly" or "quickly" (Greek, *tachos*—Revelation 1:1; 2:16; 3:11; 11:14; 22:6-7,12,20), "near" or "at hand" (Greek, *engys*—1:3; 22:10), and "about to" (Greek, *mellō*—1:19; 3:10), preterists take literary license to locate the fulfillment of most of John's prophecies in the events surrounding the fall of Jerusalem in AD 70.[20] Because Revelation is a prophecy about AD 70, they erroneously conclude the book must date prior to AD 70.

Also, preterists claim Revelation 11:1-2 points to Revelation being dated prior to AD 70.[21] They believe these verses refer to the Second Temple. If the Second Temple were still standing when Revelation was written, then it must date to before AD 70, for that's when the Second Temple was destroyed by the Roman legions under Titus.

In addition, preterists identify the beast in Revelation as Nero.[22] For Revelation to predict the end of the Neronian reign, then, it must have been written prior to this time, which would date it to the mid-60s. The main selling point for the Neronian identification of the beast is *gematria*, which states the alphabets of the ancient world not only had linguistic purpose, but numerical significance as well. Thus, a person's name could be converted into a number simply by adding up the numerical values of the letters in his name. Transliterating the Greek title *Caesar Nero* into Hebrew yields the name *nwrn rsq*. The numerical sum of these Hebrew letters yields the total 666, which preterists use to allege Nero was the beast.

Also, preterists claim Revelation 17:9-10 furnishes an important clue that enables Revelation to date prior to AD 70.[23] These verses say, "Here is the mind which has wisdom: The seven heads are seven mountains on which the woman sits. There are also seven kings. Five have fallen, one is, and the other has not yet come. And when he comes, he must continue a short time" (Revelation 17:9-10). Here, the seven heads represent seven kings. According to preterists, verse 9 identifies the geography of Rome, and these kings are all Roman kings. Verse 10 says five of them have fallen. John used the past tense of the Greek verb *piptō* ("to fall") to indicate these kings were no longer in power when he wrote. John then used the present tense of the verb *eimi* ("to be") to indicate the sixth king was currently in power when he wrote. Because the sixth king was in authority when John wrote, preterists believe that determining who he was and when he reigned will reveal an accurate date for the writing of Revelation. Because records from John's era show that Julius was commonly recognized as the first emperor of Rome,[24] preterists claim it is easy to determine the identity of these seven kings: Julius Caesar (40–44 BC), Augustus (31 BC–AD 14), Tiberius (AD 14–37), Caligula (AD 37–41), Claudius (AD 41–54), Nero (AD 54–68), and Galba (AD 68–69). Thus, Nero, it is alleged, was the sixth king in power when John wrote. Because he reigned from AD 54 to 68, it is impossible, they say, to date Revelation after AD 68.

Moreover, according to preterists, the relationship between the Jews and Gentiles as depicted in Revelation was not yet distinct. For example, in Revelation 2:9 and 3:9, John indicated Jews were in two of the seven churches (Smyrna and Philadelphia). Not only is the language in Revelation Hebraic,[25] but the Apocalypse often employs Hebrew words (Revelation 9:11; 16:16). According to preterists, the Jews and Gentiles became distinct after the Jewish War that culminated in the destruction of the temple in AD 70.[26] Thus, because Revelation reflects a situation where Christianity was not yet distinct from Israel, it must have been composed prior to AD 70.[27] Finally, preterists contend Revelation could not have been written after AD 70 because the book has no mention of what happened in AD 70 by way of remembrance. Hanegraaff notes:

> ...if the apostle John were indeed writing in AD 95, it seems incredible that he would make no mention whatsoever of the most apocalyptic event in Jewish history—the demolition of Jerusalem and the destruction of the Temple at the hands of Titus. This would be tantamount to writing the history of New York City today and making no mention of

the destruction of the World Trade Center at the
hands of terrorists on September 11, 2001.[28]

However, these aforementioned internal evidence arguments do not convincingly support an early date for Revelation. Regarding Revelation's so-called "time texts," rather than
understanding them chronologically as indicating *when* Christ
will return, as preterists assume, it is also possible to understand them adverbially or qualitatively, indicating the *manner* of Christ's return. In other words, when the action comes,
it will come suddenly or with great rapidity.[29] The New Testament allows for such a usage. For example, while it is true
Scripture often uses "shortly" or "quickly" (Greek, *tachos*) in a
chronological sense to indicate *when* (1 Timothy 3:14), Scripture also uses the same word in a qualitative sense to indicate
how. For instance, Acts 22:18 uses *tachos* to indicate manner:
"Make haste, and get out of Jerusalem quickly, because they
will not accept your testimony about me." It is also possible
to understand *engys* (Philippians 4:5) and *mellō* (1 Peter 5:1)
in terms of imminency. In other words, rather than connoting chronology, these terms could be communicating that the
prophesied events could happen at any moment.[30]

What about the argument that mention of the Second
Temple in Revelation 11:1-2 means the book must have been
written before the temple was destroyed in AD 70? This view
is problematic because it is possible for biblical writers to refer
to a temple that is yet future from the perspective of the writer.
For example, both Ezekiel and Daniel wrote during the days
of the Babylonian captivity subsequent to the destruction of
the temple by Nebuchadnezzar (586 BC) but before the temple had been rebuilt by the Jewish exiles who returned from
captivity (515 BC). Despite the fact no Jewish temple was in
physical existence at the time Daniel and Ezekiel wrote, both
prophets made reference to a temple (Daniel 8:11-14; 9:27;
11:31; 12:11; Ezekiel 40–48). Thus, it is possible that John,
while writing Revelation after the destruction of the temple in
AD 70, was also referring to a future temple.[31]

Moreover, the attempt to identify the beast as Nero based

upon the *gematria* calculation is fraught with problems.[32] First, the transliteration from Greek into Hebrew is problematic given the fact Revelation was written to a Greek-speaking audience (2–3). Although Revelation exhibits Hebraic character,[33] when John used Hebrew words, he made special note of them in order to bring them to his readers' attention (9:11; 16:16). Yet no similar special designation is even hinted at in Revelation 13:18 regarding the number 666.[34] Second, the Neronic calculation was never suggested as a solution by any of the ancient commentators,[35] including Irenaeus, who was discipled by Polycarp who in turn was discipled by John.[36] Third, it appears that preterists have cherry picked a peculiar Neronic spelling in an attempt to reach an ordained result given the fact that Nero had many other names and titles[37] and that *rsq* can also be spelled with the Hebrew letter yod (*rsyq*).[38]

Moreover, Nero's life does not fulfill the biblical predictions concerning the coming Antichrist. For example, Nero never visited Jerusalem nor had his image placed in the Jerusalem temple (Daniel 9:27; Revelation 13:14-15). To try to claim 2 Thessalonians 2:8-12 and Revelation 13 were fulfilled by Roman soldiers riding in Jerusalem on horses with the insignia of Rome on a staff is a real stretch. This does not fit the prophecies of 2 Thessalonians 2:1-12 and Revelation 13. In fact, beheadings, such as those described in Revelation 20:4, were not the practice of Rome during the siege of Jerusalem in AD 70.

Preterists also believe they can assign Revelation a Neronic date due to the fact Nero was the sixth king reigning when John wrote the Apocalypse. However, this notion is problematic. The primary difficulty is uncertainty regarding exactly *where* to initiate the count of emperors, and *how many* of the emperors should be counted.

Although preterists are confident the count should begin with Julius Caesar, other scholars are not as certain. For example, perhaps the count should begin with Augustus or even Caligula, who was the first persecuting emperor. Other scholars contemplate whether all the emperors should be counted or only those who emphasized emperor worship. There is also uncertainty over whether the three minor emperors, Galba, Otho, and Vitellius, who ruled between AD 68–69, should be included.[39] A differing perspective on any of these issues prevents the interpreter from arriving at the conclusion that Nero was the sixth king.

The early date cause is further weakened by the fact the seven kings of Revelation 17:9-10 may not represent individual emperors at all, but rather kingdoms. The kingdom view is preferable because the seven kings are also referred to as seven mountains or hills (17:9). Throughout Scripture, mountains or hills typically symbolize kingdoms or empires (Isaiah 2:2; 41:15; Jeremiah 51:25; Daniel 2:35,45).[40]

As previously mentioned, preterists argue that because Revelation reflects a situation where Christianity was not yet distinct from Israel, Revelation must have been composed prior to AD 70. However, it is hardly a foregone conclusion among scholars that the events of AD 70 resulted in a permanent rift between Christianity and Judaism. According to Hebrew-Christian scholar Arnold Fruchtenbaum, Hebrew Christians continued to live among the Jews following AD 70. The permanent rift between Judaism and Christianity did not begin until the 90s and did not reach its final form until the Bar Cochba revolt in AD 135.[41]

Finally, the notion that Revelation could not have been written after AD 70 because it doesn't mention the fall of Jerusalem is inadequate. In Revelation 1:19, Christ specifically told John to write down the things that he had "seen" (the vision of the glorified Christ in chapter 1), the things that "are" (the letters to the seven churches in Asia Minor in chapters 2–3), and the things that would "take place after these things" (the futuristic section as recorded in chapters 4–22). Had John in AD 95 written instead about the fall of Jerusalem 25 years earlier, he would have been in direct violation of Christ's command, which expressly told John to write about things in his own day (1–3) and beyond (4–22), and not past events.

In sum, we have seen that the external and internal evidence for an early date is rather weak. Let us now turn our attention to the much stronger evidence for a late date.

Arguments for a Late Date

External Evidence

Unlike early-date advocates, late-date advocates are able to produce external sources written within close proximity to the apostolic age which testify that John wrote Revelation during the reign of Domitian. For example, Eusebius (AD 300–340) noted:

> ...after Domitian had reigned fifteen years, and Nerva had succeeded to the empire, the Roman Senate, according to the writers that record the history of those days, voted that Domitian's honors should be cancelled, and that those who had been unjustly banished should return to their homes and have their property restored to them. It was at this time that the apostle John returned from his banishment in the island and took up his abode at Ephesus, according to an ancient Christian tradition.[42]

The key phrase here is, "according to the writers that record the history of those days." Mark Hitchcock explains the significance of this statement: "To whom is Eusebius referring? The context indicates that he is referring to Hegesippus, whom he has just referred to twice as a source for his information."[43] Thus, Eusebius makes reference to an early writer, Hegesippus (AD 150), who credited Domitian for John's banishment to Patmos, where Revelation was written.

Moreover, while commenting on Revelation 13:18 in his work *Against Heresies* (AD 180), Irenaeus observed, "If it were necessary that the name of him [Antichrist] should be distinctly revealed in the present time, it would have been told by him who saw the apocalyptic vision. For it was seen no long time ago, but almost in our generation, toward the end of Domitian's reign."[44] In this passage, a clear relationship exists between the verb "was seen" and the noun "apocalyptic vision." Therefore, the passage indicates Irenaeus believed John saw the apocalyptic vision at the end of Domitian's reign. Thus, Revelation should be assigned a date of AD 95 or 96.

Irenaeus' testimony regarding this matter is particularly compelling because he was a disciple of Polycarp, who in turn was a disciple of the apostle John, the author of Revelation. Elsewhere Irenaeus recalled how he listened to and treasured the things Polycarp conveyed to him directly from John's own ministry and teaching.[45]

Because of the threat Irenaeus' testimony poses to the early date of Revelation, preterists attempt to attack the credibility of his testimony in a variety of ways. For example, they reinterpret Irenaeus' statement by arguing that John is the subject of the verb "it was seen" rather than the apocalyptic vision.[46] In other words, it was John who was seen at the end of Domitian's reign rather than the vision. Thus, Irenaeus was merely commenting on how long John lived rather than when John saw the Apocalypse. Preterists also attempt to impeach Irenaeus' credibility by pointing out some factual errors he made elsewhere in his writings.[47] For example, Irenaeus claimed that Jesus lived to be over 50 years of age.[48]

Several responses can be given. First, numerous well-known reasons militate against interpreting Irenaeus' statement as indicating how long John lived rather than when he saw the Apocalypse. To begin with, the majority of patristic writers, subsequent commentators,[49] and modern scholars[50] have understood Irenaeus' statement as referring to the time when the Apocalypse was seen. Furthermore, the verb "was seen" fits best with the noun "apocalyptic vision" because the apocalyptic vision is something John saw.[51] Moreover, David E. Aune observes the passive verb "it was seen" is not the best way of describing the length of a person's life. Therefore, it is more likely this verb refers to the time when John saw the Apocalypse.[52] Finally, the nearest antecedent to the verb "it was seen" is "the apocalypse" and not "him."[53]

Many reputable scholars have rejected various attempts to impeach the credibility of Irenaeus.[54] For example, Philip Schaff supports the credibility, reliability, and trustworthiness of Irenaeus.[55] In fact, Schaff said Irenaeus' testimony regarding the Domitianic date for the composition of Revelation as "clear and weighty testimony."[56]

Early-date advocates also face the daunting task of dismissing the Domitianic evidence found in the Acts of John (fifth to sixth century) as well as the writings of Clement of Alexander (AD 150–215), Origen (AD 185–254), Victorinus (AD 304), Eusebius (AD 260–340), Jerome (AD 340–420) and Andreas of Cappadocia (sixth century).[57] Although preterists believe they have successfully refuted such evidence,[58] the staggering fact remains that the only uncontested and unambiguous testimony early-date advocates are able to produce favoring a Neronic date comes from late external sources.

Internal Evidence

Just as the external evidence for dating the book of Revelation leans heavily in favor of assigning a Domitianic date (AD 95), the internal evidence is sufficient to warrant the same conclusion. This evidence includes the condition of the churches of Asia Minor (Revelation 2–3) as well as the penalty imposed upon John, which was his banishment on Patmos. Many have observed that the condition of the churches in Revelation 2–3 are quite different from the condition of these same churches as described in various Pauline epistles written in the 60s, such as Ephesians and 1 and 2 Timothy. If Revelation was written in the 60s, as preterists allege, we would not expect to find such disparate spiritual conditions, but rather virtually the same conditions.

For example, if John wrote Revelation in the mid-60s as preterists contend,[59] then the letter to the church at Ephesus (2:1-7) would have been written in close chronology to Paul's letters to the Ephesians (AD 60–62) and to Timothy (AD 62–67), who was pastoring in Ephesus at the time. Yet Paul's letters contain no mention of the destructive elements found in Revelation 2:1-7, such as the threat of false apostles (2:2), the loss of first love (2:4), and the heresy of the Nicolaitans (2:6).[60] Because of the magnitude and severity of these problems, it is unthinkable that Paul would have omitted mention of them. Such conditions would have taken more than just a few years to develop.[61] It would have taken at least a generation for many of these problems to emerge.[62] The only logical explanation for this discrepancy is that an extended period of time elapsed between the Ephesian and Timothy letters and the composition of Revelation 2:1-7. Such an extended period of time favors a late date for the composition of Revelation.[63]

A similar problem relates to Christ's description of the church at Laodicea, which was spiritually arrogant on account of her material prosperity (Revelation 3:17). Yet, Christ's assessment would make little sense if it was aimed at the Laodicean church in the 60s as preterists assume. It remains a well-recorded historical fact that Laodicea experienced a severe earthquake in the early 60s, which took the city a generation to recover from.[64] How could Laodicea be materially prosperous in the wake of a severe earthquake that had impoverished her? However, a Domitianic date as the background for Christ's statement in 3:17 is far more credible, as this would allow at least three decades to elapse between the earthquake and Christ's statement. That would have allowed time for Laodicea to materially recover and return to her former prosperity.

Another substantial problem for the early-date view is that the church of Smyrna (Revelation 2:8-11) was not yet in existence in the 60s. Note the words of Polycarp, Bishop at Smyrna, to the Philippians:

> ...I have not observed or heard of any such thing among you, in whose midst the blessed Paul labored, and who were his letters of recommendation in the beginning. For he boasts about you in all the churches—those alone, that is, which at that time had come to know the Lord, for we had not yet come to know him.[65]

R.H. Charles explains the relevance of Polycarp's statement for the dating of Revelation: "The church in Smyrna did not exist in A.D. 60–64 at a time when St. Paul was boasting of the Philippians in all the Churches."[66] In other words, it remains difficult to date Revelation in the 60s when one of the churches in the letter was not yet in existence.

A final internal evidence argument for a Domitianic date

relates to John's punishment of banishment. If Revelation was written during the reign of Nero, then why would he execute Peter and Paul, as church history amply testifies, but at the same time banish John? Mark Hitchcock observes,

> The different punishments of Peter and Paul as compared with John argue for the fact that they were persecuted under different rulers. Moreover, there is no evidence of Nero's use of banishment for Christians. Since Domitian was the second Roman emperor after Nero to persecute Christians, and since banishment was one of his favorite modes of punishment, John's exile to Patmos is much more likely under Domitian than Nero.[67]

A Final Word Regarding Preterism

As this chapter has demonstrated, the external and internal evidence arguments for Revelation's date lean far more heavily in the direction of a late Domitianic date (AD 95) rather than an early Neronian date (AD 65). This makes the preterist perspective, or the notion that Revelation is a prophecy about the events of AD 70, a specious proposition. While many other problems with the preterist perspective could be identified,[68] the dating issue alone should cause believers who are serious about discovering God's end-time program to look elsewhere when building their eschatological system. Those who adopt preterism do so against the weight of both the external and internal evidence.

21

What to Do If
You've Been Left Behind

Tim LaHaye

I f you wake up one morning and discover your underage children missing and the 911 emergency line constantly busy, then turn on the TV to discover all channels are featuring a special news alert announcing that millions of people are missing all over the world, don't be surprised if your first thought is, *Could this be the rapture I have heard Christians talk about? If so, then I've been left behind!*

The news bulletins show unbelievable chaos everywhere: airplanes without pilots crashing or glutting the tarmacs. Runaway trains without engineers and cars without drivers wreaking havoc on the rails and roads everywhere. Many have suddenly disappeared, leaving behind their clothes, purses, wallets, medical devices, and whatever other belongings they had on their person in that fraction of a second during which millions vanished. Unimaginable turmoil and tragedy has affected everyone.

You think of a Christian friend you know, who had asked you several times if you would like to invite Jesus into your heart. But you had refused. Fortunately you have that person's phone number so you call his or her cell, but there's no answer! Your heart sinks as you realize this friend was raptured.

You race into the other bedrooms to find your three children's beds rumpled yet empty—they too are gone! Because they were below the age of accountability they were taken in the rapture—just as your friend warned. Suddenly you realize the only way you will ever see them again is to turn to faith in Jesus and invite Him into your heart.

You then call your husband at work. He answers and reports that few people showed up for work. You ask, "Roger, do you know what this is?" "Yes, it's probably that rapture our friends have been warning us about…and we were not ready. So Jesus Christ really was the Son of God, and He died for our sins on the cross and that He rose again from the dead, just like they tried to convince us. I was so blind, Sue, but I now believe! Do you think it is too late for us to accept Him?"

You feel the sting of tears on your cheeks as you reply, "I hope not!"

"Let's drop to our knees and admit to Jesus right now that we were wrong. If I remember correctly, we need to confess our sin of rejecting Christ and ask Him to come into our heart."

You readily accept your husband's suggestion, and together you pray to receive Christ as your God and Savior.

The Big Question

Will God hear such a last-minute call for salvation and save the soul of a person who once rejected Him? Absolutely! God is a merciful and forgiving God. He said this to Moses over 3500 years ago:

> The LORD, the LORD God, merciful and gracious, longsuffering, and abounding in goodness and truth, keeping mercy for thousands, forgiving iniquity and transgression and sin, by no means clearing the guilty (Exodus 34:6-7).

The apostle Peter said this about the Lord in 2 Peter 3:9: "The Lord is not slack concerning His promise, as some count slackness, but is longsuffering toward us, not willing that any should perish but that all should come to repentance."

When the rapture occurs, many will call upon the Lord for salvation. As we saw earlier in this book, according to Revelation 7:9-15, after the rapture the 144,000 special Jewish witnesses will begin reaching a "great multitude" that no man can number, from "all nations, tribes, peoples, and tongues" (verse 9). With the preaching of the two witnesses in Revelation 11, and the proclamations of the "angel...having the everlasting gospel" mentioned in Revelation 14:6-7, and other acts of God's grace, millions will hear the salvation message and receive Christ.

The Rapture Will Change Everything

The rapture will be the single most earthshaking event in human history. While the world will continue to function, it will reel from the impact of so many people missing. Every segment of society will be affected. Even non-Christian countries like China, where it is estimated that 30 million people attend secret house-churches, will be affected.

Can you imagine the turmoil that will hit in America, where the Gallup poll and others indicate that as much as 35 to 40 percent of the population professes to have had a born-again experience of receiving Christ? If that is true, this country will come to a screeching halt. With large numbers of doctors, nurses, health-care providers, emergency personnel, and teachers and other public employees missing, life as we know it will come to a standstill. Businesses and companies will be severely crippled as large portions of their workforces disappear altogether.

Officials in every country will be speechless as they try to explain away the missing multitudes. Some even today are prepared to fabricate stories about "aliens snatching them all away" and other preposterous notions. Theories will abound. And you can be assured that Satan, the master deceiver, will think of an explanation and pass it on to his servant, the Antichrist.

The Bible says this talented deceiver will sign a seven-year covenant with the unsaved leaders of Israel. He will then break that covenant in the middle of the seven-year Tribulation. By that time the Jewish temple will have been rebuilt and the

Antichrist will desecrate it by having his false prophet set up an image of himself in the temple and demanding that people bow down and worship him. Those who refuse will be killed, and the Antichrist will cause all, "both small and great, rich and poor, free and slave, to receive a mark on their right hand or on their foreheads, and that no one may buy or sell except one who has the mark" (Revelation 13:16-17).

Now Is the Day of Salvation

While there will be many converted to Christ during the seven-year Tribulation, the fact is they will have missed the rapture, the "blessed hope." That means they will have to live through the most horrific period in world history. Evil will flourish as never before, and God's wrath will pour out upon the earth to bring about unprecedented devastation.

Several years ago a young man wrote to tell me he would not accept Christ now because he wanted to wait until the Tribulation so he could witness for the Lord then—a rather cavalier attitude, to say the least. I wrote back and said he had no idea how awful those seven years will be. Besides, neither he or anyone else knows whether they will live that long. As the Bible says, "*Now* is the accepted time; behold, *now* is the day of salvation" (2 Corinthians 6:2, emphasis added).

If You Have Been Left Behind

If the rapture has taken place and you've been left behind, the best thing you can do is fall on your knees, repent of your unbelief and your rejection of Christ, confess your sin, and pray along these lines:

> Lord, I have sinned against You. I have never accepted You as my Lord and Savior. I now believe Jesus is the sinless Son of God who died for my sins and rose the third day as He said He would. And today, I invite You into my heart as Lord and Savior. Today I surrender to You the rest of my life, to do with it as You see fit.

God's Promise to Those Who Call on Him

In Romans 10:9-13 the apostle Paul wrote,

> If you confess with your mouth the Lord Jesus and believe in your heart that God has raised Him from the dead, you will be saved. For with the heart one believes unto righteousness, and with the mouth confession is made unto salvation. For the Scripture says, *"Whoever believes on Him will not be put to shame."* For there is no distinction between Jew and Greek, for the same Lord over all is rich to all who call upon Him. For *"whoever calls on the name of the* LORD *shall be saved."*

NOTES

Chapter 5—A History of the Rapture Teaching

1. Charles C. Ryrie, *Dispensationalism* (Chicago: Moody, 1995), 15-16.

2. Norman L. Geisler, "Review of Hank Hanegraaff's *The Apocalypse Code*," www.ses .edu/NormGeisler/ReviewApocalypseCode.html.

3. William E. Bell, "A Critical Evaluation of the Pretribulation Rapture Doctrine in Christian Eschatology" (PhD diss., New York University, 1967), 26-27.

4. *The Shepherd of Hermas;* 1.4.2.

5. John F. Walvoord, *The Rapture Question*, rev. ed. (Grand Rapids: Zondervan, 1979), 51.

6. Alexander Roberts, James Donaldson, and A. Cleveland Coxe, *The Ante-Nicene Fathers: Translations of the Writings of the Fathers Down to* A.D. *325* (Grand Rapids: Eerdmans Publishing Co., 1985), 558.

7. Charles C. Ryrie, *Come Quickly, Lord Jesus: What You Need to Know About the Rapture* (Eugene, OR: Harvest House, 1996), 21-22.

8. Larry Crutchfield says, "Many of them, especially in the first century, did indeed make explicit statements which indicated a belief in the imminent return of Christ. The doctrine of imminency is especially prominent in the writings of the apostolic fathers. It is on the basis of Christ's impending return (e.g., *Didache*) and on the strength of the literal fulfillment of past prophecy (e.g., *Barnabas*), that they exhorted the Christian to live a life of purity and faithfulness." Crutchfield supports this statement with the following: "See for example Clement of Rome (*I Clement* XXIII; XXXIV-XXXV); Ignatius (*Epist. to Polycarp* I and III); *Didache* (XVI, 1); Hermas (*Shepherd: Similitudes* IX, Chaps. V, VII, and XXVI); *Barnabas* (XXI). For fathers of the second century see Tertullian (*Apology* XXI); and Cyprian (*Treatises I*, 27). There are expressions of imminency even in those who expected certain events to occur before the end, as in "Hippolytus (*Treat. On Christ and Antichrist* 5); and Lactantius (*Div. Instit.* XXV)." Larry V. Crutchfield, "The Early Church Fathers and the Foundations of Dispensationalism: Part VI—The Conclusion: Evaluating the Content of Early Dispensational Concepts," *The Conservative Theological Journal* (vol. 3, no. 9; August 1999), 194.

9. Crutchfield, "Early Church Fathers—Part VI," 195-96. Crutchfield adds: "Some of the fathers like Hippolytus, Tertullian, Lactantius, and others, clearly had posttribulational elements in their views concerning the end times. But we have been unable to find an instance of the unequivocal classic posttribulationism taught today. Walvoord's assessment of the fathers' views on the tribulation is essentially correct. He says, 'The preponderance of evidence seems to support the concept that the early church did not clearly hold to a rapture as preceding the end time tribulation period. Most of the

early church fathers who wrote on the subject at all considered themselves already in the great tribulation. Accordingly Payne, as well as most other posttribulationists, takes the position that it is self-evident that pretribulationism as it is taught today was unheard of in the early centuries of the church. Consequently the viewpoint of the early church fathers is regarded by practically all posttribulationists, whether adherents of the classic view or not, as a major argument in favor of posttribulationism. However, the fact that most posttribulationists today do not accept the doctrine of imminency as the early church held it diminishes the force of their argument against pretribulationism'" [see John F. Walvoord, *The Blessed Hope and the Tribulation* (Grand Rapids: Zondervan Publishing House, 1976), 24], (196).

10. Kurt Aland, *A History of Christianity: From the Beginnings to the Threshold of the Reformation,* vol. 1 (Philadelphia: Fortress Press, 1985), Vol. I, 87.

11. Aland, *History of Christianity,* Vol. I, 92.

12. J. Barton Payne, *The Imminent Appearing of Christ* (Grand Rapids: Eerdmans, 1962), 102.

13. Paul J. Alexander, *The Byzantine Apocalyptic Tradition* (Berkeley: University of California Press, 1985), 136.

14. An English translation of the entire sermon can be found at www.pre-trib.org/article-view.php?id=169.

15. Timothy J. Demy and Thomas D. Ice, "The Rapture and Pseudo-Ephraem: An Early Medieval Citation," *Bibliotheca Sacra* 152 (July–September 1995), 12.

16. Scholar Jonathan David Burnham said, "Until at least 1845 Darby taught that the rapture would occur three-and-a-half years before the second coming. He connected the rapture with the casting out of Satan from heaven in Revelation 12, an event he believed triggered the 'great tribulation' period." Burnham, "The Controversial Relationship Between Benjamin Wills Newton and John Nelson Darby" (PhD diss., Oxford University, 1999), 128, f.n. 126.

17. Bob Gundry, *First the Antichrist: Why Christ Won't Come Before the Antichrist Does* (Grand Rapids: Baker, 1997), 188.

18. Paul J. Alexander, *The Byzantine Apocalyptic Tradition,* ed. Dorothy deF. Abrahamse (Berkeley: University of California, 1985), 210.

19. Thomas Ice, "Afterword: A Response by Thomas Ice to the Gundry Critique" in Thomas Ice and Timothy J. Demy, eds., *The Return: Understanding Christ's Second Coming* (Grand Rapids: Kregel, 1999), 72.

20. Most of the material on Brother Dolcino has been gleaned from Francis Gumerlock, "A Rapture Citation in the Fourteenth Century," *Bibliotheca Sacra* (vol. 159, no. 635; July–September 2002), 349-62. For more on Brother Dolcino see L. Mariotti, *A Historical Memoir of Fra Dolcino and His Times: Being an Account of a General Struggle for Ecclesiastical Reform, and of An Anti-Heretical Crusade in Italy, in the Early Part of the Fourteenth Century* (London: Longman, Brown Green and Longmans, 1853). Decima L. Douie, *The Nature and the Effect of the Heresy of the Fraticelli* (Manchester: The University of Manchester Press, 1932). Marjorie Reeves, *The Influence of Prophecy in the Later Middle Ages: A Study in Joachimism* (Oxford: Oxford University Press, 1969), 243-48, 318, 414-15, 487.

21. Gumerlock, "A Rapture Citation," 354-55.

22. Gumerlock, "A Rapture Citation," 356-59.

23. Gumerlock, "A Rapture Citation," 361.

24. Reeves, "Influence of Prophecy," 246.

25. Frank Marotta, *Morgan Edwards: An Eighteenth-Century Pretribulationist* (Morganville, NJ: Present Truth Publishers, 1995), 10-12.

26. Thomas Collier, *The Body of Divinity, Or, a Confession of Faith, Being the Substance of Christianity: Containing the Most Material Things Relating to Matters both of Faith and Practise* (London: Nath. Crouch, 1674), 606 pages. This writer found a copy at the British Library.

27. Collier, *Body of Divinity*, 585-86.

28. Marotta, *Morgan Edwards*, 10.

29. The entire title of Asgill's work is as follows: *An argument proving, that according to the covenant of Eternal Life revealed in the Scriptures, Man may be translated from hence into that Eternal Life, without passing through Death, although the Human Nature of Christ himself could not be thus translated till he had passed through Death* (London: n.p., 1700), 87 pages. This writer found a copy in the Bodleian Library, Oxford.

30. William Bramley-Moore, *The Church's Forgotten Hope, or, Scriptural Studies on the Translation of the Saints* (Glasgow: Hobbs & Co., 1905), 322.

31. Bramley-Moore, *The Church's Forgotten Hope*, 322.

32. Thomas R. McKibbens, Jr. and Kenneth L. Smith, *The Life and Works of Morgan Edwards* (New York: Arno, 1980), 2.

33. McKibbens and Smith, *Morgan Edwards*, 5-6.

34. McKibbens and Smith, *Morgan Edwards*, 5-6.

35. "Edwards, Morgan" in John McClintock & James Strong, *Cyclopedia of Biblical, Theological, and Ecclesiastical Literature*, XII vols. (Grand Rapids: Baker, 1981 [1867-87]), Vol. III, 69.

36. McKibbens and Smith, *Morgan Edwards*, 13-14.

37. McKibbens and Smith, *Morgan Edwards*, 16.

38. McKibbens and Smith, *Morgan Edwards*, 31.

39. McKibbens and Smith, *Morgan Edwards*, 33-35.

40. McKibbens and Smith, *Morgan Edwards*, 31.

41. Robert G. Torbet, *A History of the Baptists* (Philadelphia: The Judson Press, 1950), 243-44.

42. Henry C. Vedder, *A Short History of the Baptists* (Philadelphia: The American Baptist Publishing Society, 1907), 232.

43. McKibbens and Smith note that Edwards first wrote his work on eschatology in Latin, which is dated at 1742. Edwards attended Bristol College from 1742 till 1744. Edwards says at the beginning of his essay: "Thousand pities, sir, that you had not allotted the task to one of these older and abler students!" This supports the notion that he wrote the essay during his first year at Bristol since he identifies himself as one of the younger students.

44. Morgan Edwards, *Two Academical Exercises on Subjects Bearing the Following Titles; Millennium, Last-Novelties* (Philadelphia: Dobson and Lang, 1788), 5-6. The English has been modernized. This entire book is available on the Internet at www.pre-trib .org/article-view.php?id=178.

45. McKibbens and Smith, *Morgan Edwards*, 33.

46. Edwards was between the ages of 20-22, while Darby was about 27 years old. Both men held their view throughout their lives.

47. Emphasis added. Edwards, *Two Academical Exercises*, 7.

48. See footnote 16.

49. Edwards, *Two Academic Exercises*, compare with page 7.

50. Edwards, *Two Academical Exercises*, 21.

51. Edwards, *Two Academical Exercises*, 24.

52. Edwards, *Two Academical Exercises*, 25.

53. McKibbens and Smith, *Morgan Edwards*, iv.

54. McKibbens and Smith, *Morgan Edwards*, 51.

55. William Henry Allison, "Baptist Councils in America: A Historical Study of Their Origin and the Principles of their Development," (PhD thesis, University of Chicago, 1906), 20-26.

56. John L. Bray, *The Origin of the Pre-Tribulation Rapture Teaching* (Lakeland, FL: John L. Bray Ministry, 1982), p. 31. Lacunza is a reference to the Jesuit priest Manual de Lacunza (1731–1801), who wrote under the pseudonym of Juan Josafat Ben-Ezra, a converted Jew, *The Coming of Messiah in Glory and Majesty*, Translated from the Spanish, with a Preliminary Discourse, by The Rev. Edward Irving, A.M., 2 vols. (London: L. B. Seeley and Son, 1827).

57. John L. Bray, *Morgan Edwards and the Pre-Tribulation Rapture Teaching (1788)* (Lakeland, FL: John L. Bray Ministry, 1995), 15.

58. Burnham, "The Controversial Relationship," 129.

59. Libraries personally searched in the UK include the following: The British Library in London, The Bodleian Library in Oxford, The Cambridge University Library, Kings College in London, The Queens College in London, The University of London Library, The University of Wales, Lampeter, The New College Library at the University of Edinburgh, The University of Glasgow in Scotland, Trinity College in Dublin, Ireland. Not even Bristol Baptist College, where Edwards attended, had a copy of his book on eschatology. However, with the help of the librarian at the University of Wales, Lampeter, we were able to locate a copy at the Scottish National Library in Edinburgh on microfilm. Thus, it may still be true that there is not an actual copy of the book in the libraries of the entire UK.

60. In addition to the Library of Congress, Bray cites the following libraries in the US that have Edwards' eschatology work: Ambrose Swasey Library, Colgate Rochester Divinity School, Rochester, NY; American Baptist Historical Society, Rochester, NY; The John Carter Brown Library, Brown University, Providence, RI; Historical Commission of the Southern Baptist Convention, Nashville, TN; the Library at Southern Baptist Theological Seminary, Louisville, KY. Bray, *Morgan Edwards*, 8.

61. This writer personally visited Bristol Baptist College in Bristol, England, and inquired about their former student, Morgan Edwards. While the school did have a record of his attendance there as a student, they had no copies of any of his work from his student days, nor did they have any of his published works. Edwards would likely have received back the only handwritten copy of his eschatology paper (1742) that he would have published later in Philadelphia (1788).

62. Geisler, "Review of Hank Hanegraaff's *The Apocalypse Code*," www.ses.edu/NormGeisler/ReviewApocalypseCode.html.

Chapter 6—The Doctrine of an Imminent Rapture

1. For discussions of various issues regarding a definition of imminency, see John

Walvoord, *The Blessed Hope and the Tribulation* (Grand Rapids: Zondervan, 1976), 71; Wayne Grudem, *Systematic Theology* (Grand Rapids: Zondervan, 1994), 1096, n. 7; and John A. Sproule, *In Defense of Pretribulationism* (Winona Lake, IN: BMH Books, 1980), 12.

2. Renald Showers, *Maranatha Our Lord, Come!* (Bellmawr, NJ: Friends of Israel, 1995), 127.

3. Ibid., 127-28.

4. Douglas J. Moo, "The Case for the Posttribulation Rapture Position," in *Three Views on the Rapture* (Grand Rapids: Zondervan, 1996), 208.

5. Some of the following passages are discussed more fully in Wayne A. Brindle, "Biblical Evidence for the Imminence of the Rapture," *Bibliotheca Sacra* 158/630 (April-June 2001): 138-51.

6. The idea that Christ "comes" to believers at the time of their deaths is not found in the Bible.

7. A possible cultural background for this statement may be found in the fact that fathers and soon-to-be-married sons normally added small apartments ("dwelling places" or *insulae*) to their homes so that they could join together in an ever-increasing expanded family.

8. Contrast this with Jesus' counsel to those present on earth during the Tribulation to flee from persecution (Matthew 24:15-22).

9. Brindle, "Biblical Evidence," 141-42.

10. Cf. John F. Walvoord, *The Rapture Question* (Grand Rapids: Zondervan, 1957), 76.

11. The word *tachu*, "quickly," is also used of Christ's coming in 2:16 and 3:11.

12. Walter Bauer, Frederick W. Danker, William F. Arndt, and F. Wilbur Gingrich, *A Greek-English Lexicon of the New Testament and Other Early Christian Literature*, 3d ed., rev. and ed. Frederick W. Danker (Chicago: University of Chicago Press, 2000), 993.

13. In fact, a whole industry of preterist writers has sprung up to explain that Jesus has already returned and most Christians have failed to realize it.

14. See the following for some interesting attempts: Robert H. Mounce, *The Book of Revelation*, New International Commentary on the New Testament, rev. ed. (Grand Rapids: Eerdmans, 1998), 404; Robert W. Wall, *Revelation*, New International Biblical Commentary (Peabody, MA: Hendrickson, 1991), 263.

15. G.K. Beale, *The Book of Revelation*, New International Greek Testament Commentary (Grand Rapids: Eerdmans, 1999), 1135.

16. Johannes P. Louw and Eugene A. Nida, *Greek-English Lexicon of the New Testament Based on Semantic Domains* (New York: United Bible Societies, 1988), 1:296, which also translates it as "await eagerly or expectantly," "look forward eagerly."

17. Bauer, Danker, Arndt, and Gingrich, *A Greek-English Lexicon of the New Testament*, 100.

18. Gordon D. Fee, *The First Epistle to the Corinthians* (Grand Rapids: Eerdmans, 1987), 42, n. 36.

19. Cf. William K. Harrison, "The Time of the Rapture as Indicated in Certain Scriptures—Part I," *Bibliotheca Sacra* 114/456 (October 1957): 319.

20. See Daniel B. Wallace, "A Textual Problem in 1 Thessalonians 1:10: Ἐκ τῆς Ὀργῆς vs. Ἀπὸ τῆς Ὀργῆς," *Bibliotheca Sacra* 147/588 (October 1990): 478, for a convincing argument that the best manuscript reading supports the statement that Christ will

not simply rescue believers "out of" the coming wrath, but will keep them "away from" that wrath.

21. D. Edmond Hiebert, *The Thessalonian Epistles* (Chicago: Moody, 1971), 75.

22. Hiebert, *The Thessalonian Epistles*, 72.

23. F.F. Bruce, *1 & 2 Thessalonians*, Word Biblical Commentary (Waco, TX: Word, 1982), 19-20.

24. Cf. John F. Walvoord, *The Blessed Hope and the Tribulation* (Grand Rapids: Zondervan, 1976), 117.

25. Paul D. Feinberg, "The Case for the Pretribulation Rapture Position," in *Three Views on the Rapture* (Grand Rapids: Zondervan, 1996), 53-54.

26. Bruce, *1 & 2 Thessalonians*, 111-12.

27. As Walvoord puts it, "The implication is quite clear that believers are in a different time reference, namely, that they belong to the day that precedes the darkness" (*The Blessed Hope and the Tribulation*, 117).

28. Bauer, Danker, Arndt, and Gingrich, *A Greek-English Lexicon of the New Testament*, 610.

29. As Earl Radmacher says, "If...there are specific prophesied signs, in reality we would not be looking for the Savior at any moment but instead should be watching for the revelation of the Man of Sin, the Great Tribulation, etc." ("The Imminent Return of the Lord," *Chafer Theological Seminary Journal* 4.3 [July 1998]: 20).

30. Zane C. Hodges, *The Epistle of James: Proven Character Through Testing* (Irving, TX: Grace Evangelical Society, 1994), 110-11.

31. D. Edmond Hiebert, *The Epistle of James: Tests of a Living Faith* (Chicago: Moody, 1979), 301.

32. Hodges, *The Epistle of James*, 111.

33. Radmacher, "Imminent Return," 20.

34. Walvoord says, "The teaching of the coming of the Lord for the church is always presented as an imminent event which should occupy the Christian's thought and life to a large extent" (Walvoord, *The Rapture Question*, 81). Gleason Archer suggests that a comparison of this passage with Revelation 19:7-8,14 proves that by the time Jesus leaves heaven for earth at His second coming the church will have been raptured, purified, and glorified, and have joined Christ's armies (dressed in white clothing) for His victorious return to earth ("The Case for the Mid-Seventieth-Week Rapture Position," in *Three Views on the Rapture* [Grand Rapids: Zondervan, 1996], 119-20).

35. Stephen S. Smalley, *1, 2, 3 John*, Word Biblical Commentary (Waco, TX: Word, 1984), 147.

36. Feinberg, "Case," in *Three Views on the Rapture*, 80.

Chapter 7—Three Foundational Rapture Passages

1. Daniel's seventieth week refers to the last seven years God decreed for Israel as outlined in the chronology for Israel recorded by Daniel (Daniel 9:24-27). In this paper, the final seven-year period prior to the second coming of Jesus Christ, usually referred to as the Tribulation, will also be described by the more precise term Daniel's seventieth week, which is also equivalent to the Day of the Lord.

2. Since a legitimate offer of the kingdom was still to be made to Israel by Peter in Acts 2 and 3, and their acceptance would have brought in the kingdom, our Lord

was intentionally silent at this point to give Israel a second legitimate chance to accept Him as their Messiah before the judgment of AD 70. Alva J. McClain, "The Greatness of the Kingdom, Part IV: The Mediatorial Kingdom from the Acts Period to the Eternal State," *Bibliotheca Sacra*, 112:148 (Dallas: Dallas Theological Seminary), 305-07.

3. Gerald B. Stanton, *Kept From the Hour: Biblical Evidence for the Pretribulational Return of Christ* (Miami Springs, FL: Schoettle, 1991), 84. The term "Day of the Lord" is much discussed. Even those who believe it is sometimes used to describe some historic judgments of God, all see it as a term for God's end-time judgments against His enemies. Among pretribulationists some believe it refers only to the seven-year period of the Tribulation (Arnold Fruchtenbaum, *The Footsteps of the Messiah* [Tustin, CA: Ariel Ministries, 1982]), and others also include the Millennial kingdom as well. At the very least, almost all agree it refers to the entire seven-year Tribulation.

4. Colin Brown, *New International Dictionary of New Testament Theology*, vol. 2 (Grand Rapids: Zondervan, 1986), 2:241.

5. The Greek word *koimao* is often attested in extrabiblical literature as a euphemism for death. In Scripture it is used only for believers. This word does not refer to the nonscriptural doctrine of "soul sleep" but to the rest of the physical body of the believer after physical death.

6. Both "voice" and "archangel" lack the article in the Greek text. This anarthrous construction often emphasizes the quality of the nouns and does not indicate the same thing as an indefinite pronoun in English. This should be understood to refer to Michael, *the* archangel.

7. The grammatical structure here uses a double negative (*ou me*) with a subjunctive mood verb, the strongest way to emphasize the impossibility of an action.

8. William Arndt, Frederick W. Danker, and Walter Bauer, *A Greek–English Lexicon of the New Testament and Other Early Christian Literature*, 3d ed. (Chicago: University of Chicago Press, 2000), 361.

   NOTE: English translations are from the NKJV. Greek words are inserted along with their English transcription from *The Complete Word Study Dictionary*, *New Testament* Logos Bible Software (Logos 4th edition).

9. The text of the Latin Vulgate translates the Greek verb *harpazo* with the Latin verb *rapio*. In this context the form *rapiemur* (future active indicative, first person plural) is used. Over time, *rapturo*, the future active participle was used in theological writings which then developed into the English word, "rapture." S.v. *rapio*, *A Latin Dictionary*. Founded on Andrews' edition of Freund's Latin dictionary. Revised, enlarged, and in great part rewritten by Charlton T. Lewis, PhD and Charles Short, LLD. Oxford. Clarendon Press. 1879. On the Perseus website, http://www.perseus.tufts.edu/hopper/text?doc=Perseus:text:1999.04.0059:alphabetic%20letter=R:entry%20group=2:entry=rapio&toc=Perseus%3Atext%3A1999.04.0059%3Aalphabetic+letter%3DR%3Aentry+group%3D3.

10. Robert L. Dean, Jr. "Chronological Issues in the Book of Revelation," *Bibliotheca Sacra* 168:670 (Dallas: Dallas Theological Seminary, April-June, 2011), 217-26. A version of this paper is also available on the www.pre-trib.org website.

11. Renald Showers cites the following individuals who see a connection between John 14:1-3 and 1 Thessalonians 4:13-18: J. H Bernard, James Montgomery Boice, Arno C. Gaebelein, Arthur Pink, Rudolf Schnackenburg, F.F. Bruce, R.V.G. Tasker, and W.E. Vine in *Maranatha: Our Lord, Come!* (Bellmawr, NJ: Friends of Israel, 1995), 162.

12. Smith wrote, "Hence it is impossible that one sentence or even one phrase can be alike in the two lists…And finally not one word in the two lists is used in the same relation or connection." J.B. Smith, *A Revelation of Jesus Christ: A Commentary on the Book of Revelation* (Scottdale, PA: Herald, 1961), 312.

13. Smith, *A Revelation of Jesus Christ*, 312: "The words or phrases are almost an exact parallel. They follow one another in both passages in exactly the same order. Only the righteous are dealt with in each case. There is not a single irregularity in the progression of words from first to last. Either column [passage] takes the believer from the troubles of earth to the glories of heaven."

14. *Theological Dictionary of the New Testament*, eds. Gerhard Kittel, Geoffrey William Bromiley, and Gerhard Friedrich, electronic ed. (Grand Rapids: Eerdmans, 1964–1976). 5:121, 132. Gerald L. Borchert, vol. 25B, *John 12–21*, electronic ed., Logos Library System; *The New American Commentary* (Nashville: Broadman & Holman, 2003), 103.See also *NIDNTT* II, 250 as well as George Gunn, "John 14:1-3 The Father's House: Are We There Yet?" Unpublished paper www.pre–trib.org.

15. Old Testament usage of the phrase "Father's house" indicates a place that was previously left while the person went away on a trip. In this analogy, Jesus left the Father's house for a sojourn on earth and then returned at His ascension—cf. Genesis 12:1; 20:13; 24:7; 28:21; 31:30, 34; 38:11 50:22; Leviticus 22;12-13; 1 Samuel 18:1-4.

16. Gerald L. Borchert, vol. 25B, *John 12–21*, electronic ed., Logos Library System; *The New American Commentary* (Nashville: Broadman & Holman Publishers, 2003), 104. Also, TDNT cites the Pausanius, who uses the word for an inn or place of halt on a journey; E.J. Goodspeed who cites it as used for a watch-house in a police district, and the *Papyrus Grecs d'époque Byzantine*, ed. J. Maspéro, 1911ff. which uses it for a shepherd's hut in a field: *Theological Dictionary of the New Testament*, eds. Gerhard Kittel, Geoffrey W. Bromiley, and Gerhard Friedrich, electronic ed. (Grand Rapids: Eerdmans, 1964–1976).

17. Daniel B. Wallace, *Greek Grammar Beyond the Basics—Exegetical Syntax of the New Testament* (Zondervan Publishing House and Galaxie Software, 1999; 2002), 536.

18. Other illuminating phrases are "body of Christ" (Colossians 1:24), which is composed of those who have put off the body of the sins of the flesh by the circumcision of Christ" (Colossians 2:11).

19. Five discrete resurrections are identified in Scripture. The first four are combined as one event, the *first* resurrection (Revelation 20:5). These four resurrrections are: (1) the resurrection of Jesus Christ (Matthew 28:1-8); (2) the resurrection of the "dead in Christ" at the time of the rapture (1 Thessalonians 4:13-18); (3) the resurrection of Old Testament saints, for they must be resurrected to participate in the future Kingdom of Christ (Psalm 50:1-6; Isaiah 26:19); (4) the resurrection of Tribulation saints (Revelation 20:4). The fifth resurrection is the resurrection of the unbelievers of all the ages to appear before the Great White Throne (Revelation 20:12).

20. The resurrection of distinct groups at different times is indicated by the word *tagma* ("order"), a word which often has military application, meaning divisions, companies, groups, or ranks.

21. John F. Walvoord, *The Rapture Question: Revised and Enlarged Edition*, 248.

Chapter 8—The Pretribulation Rapture Teaching in the Early Church

1. George E. Ladd, *The Blessed Hope* (Grand Rapids: Eerdmans, 1956), 31.

2. Dave MacPherson, *The Great Rapture Hoax* (Fletcher, NC: New Puritan Library, 1983), 15.

3. Grant R. Jeffrey, *Final Warning* (Toronto: Frontier Research Publications, 1995), 304-10.

4. Paul J. Alexander, "The Diffusion of Byzantine Apocalypses in the Medieval West and the Beginnings of Joachimism," in *Prophecy and Millenarianism: Essays in Honour of Marjorie Reeves,* ed. Ann Williams (Essex, UK: Longman, 1980), 59.

5. W. Bousset, *The Antichrist Legend,* trans. A.H. Keane (London: Hutchinson, 1896), 33-41.

6. E.A. Wallis Budge, *The Book of the Cave of Treasures* (London: The Religious Tract Society, 1927), 267-70.

7. Nathaniel Lardner, *Works of Nathaniel Lardner,* vol. 4 London: J. Johnson, 1767), 434.

8. Paul J. Alexander, *The Byzantine Apocalyptic Tradition* (Berkeley: University of California, 1985), 2.10.

9. *Briefe, Abhandlungen und Predigten aus den zwei letzten Jahrhunderten des kirchlichen Altertums und dem Anfang des Mittelaters,* C.P. Caspari, ed. (Christiania, 1890), 208-20.

Chapter 9—The Purpose and Role of the Tribulation

1. Edward E. Hindson, *Revelation: Unlocking the Future* (Chattanooga, TN: AMG, 2002), 97-128.

2. Merrill Tenney, *Interpreting Revelation* (Grand Rapids: Eerdmans, 1988), 80.

3. Arthur Levine, *When Dreams and Heroes Died* (San Francisco: Jossey-Bass, 1980).

4. John Phillips, *Only God Can Prophesy!* (Wheaton, IL: Harold Shaw, 1975), 111-12.

5. Alfred Edersheim, *The Temple* (Grand Rapids: Eerdmans, 1963), 162-68.

6. Bruce Metzger, *Breaking the Code: Understanding the Book of Revelation* (Nashville: Abingdon, 1993), 63.

7. Phillips, *Only God Can Prophesy!,* 113.

8. Leon Morris, *The Revelation of St. John* (Grand Rapids: Eerdmans, 1969), 124.

9. John Walvoord, *The Revelation of Jesus Christ* (Chicago: Moody Press, 1966), 139.

10. Walvoord, *The Revelation,* 142-49.

11. Cf. Robert Thomas, *Revelation 1-7* and *Revelation 8-22: An Exegetical Commentary* (Chicago: Moody, 1992), on these sections of Revelation.

Chapter 11—How to Avoid Being Left Behind

1. Joseph Stowell, "Set Your Mind on Heaven," in *10 Reasons Why Jesus Is Coming Soon* (Sisters, OR: Multnomah Books, 1998), 252.

Chapter 12—Is the Rapture Found in 2 Thessalonians 2:3?

1. *City of God,* 20.19 (NPNF 1.2. 437).

2. Donald Bloesch, *Essentials of Evangelical Theology,* Vol. 2 (San Francisco: Harper & Row, 1978), 182.

3. Charles C. Ryrie, *Dispensationalism Today* (Chicago: Moody, 1965), 151; Louis Berkhof, *Systematic Theology* (Grand Rapids: Eerdmans, 1941), 718.

4. Martin Rosenthal, *The Pre-Wrath Rapture of the Church* (Nashville: Thomas Nelson, 1990), 198.

5. C.F. Hogg and W.E. Vine, *The Epistles to the Thessalonians*, reprint (Grand Rapids: Kregel, 1959), 247; Lewis Sperry Chafer, *Systematic Theology*, Vol. VI (Dallas: Dallas Seminary Press, 1948), 86.

6. A.L. Moore, ed., *I and II Thessalonians* (London: Marshall, Morgan & Scott, 1969), 100-01.

7. David Williams, *1 & 2 Thessalonians*, New International Bible Commentary Series, vol. 12 (Peabody, MA: Hendrickson, 1992), 124.

8. F.F. Bruce, *1 and 2 Thessalonians*, Word Biblical Commentary (Waco, TX: Word, 1982), 167.

9. Stanley Ellisen, *A Biography of a Great Planet* (Wheaton, IL: Tyndale, 1975), 121.

10. Gordon R. Lewis, "Biblical Evidence for Pretribulationism," *Bibliotheca Sacra*, vol. 125, no. 499 (1968): 218.

11. This speaks only of the Holy Spirit in His specific work in the church, not of His omnipresence, nor of His other works that preceded the origin of the church and during the Tribulation.

12. See Thomas Ice and Timothy Demy, eds., *When the Trumpet Sounds: Today's Foremost Authorities Speak Out on End-Time Controversy* (Eugene, OR: Harvest House, 1995), 291-94.

13. John Walvoord, *The Blessed Hope and the Tribulation* (Grand Rapids: Zondervan, 1976), 125.

Chapter 13—"Departing" Rather than "Falling Away" in 2 Thessalonians 2:3

1. Thomas Ice and Timothy Demy, *When the Trumpet Sounds*(Eugene, OR: Harvest House, 1995), 268.

2. Ice and Demy, *When the Trumpet Sounds*, 268.

3. Ice and Demy, *When the Trumpet Sounds*, 269, note 26.

4. This is taken from an email letter from Dr. Larry Crutchfield to Tim LaHaye and used with permission.

5. Henry George Liddell and Robert Scott, *Greek-English Lexicon*, rev. ed. (Oxford: Clarendon Press, 1973). While this lexicon pertains to Classic Greek rather than to New Testament Greek, this fact in no way detracts from its authority in respect to the root meaning of words.

6. William Tyndale's version of the New Testament, translated and published at Worms, c. 1526, renders *hee apostasia* "a *departynge*." Coverdale (1535), Cranmer (1539), and the Geneva Bible (1557) render it the same way. Beza (1565) translates *apostasia* "departing."

7. Such a noted scholar as Dr. George Milligan, in his commentary on the Greek text of the Thessalonian epistles (New York: Macmillan), although holding to the traditional translation of *apostasia*, states that "the use of the definite article proves [that the *apostasia* referred to is one] regarding which the apostle's readers were already fully informed."

8. Hart Armstrong, *When Is the Rapture?* (Wichita, KS: Christian Communications, 1995), 60.

9. Armstrong, *When Is the Rapture?*, 60-61.

Chapter 14—The End-time Apostasy Is Already Here

1. See "Harry Emerson Fosdick" at http://en.wikipedia/wiki/Harry_Emerson_Fosdick.

2. See "Harry Emerson Fosdick: Liberalism's Popularizer" at www.christianitytoday.com/ch/131 christians/pastorsandpreachers/fosdick.html.

3. See "Norman Vincent Peale: Apostle of Self-Esteem" at www.inplainsight.org/html/norman_vincent_peale.html.

4. Dave Hunt, "Revival or Apostasy," *The Berean Call* (October 1997), 2.

5. Rick Miesel, "Robert Schuller: General Teachings/Activities," http://www.rapidnet.com/~jbeard/bdm/exposes/schuller/general.htm, 8. See also Miesel's article on Norman Vincent Peale at http://www.rapidnet.com/~jbeard/bdm/ Psychology/guide po/peale.htm.

6. Robert Schuller, *Self-Esteem: The New Reformation* (Waco, TX: Word, 1982), 39. An insightful review of Schuller's writings can be found in an article by Joseph P. Gudel entitled "A New Reformation?" Published in *Passport Magazine* (January-February 1988), it is available at http://www.issuesetc.org/resource/archives/guide12.htm. Other excellent summaries of Schuller's thought can be found on the Internet, including David W. Cloud's article entitled "Evangelicals and Modernist Robert Schuller" at http://cnview.com/on_line_resources/evangelicals_and_modernist_robert_schuller.htm and the analysis is entitled, "The God of the Bible Versus the God of Multi-level Marketing: Positive Thinking" at http://www.users.fast.net/~gospeltruth/positive.htm.

7. Schuller, *Self-Esteem*, 19.

8. Schuller, *Self-Esteem*, 80.

9. Schuller, *Self-Esteem*, 14.

10. Schuller, *Self-Esteem*, 68.

11. Robert Schuller, "Dr. Schuller Comments" (letter to the editor), *Christianity Today* (October 5, 1984), 12-13.

12. Richard Stengel, "Apostle of Sunny Thoughts," *Time* (March 18, 1985), 70.

13. John Shelby Spong, *Rescuing the Bible from Fundamentalism: A Bishop Rethinks the Meaning of Scripture* (San Francisco: Harper, 1992). Another revealing book by Bishop Spong is *Why Christianity Must Change or Die: A Bishop Speaks to Believers in Exile* (San Francisco: Harper, 1999). A good summary of Bishop Spong's views can be found on the Internet in his "Call for a New Reformation," http://www.diocese ofnewark.org/jsspong/reform.htm.

14. Dave Hunt, "What's Happening to the Faith?" *The Berean Call* (May 1998), 1. Dr. Godsey's views can be found in the book *When We Talk About God, Let's Be Honest* (Macon, GA: Smyth & Helwys, 1996).

15. R. Albert, "The Immoderator," *World* (March 1998), 18.

16. See "The Jesus Seminar: The Search for Authenticity" at http://home.fireplug.net/~rshand/reflections/messiah/seminar.htm.

17. In April 1996, *Time* magazine featured the Jesus Seminar on its cover under the title "The Search for Jesus." The cover article presented a comprehensive survey of the seminar's organization, methodology, and conclusions. See David Van Biema, "The Gospel Truth—The iconoclastic and provocative Jesus Seminar argues that not much of the New Testament can be trusted. If so, what are Christians to believe?" *Time* (April 8, 1996).

18. Craig L. Blomberg, "The Seventy Four 'Scholars: Who Does the Jesus Seminar Really Speak For?" *Christian Research Journal* (Fall 1994), 32, http://www.rim.org/muslim/jesusseminar.htm.

19. Robert W. Funk and Roy W. Hoover, *The Five Gospels*, reprint (San Francisco: Harper, 1997). A good review of this book can be found in an article by D.A. Carson, "Five Gospels, No Christ" in *Christianity Today* (April 25, 1994), 30-33.

20. See "The United Church of Canada and Homosexuality" at www.religioustolerance .org/ hom_ucc.htm.

21. Mark Tooley, "Church Gathering Features Radical Speakers," *AFA Journal* (June 1997), 19. See also Jackie Alnor, "Invasion of the Sophia Women," *Christian Sentinel* (Spring 1999), 24-25.

22. *Daily Mail*, "Archbishop of Canterbury: Doubts Resurrection of Jesus" (August 4, 1999).

23. Shaila Dewan, "United Church of Christ Backs Same-Sex Marriage," *The New York Times* (July 5, 2005).

24. George Conger, "'Jesus is not the only way to God,' says Presiding Bishop," www .religiousintelligence.co.uk/news/?NewsID'4282.

25. Albert Mohler, "The Amazing Technicolor Multifaith Theology School," www. albertmohler.com/2010/06/11/ claremont-and-the-amazing-technicolor-multifaith -theology-school.

26. Thomas Nelson Publishers, "The Remnant Study Bible: The Last Study Bible You'll Ever Need," www.theremnantstudybible.com/component/content/article/3-news flash/4-newsflash-3.html.

27. Adela Yarbro Collins, "Is Hershel Doomed to the Lake of Fire?" *Biblical Archaeology Review* (January/February 2011), 26.

28. Denny Burk, "Brian McLaren: DaVinci Code Not as Dangerous as Left Behind," www .dennyburk.com/brian-mclaren-davinci-code-not-as-dangerous-as-left-behind/?cat'6.

29. Brian McLaren, "A Generous Orthodoxy," www.brianmclaren.net/archives/books/ brians-books/a-generous-orth.html.

30. Rob Bell, *Velvet Elvis: Repainting the Christian Faith* (Grand Rapids: Zondervan, 2006), 27.

31. Bell, *Velvet Elvis*, 68.

32. Bell, *Velvet Elvis*, 21.

33. Rob Bell, *Love Wins: A Book About Heaven, Hell, and the Fate of Every Person Who Ever Lived* (New York: HarperOne, 2011).

34. Bell, *Love Wins*, viii.

35. Bell, *Velvet Elvis*, 118.

36. See "Christianity Today" at http://en.wikipedia.org/wiki/Christianity_Today#cite_ note-Press-1.

37. Phil Johnson, "Christianity Astray: Is 'New Evangelicalism' Really *Pseudo*-Evangelicalism?" at http://www.spurgeon.org/~phil/articles/ca.htm.

38. National Council of Churches, "Dangers of 'Christian Zionism' are cited in new NCC brochure," www.ncccusa.org/news/081202christianzionismbrochure.html. A copy of the NCC brochure can be downloaded at this site.

39. "Interview with Rob Bell," *Relevant* (January/February, 2008).

40. Brian McLaren, "Four Points Toward Peace in the Middle East," *Sojourners* (April 16, 2009, http://blog.sojo.net/2009/04/16/four-points-toward-peace-in-the-middle-east.

41. McLaren, "Four Points."

42. Brian McLaren, *Everything Must Change* (Nashville: Thomas Nelson, 2009), 144.

43. Assist News Service, "Rick Warren's 'Sermon on the Mound' at Angel Stadium…" (April 4, 2010), www. assistnews.net/Stories/2010/s10040017.htm. The acronym PEACE stands for Promote reconciliation, Equip servant leaders, Assist the poor, Care for the sick, and Educate the next generation. Note that there is no mention of proclaiming the gospel. A detailed presentation of this plan can be found at http:// thepeaceplan.com.

44. For evidence of the overwhelming biblical illiteracy that exists among professing Christians today, including evangelicals, see the polls conducted by the Barna Group at www. barna.org.

45. Some of the opening paragraphs of this chapter were taken in rewritten form from Dr. Reagan's book *Living for Christ in the End Times* (Green Forest, AR: New Leaf, 2000).

Chapter 15—The Literal Interpretation of Scripture and the Rapture

1. David L. Cooper, *The World's Greatest Library: Graphically Illustrated* (Los Angeles: Biblical Research Society, 1970), 11.

2. Tim LaHaye and Jerry B. Jenkins, *Are We Living in the End Times? Current Events Foretold in Scripture…And What They Mean* (Wheaton, IL: Tyndale House, 1999), 6.

3. *Webster's New Twentieth Century Dictionary*, unabridged, 2d ed. (Cleveland: World, 1962), 1055.

4. *The Compact Edition of The Oxford English Dictionary* (New York: Oxford Press, 1971), s.v., "literal."

5. Paul Lee Tan, *The Interpretation of Prophecy* (Winona Lake, IN: Assurance Publishers, 1974), 29.

6. Bernard Ramm, *Protestant Biblical Interpretation: A Textbook of Hermeneutics*, 3d ed. (Grand Rapids: Baker, 1970), 119.

7. This is essentially the interpretation given by John Calvin in his commentary. John Calvin, *Commentary on the Book of the Prophet Isaiah*, Vol. 1, translated from the original Latin by Rev. William Pringle (Grand Rapids: Baker, 1979), 89-103.

8. *Tim LaHaye Prophecy Study Bible*, KJV (Chattanooga, TN: AMG, 2000), 691.

9. Charles C. Ryrie, *Dispensationalism* (Chicago: Moody, [1966], 1995), 80.

10. Roy B. Zuck, *Basic Bible Interpretation: A Practical Guide to Discovering Biblical Truth* (Wheaton, IL: Victor, 1991), 100.

11. Zuck, *Basic Bible Interpretation*, 100-1.

12. Tan, *Interpretation of Prophecy*, 103.

13. Zuck, *Basic Bible Interpretation*, 77.

14. Ryrie, *Dispensationalism*, 80-81.

15. Elliott E. Johnson, *Expository Hermeneutics: An Introduction* (Grand Rapids: Zondervan, 1990), 9.

16. Hank Hanegraaff, *The Apocalypse Code* (Nashville: Thomas Nelson, 2007).

17. Ramm, *Protestant Biblical Interpretation*, 126.

18. Floyd E. Hamilton, *The Basis of Millennial Faith* (Grand Rapids: Eerdmans, 1942), 38.

19. Oswald T. Allis, *Prophecy and the Church* (Phillipsburg, NJ: Presbyterian & Reformed, [1945] 1947), 238.

20. Tan, *Interpretation of Prophecy*, 63.

21. Ryrie, *Dispensationalism*, 81.

22. For example Proverbs 5:4,11; 14:12-13; 16:25; 18:18; 20:21; 25:8; 29:21.

23. Bernard Ramm, *Protestant Biblical Interpretation: A Textbook of Hermeneutics*, 3d ed. (Grand Rapids: Baker, 1970), 49.

24. Joseph W. Trigg, "Introduction," in R.P.C. Hanson, *Allegory & Event: A Study of the Sources and Significance of Origen's Interpretation of Scripture* (Louisville: Westminster John Knox, 2002), vi.

25. Ronald E. Diprose, *Israel in the Development of Christian Thought* (Rome: Instituto Biblico Evangelico Italiano, 2000), p. 87. Frederic W. Farrar explains further: "The Bible, he [Origen] argued, is meant for the salvation of man; but man, as Plato tells us, consists of three parts—body, soul, and spirit. Scripture therefore must have a threefold sense corresponding to this trichotomy. It has a literal, a moral, and a mystic meaning analogous to the body, to the soul, to the spirit…But of two of these three supposed senses Origen makes very little use. To the moral sense he refers but seldom; to the literal sense scarcely at all." Frederic W. Farrar, *History of Interpretation* (Grand Rapids: Baker, [1886] 1961), 196-97.

26. Diprose, *Israel*, 87-88.

27. Hanegraaff, *Apocalypse Code*, 21.

28. Hanegraaff, *Apocalypse Code*, 23.

29. Hanegraaff, *Apocalypse Code*, 22.

30. Hanegraaff, *Apocalypse Code*, 23.

31. Ramm, *Protestant Biblical Interpretation*, 49.

32. R.H. Charles, *Studies in the Apocalypse* (Edinburgh: T & T Clark, 1913), 11.

33. Diprose, *Israel*, p. 89 (emphasis original).

34. See for example, Hanegraaff, *Apocalypse Code*, 116, 124, 127, 180, 199, 200, 221.

35. Diprose, *Israel*, 90.

36. Hanegraaff, *Apocalypse Code*, 115-16, 117-24, 233-35.

37. Hanegraaff, *Apocalypse Code*, 116, 124-28, 135-36.

38. Hank Hanegraaff, "Response to *National Liberty Journal* article on *The Apocalypse Code*," www.equip.org/site/apps/nl/content2.asp?c=muI1LaMNJrE&b=2616123&ct=3839317.

39. Geisler, "Review of Hank." It is interesting that Hanegraaff does not understand his own model within a historical context of what the church has believed throughout her history. Thinking that he does not hold to any form of Replacement Theology he says, "God has only ever had one chosen people who form one covenant community… As such, the true church is true Israel, and true Israel is truly the church—one cannot replace what it already is." Hanegraaff, "Response."

40. Henry Preserved Smith, *Essays in Biblical Interpretation* (Boston: Marshall Jones Company, 1921), 58.

41. Frederic W. Farrar, *History of Interpretation* (Grand Rapids: Baker, [1886] 1961), 245-46.

42. Ramm, *Protestant Biblical Interpretation*, 51.

43. Ramm, *Protestant Biblical Interpretation*, 52.

44. Martin Luther cited in Ramm, *Protestant Biblical Interpretation*, 54.

45. John Calvin cited in Ramm, *Protestant Biblical Interpretation*, 58.

46. Jeffrey K. Jue documents how Joseph Mede and a host of many others among the

English began adopting a millennialist view of eschatology. Jue says, "By the mid-seventeenth century the most popular eschatological position in England was millenarianism." *Heaven Upon Earth: Joseph Mede (1586–1638) and the Legacy of Millenarianism* (Dordrecht, Holland: Springer, 2006), 4.

47. Jue notes that, "the majority of New England puritans held to the doctrine of a future national conversion of ethnic Jews." *Heaven Upon Earth*, 191. "The doctrine of the national conversion of the Jews was an integral part of the eschatology of the New England settlers." Jue, *Heaven Upon Earth*, 193. "Virtually all seventeenth- and early eighteenth-century millennialists on both sides of the Atlantic agreed that even though the Jews were still languishing in their Diaspora, Jehovah had not forgotten his chosen people and would, in due time, restore them to their once-elevated position among the nations." Reiner Smolinski, *The Threefold Paradise of Cotton Mather: An Edition of "Triparadisus"* (Athens, GA: University of Georgia Press, 1995), 21.

48. Wallis tells us: "The rediscovery of the last five chapters of Irenaeus about 1570 may have contributed to Alsted's formulation of premillennialism, since he and others used the writers of the ancient church. We may feel that the intensive Bible study of the Reformation, combined with the knowledge of antiquity, was beginning to swing the pendulum back to the primitive premillennialism of Irenaeus which had been rejected by Augustine." Wilber B. Wallis, "Reflections on the History of Premillennial Thought," in R. Laird Harris, Swee-Hwa Quek, & J. Robert Vannoy, eds., *Interpretation & History: Essays in Honour of Allen A. MacRae* (Singapore: Christian Life, 1986), 229. Early Puritan Joseph "Mede observed a similarity between Patristic chiliasm and his own millenarianism, especially the writings of the Ante-Nicene Fathers. However, in the early sixteenth century any appeal to the Ante-Nicene Fathers' views on the Apocalypse was discouraged for fear of encouraging their chiliasm." Jue, *Heaven Upon Earth*, 110.

49. In a note on Romans 11:25, the Geneva Bible says, "The blindness of the Jews is neither so universal that the Lord hath no elect in that nation, neither shall it be continual for there shall be a time wherein they also (as the Prophets have forewarned) shall effectually embrace that which they do now so stubbornly for the most part reject and refuse." *The 1599 Geneva Bible* (White Hall, WV: Tolle Lege Press, 2006), 1155. Notice that this note believes that the Old Testament prophets also taught a future for Israel as well.

50. Jue, *Heaven Upon Earth*, 199.

51. Ramm has entitled his presentation of literal interpretation or the historical, grammatical, and contextual method as Protestant Biblical Interpretation in his book with that title. Bernard Ramm, *Protestant Biblical Interpretation: A Textbook of Hermeneutics*, 3d ed. (Grand Rapids: Baker, 1970).

52. Wallis, "Reflections," 229.

53. Wallis, "Reflections," 232-34.

54. Wallis, "Reflections," 234.

55. Beryl Smalley, *The Study of the Bible in the Middle Ages* (Notre Dame, IN: University of Notre Dame Press, [1964], 1982), 358.

56. Smalley, *The Study*, 359.

57. Smalley, *The Study*, 360. Traditionally non-literal interpretation has been an old garment that has been labeled "spiritualizing." In this approach the words of the author are clothed with some deeper spiritual sense. With this method of interpretation,

the words of the Old Testament prophets are often explained away. A more recent and "fashionable" term is *sensus plenior*. Use of this concept involves finding a "fuller meaning" that the author did not clearly intend. The "layered look" is also finding its way into the evangelical community as some are returning to the multiple meanings of the text once held by the Schoolmen of the Middle Ages. Bruce K. Waltke suggests a fourfold approach: historical, typical, anagogical, and moral. See Bruce K. Waltke, "The Schoolmen's Hermeneutics Reconsidered," an unpublished paper given at the Northwest Evangelical Theological meeting April 1993.

58. "An Interview: Dr. John F. Walvoord Looks at Dallas Seminary," *Dallas Connection* (Winter 1994, Vol. 1, No. 3), 4.

59. Walter C. Kaiser, Jr., "Evangelical Hermeneutics: Restatement, Advance or Retreat from the Reformation?" *Concordia Theological Quarterly* 46 (1982), 167. Kaiser believes that the present-day crisis finds its historical roots in the writings of liberal existentialists like Friedrich Schleirmacher (1768–1834), Wilhelm Dilthey (1833–1911), Martin Heidegger (1889–1976), Rudolf Bultmann (1884–1976), and Hans Georg Gadamer (b. 1900). Kaiser, "Evangelical Hermeneutics," 167.

60. Kaiser, "Evangelical Hermeneutics," 167.

61. Kaiser, "Evangelical Hermeneutics," 167.

62. Geisler, "Review of Hank."

Chapter 17—Israel and the Church and Why They Matter to the Rapture

1. The Greek term *harpazo* in 1 Thessalonians 4:17 means "to snatch away." It is the Latin translation of this term that gives us the term *rapture*. The term *eschatology* comes from the Greek term *eschatos*, which refers to "last." Thus, eschatology is the study of the last things.

2. Clearly the apostles are New Testament persons. Some debate has existed as to whether the "prophets" are Old Testament or New Testament persons. But the fact that the other two references to "prophets" in Ephesians 3:5 and 4:11 are New Testament persons makes it highly likely that the reference here in Ephesians 2:20 is also on New Testament persons.

3. For more information concerning a refutation of replacement theology or supersessionism see Michael J. Vlach, *Has the Church Replaced Israel? A Theological Evaluation* (Nashville, TN: B&H, 2010). See also Barry Horner, *Future Israel: Why Christian Anti-Judaism Must Be Challenged* (Nashville, TN: B&H, 2007).

4. Walter C. Kaiser, Jr., "Kingdom Promises as Spiritual and National," in *Continuity and Discontinuity: Perspectives on the Relationship Between the Old and New Testaments* (Wheaton, IL: Crossway, 1988), 302.

5. In actuality, these three phases of God's wrath—God's abiding wrath upon the unbeliever, the Day of the Lord's wrath, and eternal wrath in the lake of fire are all related to each other. But the emphasis in 1 Thessalonians is on the Day of the Lord's wrath associated with the Tribulation.

6. Richard L. Mayhue, *Snatched Before the Storm* (Winona Lake, IN: BMH Books), 8.

Chapter 18—The Rapture, Church, and Israel in End-times Prophecy

1. Samuel Schor, *The Everlasting Nation and their Coming King*, 3d ed. (Eastbourne: Prophetic Witness, 1971), 9.

2. Schor, *The Everlasting Nation*, 87.

3. *The Works of the Most Reverend Father in God, William Laud, D.D., Vol. I: Sermons*, ed. William Scott (Oxford: John Henry Parker, 1847), 19-20.

4. Henry Finch, 'To all the seed of Jacob, far and wide dispersed. Peace and Truth be multiplied unto you', in Henry Finch, *The World's Great Restauration, or the Calling of the Jewes, and with them of all the Nations and Kingdomes of the Earth, to the Faith of Christ* (London: William Gouge, 1621), preface.

5. Robert Murray M'Cheyne, "Our Duty To Israel," in Andrew A. Bonar, *Memoir and Remains of Robert Murray M'Cheyne* (Edinburgh: The Banner of Truth Trust, 1978), 493.

6. Lewis Sperry Chafer, *He That Is Spiritual: A Classic Study of the Biblical Doctrine of Spirituality*, rev. ed. (Grand Rapids: Zondervan, 1967), 50.

7. Schor, *The Everlasting Nation*, 47-48.

8. David Baron, *Israel in the Plan of God* (Grand Rapids: Kregel, 1983), 147.

9. Arthur Skevington Wood, *Prophecy in the Space Age: Studies in Prophetic Themes* (London: Marshall, Morgan & Scott, 1964), 55.

10. John Nelson Darby, "Examination of a few Passages of Scripture (1850)," in *The Collected Writings of J.N. Darby, Volume 4*, ed. William Kelly (Kingston-on-Thames: Stow Hill Bible & Tract Depot, n.d.), 254-55.

11. Wood, *Prophecy in the Space Age*, 56.

12. John Nelson Darby, *Synopsis of the Books of the Bible, Volume 2: Ezra-Malachi* (London: G. Morrish, n.d.), 472.

13. James Ayre, *In That Day: An Exposition of the Final Destiny of Israel According to Zechariah* (Cheadle: Myrtle Vale, 1986), 24.

14. Thomas Newton, "The Fulfilment of the Mosaical Prophecies Concerning the Jews as Unanswerable Argument for the Truth of the Bible," in Vicesimus Knox, *Elegant Extracts: or, Useful and Entertaining Passages in Prose, Selected for the Improvement of Young Persons*, 8th ed. (London: 1803), 234.

15. J.C. Ryle, *Are You Ready for the End of Time?* (Fearn: Christian Focus, 2001), 149-50.

16. Ryle, *Are You Ready for the End of Time?*, 155.

17. Ryle, *Are You Ready for the End of Time?*, 150, 157-58.

18. William Eugene Blackstone, *Jesus Is Coming* (Chicago: Fleming H. Revell, 1932), 162.

19. Christabel Pankhurst, *Pressing Problems of the Closing Age* (London: Morgan & Scott Ltd., 1924), 73.

20. C.I. Scofield, *Prophecy Made Plain: Addresses on Prophecy* (London: Alfred Holness, n.d.), 13.

21. Scofield, *Prophecy Made Plain*, 57.

22. J.B. Webb, *Naomi; or The Last Days of Jerusalem* (Edinburgh: W.P. Nimmo, Hay, & Mitchell, 1887), 5, 7-8.

23. Francis Atterbury, "The Horrid Imprecation of the Jews, and the Justice and Wisdom of God in Fulfilling it Upon Them, Displayed," in *Sermons on Several Occasions… Published from the Originals by Thomas Moore, Vol. 1* (London: George James, 1734), 117.

24. Atterbury, "The Horrid Imprecation of the Jews," 132-33.

25. William Henry Hechler, *The Restoration of the Jews to Palestine* (London: 1884).

26. Quoted in Paul Richard Wilkinson, *For Zion's Sake: Christian Zionism and the Role of John Nelson Darby* (Paternoster: Milton Keynes, 2007), 220.

Chapter 19—The Basis of the Second Coming of the Messiah

1. Stanley Toussaint and Charles Dyer, *Essays in Honor of J. Dwight Pentecost* (Chicago: Moody, 1986), 24.
2. Toussaint and Dyer, *Essays*, 27.
3. Toussaint and Dyer, *Essays*, 22.
4. A detailed study of "The Basis of the Second Coming of the Messiah" may be found in the revised edition of *The Footsteps of the Messiah*, a book by Dr. Arnold G. Fruchtenbaum. This book may be purchased through Ariel Ministries.

Chapter 20—The Date of the Book of Revelation

1. For popular level expositions of preterism, see R.C. Sproul, *The Last Days According to Jesus* (Grand Rapids: Baker, 1998); Hank Hanegraaff, *The Apocalypse Code* (Nashville, TN: Thomas Nelson, 2007); Gary DeMar, *Last Days Madness*, 4th rev. ed. (Powder Springs, GA: American, 1999); idem, *End Times Fiction* (Nashville, TN: Thomas Nelson, 2001). However, these interpreters should be categorized as partial preterists, who are quick to distinguish themselves from full preterists by still holding to a future bodily return of Christ and final judgment (20:7-15). See Kenneth L. Gentry, "A Preterist View of Revelation," in *Four Views on the Book of Revelation*, ed. C. Marvin Pate (Grand Rapids: Zondervan, 1998), 86, 46, n. 25.
2. Sproul, *The Last Days According to Jesus*, 140.
3. For an in-depth scholarly treatment of this issue, see *Mark Hitchcock, A Defense of the Domitianic Date of the Book of Revelation* (PhD diss., Dallas Theological Seminary, 2005).
4. Kenneth Johnson, trans., "The Muratorian Canon Fragment," online: http://www .biblefacts. org/church/mcf.html, accessed April 22, 2002.
5. Richard N. Longenecker, *The Ministry and Message of Paul* (Grand Rapids: Zondervan, 1971), 85-86.
6. Kenneth L. Gentry, *Before Jerusalem Fell: Dating the Book of Revelation* (Tyler, TX: Institute for Christian Economics, 1989), 93-94.
7. Tertullian, *Exclusion of Heretics*, 36.
8. Gentry, *Before Jerusalem Fell*, 94-97.
9. Epiphanius, *The Sect Which Does Not Accept the Gospel of John or His Revelation*, 51:12:2 in Philip R. Amidon, ed. and trans., *The Panarion of St. Epiphanius, Bishop of Salamis, Selected Passages* (New York: Oxford University Press, 1990), 180.
10. F. Hort, *The Apocalypse of St. John: 1 to 111* (London: Macmillan, 1908), xviii.
11. Gentry, *Before Jerusalem Fell*, 104-05.
12. James Murdock, trans., *The Syriac New Testament*, 6th ed. (London: Marshall Bros., 1893), 442; William Wright, *Apocryphal Acts of the Apostles*, vol. 2 (London, n.p. 1871; reprint, Amsterdam: Philo, 1968), 55-57.
13. Robert Jamieson, A. Fausset, and David Brown, *A Commentary, Critical and Explanatory, on the Whole Bible* (New York: Richard R. Smith, 1930), 548.
14. R.H. Charles, *A Critical and Exegetical Commentary on the Revelation of St. John*, vol. 1, The International Critical Commentary (Edinburgh: T&T Clark, 1920), xcii.
15. Gentry, *Before Jerusalem Fell*, 105-08.
16. Brooke F. Westcott, *A General Survey of the History of the Canon of the New Testament*, 6th ed. (Grand Rapids: Baker, 1855; reprint, 1980), 536, n. 7; J. Ritchie Smith, "The Date of the Apocalypse," *Bibliotheca Sacra* 45 (April-June 1888): 302.

17. Smith, "The Date of the Apocalypse," *Bibliotheca Sacra* 45 (April-June 1888): 301.

18. Smith, "The Date of the Apocalypse, 303.

19. Smith, "The Date of the Apocalypse," 305.

20. Gentry, "A Preterist View of Revelation," 40-45.

21. Gentry, *Before Jerusalem Fell*, 165-92. These verses say, "Then I was given a reed like a measuring rod. And the angel stood, saying, 'Rise and measure the temple of God, the altar, and those who worship there. But leave out the court which is outside the temple, and do not measure it, for it has been given to the Gentiles. And they will tread the holy city underfoot for forty-two months'" (Revelation 11:1-2).

22. Kenneth L. Gentry, *The Beast of Revelation*, rev. ed. (Powder Springs, GA: American Vision, 2002).

23. Gentry, *Before Jerusalem Fell*, 146-64; idem, *The Beast of Revelation*, 137-45.

24. Flavius Josephus, *Antiquities of the Jews*, trans. William Whilston, *The New Complete Works of Josephus* (Edinburgh, Scotland: William P. Nimmo, 1867; reprint, Grand Rapids: Kregel, 1997), 18:2:2; 18:6:10.

25. Moses Stuart, *Commentary on the Apocalypse*, vol. 1 (Andover, MA: Allen, Morrill, and Wardwell, 1845), 229.

26. C. Moule, *The Birth of the New Testament*, 3d ed., Harper's New Testament Commentaries (San Francisco: Harper & Row, 1982), 59.

27. Gentry, *Before Jerusalem Fell*, 220-31.

28. Hank Hanegraaff and Sigmund Brouwer, *The Last Sacrifice* (Wheaton, IL: Tyndale, 2005), 342.

29. John F. Walvoord, *The Revelation of Jesus Christ* (Chicago: Moody, 1966), 35.

30. Hitchcock, "A Defense of the Domitianic Date of the Book of Revelation", 86-96.

31. Moreover, even if it is assumed that Revelation 11:1-2 refers to Herod's temple that was destroyed in AD 70, how is it possible to fit the rest of the contents of Revelation 11 into the events of AD 70? For example, much of the rest of Revelation 11 is devoted to a discussion of the two witnesses who perform miracles, are slain, are gazed upon by the world, lie dead for three-and-a-half days, resurrect, and ascend to heaven. These events are not even hinted at in Josephus' detailed accounts that discuss the siege of Jerusalem. Smith, "The Date of the Apocalypse," 308.

32. For a more extensive refutation of the Neronian hypothesis, see Hitchcock, "A Defense of the Domitianic Date of the Book of Revelation," 137-56; Andy Woods, "Revelation 13 and the First Beast," in *The End Times Controversy: The Second Coming Under Attack*, eds. Tim LaHaye and Thomas Ice (Eugene, OR: Harvest House, 2003), 237-50.

33. Gentry, *Before Jerusalem Fell*, 209-12.

34. Smith, "The Date of the Apocalypse," 317.

35. Smith, "The Date of the Apocalypse," 318.

36. Robert H. Mounce, *The Book of Revelation*, New International Commentary on the New Testament (Grand Rapids: Eerdmans, 1983), 35.

37. G.K. Beale, *The Book of Revelation*, New International Greek Testament Commentary, ed. I. Howard Marshall and Donald A. Hagner (Grand Rapids: Eerdmans, 1999), 719.

38. Beale, *The Book of Revelation*, 719; Mounce, *The Book of Revelation*, 264, n. 61. In addition to these aforementioned problems associated with *gematria*, the "beast equals Nero" thesis should be rejected on other grounds as well. For example, Nero did not

force the entire world to take a mark on their right hand or forehead to participate in the global economy (13:16-18), coerce the entire world to worship a singular image of him (13:15), resurrect from the dead (13:14), associate with the miracle working false prophet (13:13,15), and receive veneration from the entire planet (13:8). See Mark Hitchcock and Thomas Ice, *The Truth Behind Left Behind* (Sisters: OR: Multnomah, 2004), 216-17.

39. D.A. Carson, Douglas J. Moo, and Leon Morris, *An Introduction to the New Testament* (Grand Rapids: Zondervan, 1992), 476; Thomas, *Revelation 8–22: An Exegetical Commentary* (Chicago: Moody Press, 1992), 297.

40. Charles H. Dyer, "The Identity of Babylon in Revelation 17-18," *Bibliotheca Sacra* 144 (October-December 1987): 439; J. Seiss, *The Apocalypse: Lectures on the Book of Revelation* (New York: Charles C. Cook, 1909; reprint, Grand Rapids: Zondervan, 1977), 391-92; George Eldon Ladd, *A Commentary on the Revelation of John* (Grand Rapids: Eerdmans, 1972; reprint, 1979), 227-28. Some have suggested that the five fallen kingdoms include Egypt, Assyria, Babylon, Persia, and Greece. Rome was the kingdom reigning while John wrote. The seventh kingdom will be the revived Roman Empire under the future Antichrist. Thomas, *Revelation 8–22*, 297; John F. Walvoord, *The Revelation of Jesus Christ* (Chicago: Moody, 1966), 251-54.

41. Arnold G. Fruchtenbaum, *Hebrew Christianity: Its Theology, History, & Philosophy* (Washington, DC: Canon Press, 1974), 41-44.

42. Eusebius, *Ecclesiastical History*, 3:20.

43. Mark Hitchcock, "The Stake in the Heart: The A.D. 95 Date of Revelation," in *The End Times Controversy*, eds. Tim LaHaye and Thomas Ice (Eugene, OR: Harvest House, 2003), 127.

44. Irenaeus, *Against Heresies*, 5:30:3, http://www.ccel.org/fathers2/ANF-01/anf01-63 .htm, accessed 20 April 2002.

45. Eusebius, *Ecclesiastical History*, 5:20:4-7, http://www.ccel.org/fathers 2/NPNF2-01/ TOC.htm, accessed April 22, 2002.

46. Gentry, *Before Jerusalem Fell*, 45-67.

47. Gentry, *Before Jerusalem Fell*, 63-64.

48. Irenaeus, *Against Heresies*, 2:22:5.

49. Beale, *The Book of Revelation*, 20.

50. Smith, "The Date of the Apocalypse," 299.

51. H. Wayne House and Thomas Ice, *Dominion Theology: Blessing or Curse?* (Portland: Multnomah, 1988), 251-52.

52. David E. Aune, *Revelation 1-5*, vol. 1., ed. Ralph P. Martin, Word Biblical Commentary, (Dallas: Word Books, 1997), ix.

53. Beale, *The Book of Revelation*, 20.

54. Westcott, *A General Survey of the History of the Canon of the New Testament*, 341, 381.

55. Philip Schaff, *History of the Christian Church*, 3d ed. (Grand Rapids: Eerdmans, 1910), 2:750-51.

56. Schaff, *History of the Christian Church*, 1:834. Schaff's opinion on this matter is especially compelling in light of the fact Schaff held to an early date of Revelation. See Gentry, *Before Jerusalem Fell*, 30, 37.

57. Smith, "The Date of the Apocalypse," 300-4.

58. Gentry, *Before Jerusalem Fell*, 68-109.

59. Gentry, *Beast of Revelation*, 245.

60. Robert L. Thomas, "Theonomy and the Dating of Revelation," *Master's Seminary Journal* 5, no. 2 (Fall 1994): 201.

61. Robert L. Thomas, *Revelation 1–7: An Exegetical Commentary*, ed. Kenneth Barker (Chicago: Moody, 1992), 38.21-22; Donald Guthrie, *New Testament Introduction*, 4th rev. ed. (Downers Grove, IL: InterVarsity, 1990), 953-55.

62. Collin J. Hemer, *The Letters to the Seven Churches of Asia in Their Local Setting* (Sheffield: JSOT Press, 1986); G.K. Beale, "Review of the Seven Churches of Asia in Their Local Setting," *Trinity Journal* 7 (1986): 107-8.

63. Mounce, *The Book of Revelation*, 34.

64. Hemer, *The Letters to the Seven Churches of Asia in Their Local Setting* , 194-95.

65. Polycarp, *Letter of Polycarp to the Philippians*, 11.3.

66. Charles, *A Critical and Exegetical Commentary on the Revelation of St. John*, xciv.

67. Hitchcock, "The Stake in the Heart: The A.D. 95 Date of Revelation," 149.

68. For a fuller discussion of the many problems involving preterism, see Tim LaHaye and Thomas Ice, eds., *The End Times Controversy* (Eugene, OR: Harvest, 2003).

Books in the
Tim LaHaye Prophecy Library®
by Harvest House Publishers

Charting the End Times
Tim LaHaye and Thomas Ice

The result of decades of research and Bible study, this landmark resource provides a fascinating picture of the end times. Includes a visual foldout, 50 color charts/diagrams, explanatory text, and clear answers to tough questions.

Charting the End Times CD
Tim LaHaye and Thomas Ice

Includes all the charts from the book, a Windows/Macintosh CD-ROM. Both Windows and Macintosh compatible.

**Charting the End Times
Prophecy Study Guide**
Tim LaHaye and Thomas Ice

This standalone study guide for individuals or groups takes readers through the high points of Bible prophecy with helpful charts that offer a clear picture of what will happen and when in the last days.

**Exploring Bible Prophecy from
Genesis to Revelation**
Tim LaHaye and Ed Hindson, general editors

It's all here—clear and concise explanations for key prophetic passages from the beginning to the end of the Bible. Written by Bible scholars but created for lay-level Bible students, this includes useful charts, diagrams, and time lines that enhance one's understanding of Bible prophecy.

The Popular Encyclopedia of Bible Prophecy
Tim LaHaye and Ed Hindson, general editors

An A-to-Z encyclopedia filled with over 400 pages of facts, information, and charts about the last days.

The Rapture
Tim LaHaye

When friends and colleagues began wavering in their beliefs about the end times, LaHaye began a vast research project resulting in this complete defense of the pretribulation view. Straightforward, understandable, and informative.

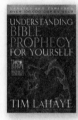

Understanding Bible Prophecy for Yourself
Tim LaHaye

Tim LaHaye's bestselling book, redesigned and updated! This easy-to-follow guide offers the tools believes need to accurately interpret biblical prophecy. Includes charts, tips for interpreting difficult passages, and summaries of Bible history, customs, and beliefs. Includes study questions great for individual or group use.

Tim LaHaye Prophecy Study Bible

Available in King James Version and New King James Version

A study Bible that is faithful to the pretribulational view of Bible prophecy, with more than 70 articles from prophecy experts and 84 charts and tables that help to make clear God's prophetic plan. Also included are a Bible concordance, center-column references, the 329 prophecies of Jesus' second coming, and textual notations on key passages.

A truly extraordinary resource for pastors, teachers, and all others who desire to better understand what the Bible says about the last days.

Available at www.timlahaye.com

About the Pre-Trib Research Center

In 1991, Dr. Tim LaHaye became concerned about the grow-ing number of Bible teachers and Christians who were attack-ing the pretribulational view of the rapture as well as the literal interpretation of Bible prophecy. In response, he wrote *No Fear of the Storm* (Portland, OR: Multnomah Publishers, 1992, now titled *The Rapture*). In the process of writing this book, Tim was impressed by the Christian leaders who, in Great Britain dur-ing the 1820s and 1830s, set up conferences for the purpose of discussing Bible prophecy. In 1992, Tim contacted Thomas Ice about the possibility of setting up similar meetings, which led to the first gathering of what is now known as the Pre-Trib Study Group in December 1992.

In 1993, Dr. LaHaye and Dr. Ice founded the Pre-Trib Research Center (PTRC) for the purpose of encouraging the research, teaching, propagation, and defense of the pretribulational rap-ture view and related Bible prophecy doctrines. It is the PTRC that has sponsored the annual study group meetings since that time, and there are now more than 200 members comprised of top prophecy scholars, authors, Bible teachers, and prophecy stu-dents.

LaHaye and Ice, along with other members of the PTRC, have since produced an impressive array of literature in support of the pretribulational view of the rapture as well as the literal interpre-tation of Bible prophecy.

To find out more about the PTRC and its publications, write to:

Pre-Trib Research Center
PO Box 21796
El Cajon, CA 92021

You can also get information at www.pre-trib.org